# The Warm Hug

# The Warm Hug

## Substance Use and How to Fix the Failure of Treatment and Recovery in America

Keith Keller

Foreword by Benjamin Westhoff

Infinite Recovery Press

**Disclaimer**

This book is licensed for your personal use and education only. While best efforts have been used, the author and publisher are not offering legal, medical, or any other professional services or advice and make no representations or warranties of any kind and assume no liabilities of any kind with respect to the accuracy or completeness of the contents and specifically disclaim any implied warranties of merchantability or fitness of use for a particular purpose, nor shall they be held liable or responsible to any person or entity with respect to any loss or incidental or consequential damages caused, or alleged to have been caused, directly or indirectly, by the information or programs contained herein.

The information, ideas, and techniques in this book are not medical advice or treatment, but rather information intended to assist the reader. It is the responsibility of the reader to seek treatment for any medical, mental, or emotional conditions that might warrant professional care.

Some names and identifying characteristics of people mentioned in this book have been changed to protect the privacy of the individuals.

**Published by Infinite Recovery Press**
**ISBN: 978-0-9600669-2-6**
**Library of Congress Control Number: 2026914317**

**Content Editor, Creative Consultant—Benjamin Westhoff**
**Copy Editor—Joni Wilson**
**Cover Design—Farah Evers**
**Administrative Support—Melody York**

## Dedication

"Men will always be mad, and those who think
they can cure them are the maddest of all."
~ Voltaire

To all the people in chaotic substance use. That was me at one time. To all the people thinking about changing. To all the people who are in the midst of change. And to all the people living in any part of the recovery process, thank you. Serving you is my life's purpose, and this book is dedicated to you.

The substance use disorder, treatment, and recovery world is full of talented, brilliant, and amazing people. There are much better nurses than me. There are countless people who understand treatment and the treatment system much better than I do. There are many people who know much more than I know about everything in this book. There are many people who know more about recovery and work better recoveries than I do. There are people smarter than me who work much harder than I do.

Lord only knows how many people are better writers than I am.

Thank you all for inspiring me to be a better man.

And—
In memory of Travis Wyant, RN, Rockstar.

# Contents

# Foreword

Ben Westhoff

If you're like me, you grew up believing drug and alcohol addiction was hopeless, that the inebriate outside the liquor store and the heroin-using person on the street were doomed forever. Nothing could save them.

This was part of the scared-straight messaging of the 1980s, a time where overdose deaths were just a fraction of what they are today. Who knows how many young impressionable kids this messaging stopped from trying drugs (certainly not me), but in the coming decades the addiction landscape got much worse. Today we know for certain that the fearmongering was wrong about at least one thing: Recovery is possible.

Just ask Keith.

Keith Keller is a man thriving in long-term recovery, who is also one of the world's foremost addiction and recovery experts. As you will read, he has not just beaten addiction but also ascended to the highest echelon of addiction treatment in a nursing practice. Today, he's part of an elite group of top-tier substance treatment nurses, who travel all over the country helping people. His goal, with this book and in his practice, is simple: to change the way people recover from addiction and substance use disorder.

Specializing in detox, clinical stabilization, and recovery coaching, he has worked in just about every facet of substance use treatment. He has also studied alternative modalities and brings a holistic perspective. He knows almost everything there is to know about medications for addiction treatment, but he also knows that medicine is just the tip of the spear, and that helping people reclaim their lives also involves providing support, education, and the skills of recovery, something anyone can learn.

Keith knows that everyone is different. Having helped thousands of people over the years, he knows where traditional detox and rehab models break down. That's what makes this book so critical right now, and why I was thrilled to serve as its editor. In an era of one-size-fits-all healthcare, Keith believes in tailoring specific programs to specific people. He explains the philosophy of this humane approach in the following pages.

I have spent the last decade chronicling how fentanyl gets into this country, how the supply chain from China to Mexico to the US and Canada created the worst drug crisis the world has ever seen. But after getting to the roots of this problem, I pondered: Now what? How do we get out of this mess?

That's where Keith comes in. This book is the most compelling account available about drug and alcohol treatment and recovery programs and models, what they get wrong and what they get right. Keith is no academic in an ivory tower, no journalist relying on experts: He is the expert. His real-life experience—complemented by a curiosity that drives him to read and incorporate into his practice addiction-focused journals, newsletters, and studies—makes him the perfect guide to treatment and recovery. Keith doesn't just offer information on how he gets people through detox treatment, but also big picture prescriptions on how to modernize our addiction medicine system.

And his personal stories are endlessly entertaining. I can picture him drumming for his cover and original bands in the 1980s, running the gamut from hard rock to grunge, all the while drunk out of his ever-loving mind. The verdict of Keith's bandmates of the day was unanimous: "good drummer, bad drinker."

His quest for the "perfect note" was inextricably tied up with his quest for the "perfect buzz." Today, Keith understands and applies the psychological and pharmacological underpinnings of his crazier-than-fiction personal addiction stories. He knows why and how chemicals once ruled his life, and how to help others escape like he did.

His hard-won expertise requires a level of knowledge that cannot be assembled only from books, or only from clinical encounters, or only from lived experience. Keith has it all. He knows the difference between someone saying they want to get better and the moment they actually do. He is hard to con, but easy to trust. My suggestion? Read this book. And then give it to someone who needs it.

Addiction is treatable. Recovery is possible. Just ask Keith.

# Introduction

"We need to have a serious talk."

I'm speaking to my client. He is a 60-year-old entrepreneur and former singer/songwriter receiving a personalized detox in his home. I'll call him John because I can't use his real name. He's having tremors and a headache, sweating, nausea... the early stages of alcohol withdrawal.

I'm here to manage treatment for that withdrawal, but it's not that simple.

John is a good-looking man, tall, toned, and well-groomed. Aside from excessive drinking, he takes care of his health. He worked in the music industry as a performer and publisher, earning several gold records. He moved on to business, but his old rock-star lifestyle didn't work in his new businessman life.

He had some successful years when he moved on to business, but alcohol fueled bad decisions, leading to a series of financial setbacks. Sober John has a future in business; drinking John does not. He still has the love and support of his children and his siblings, but it's clear that his drinking is putting that at risk.

All of this has brought him to the edge of an abyss; his options are rapidly diminishing.

John was treated by one of my colleagues, just 12 days earlier. Unfortunately, John resumed drinking one hour after my colleague departed. That's when the Uber alcohol order arrived. Within a few days, he was drinking soon after waking up, passing out during the day, and then drinking until losing consciousness at night. Unable to pull himself out of this nosedive, he reached out for help again.

I learned the complexity of John's history and relationship with substances. For 35 years, he had taken prescribed Xanax, an extraordinary duration, considering it is physically and emotionally habit-forming, and therefore typically used for short-term management.

John's situation, then, presented me with a conundrum. The alcohol detox entails managing withdrawal symptoms with diazepam, a medication from the same family as Xanax. Using both at the same time would be ill-advised, unpredictable, and potentially dangerous. Therefore, I asked John to turn over his Xanax, which he did. Still, I suspected there was more.

"The other nurse told me there was a second bottle," I said.

He said he'd put the medication somewhere while he was intoxicated and couldn't remember where. "I was out of it, that's everything I can find."

"People don't tend to misplace medication that important to them," I respond.

He becomes defensive in an over-the-top way. He knows I'm smelling the BS. "Well then, we can finish this right now. You can get the fuck out and I'm going to drink."

When I had arrived two hours earlier, we'd set the ground rules for the treatment. Receiving treatment at home comes with both privileges and responsibilities. John could sleep in his own bed, eat his own food, have his phone, and basically do as he pleases. But because there is no way for me to completely ensure the absence of alcohol or other intoxicating substances, there needed to be trust.

John had said he understood and committed to working within this framework. I had stated plainly that if he drank during the detox, the treatment plan would be reevaluated and told him I'd need to hold his other medications. He'd agreed at the time but now seemed to be reneging. Fortunately, the medication I'd administered earlier to proactively manage the withdrawal symptoms began to take effect, and John calmed down. He lay down to rest, before getting up a short while later and eventually producing a bottle of Xanax.

Still, things felt contentious. John's body language seemed furtive, and I knew I would have to initiate a difficult conversation, one that would make or break the treatment.

John's significant other arrived, watching as the situation unfolded and becoming alarmed at John's threat to resume drinking. "You can't. Look what's been happening for the last week. You'll go right back to that."

"John, this is about your safety," I added. "I'm responsible for that. I understand how hard this is for you, and believe me, this conversation is terribly uncomfortable for me too. It's the absolute worst part of my job. But your safety matters."

Another long silence. The tension was high.

I pressed on, hoping for the best. "What really matters is what we do moving forward. I give you my word, this is no harm, no foul, if we can just get past this."

Yet another long moment of silence. Then, John reached in his pocket and took out a small metal pillbox. It contained six Xanax. This was a turning point.

I thanked him, and told him, in all seriousness, that what he had done was downright heroic.

John expressed relief; a significant weight had been lifted from his shoulders. He had realized how the treatment, and therefore his new recovery, would be undermined had he chosen to proceed on a faulty basis. From that moment forward, our rapport was strengthened, but more important, we established trust.

John did something incredibly hard. I know this because I've been working in facilities and treatment programs—observing nurses and clinicians navigate these dynamics—for over 30 years.

About 10 or 15 years ago I wouldn't have initiated the conversation. Today, understanding substance use, treatment, and recovery on multiple levels—medically, neurologically, psychosocially, and through lived experience—is my gift.

As a registered nurse, my substance use disorder experience includes inpatient detox/clinical stabilization, residential treatment of adolescents, outpatient methadone treatment, intensive outpatient program facilitation, and office-based addiction treatment in a primary care setting. My general nursing background includes operating room, pediatrics, geriatrics, IV therapy, dialysis, acute care and community mental health, hospice, and allied health program teaching. Hiring managers would sometimes look at my résumé and suggest that I decide what I want to be when I grow up. I did, and it's my current role, where I use experience from everything that came before.

But wait, there's more!

I studied alternative, complementary, and energy medicine, earning an associate's degree in a healing modality called polarity therapy. From this work, I derive my holistic perspective on healthcare. I then devoted years to learning science-focused approaches to change and personal transformation.

Also, I'm a person in long-term recovery from substance use disorder.

All of that supports my qualification to make the following observation: Addiction in America is pitifully misunderstood. Treatment, as commonly practiced, is pathetically ineffective. Recovery is haphazard and largely archaic. I'm advocating for radical reconsideration of how we do things.

Treatment has barely changed in 60 or 70 years. While the incorporation of the disease model is significant, medical management and psychoeducation, the substance of substance use treatment, are not getting the job done. An outgrowth of our free-market healthcare industrial complex, the current system includes everything from essential services in community medical practices to propositions in private equity-based venture capitalism. Those trying to get addiction care are like pawns on chessboards, and their highest interest is not the focus of the game.

Recovery is perceived by many as a life of endless daily meetings, the supervision of an iron-fisted taskmaster, otherwise known as a sponsor, and living in constant fear of failure. To many in the throes of addiction, recovery seems like a mysterious riddle on the other side of a painful ordeal—unattainable or next to it. The image held by the public at large is of a depressing church basement with chairs in a circle and sad-looking people intoning "I'm Keith, I'm an *alcoholic*."* The reality is that there aren't enough options, and the chances are slim that a given individual will find one well suited to their needs. The traditional model of 12-Step peer support like Alcoholics Anonymous, AA, and Narcotics Anonymous, NA, the most widely accessible options, is like spinning the roulette wheel to see if you're one of the few who can succeed in a 90-year-old approach that has intentionally avoided changing with the times.

Now, if you are a dedicated professional working in the treatment and recovery sectors, first and foremost—thank you! I appreciate you, but let's be honest. We are losing.

I'm not throwing stones while giving myself a pass. Over the last 10 years, I've needed to upgrade my practice and understanding in

* The reason the word alcoholic is in italics is discussed in Chapter 16.

numerous areas. I don't think this can be a self-righteous rant while I'm owning my mistakes, the things I was wrong about, and how I've learned to do better personally. Harm reduction versus abstinence; smoking in treatment; person-first, strength-based language; to name a few, are areas that I viewed much differently scant years ago.

"ADDICTION."

How does it feel when you say it out loud? People need to be able to say the word without feeling uncomfortable, at least no more so than saying cancer or diabetes. People fear and stigmatize what makes them feel uncomfortable and what they do not understand. We need to better understand addiction. We need to better understand the difference between substance use and addiction. This requires modeling of behaviors and examples on the part of people such as me with lived experience, people in the recovery field, and everyday people who have been directly or indirectly affected. When people don't understand something, they take their cues from those who do understand.

Addiction is unique to each individual, and treatment needs to reflect that. A person's history, circumstances, and behavior patterns bring them to seek treatment. Treatment needs to better value that as holding potential to help each person. More attention to assessment of readiness and motivation to change is the first step in individualizing treatment. Acknowledging that people can only accept the level of treatment they are personally ready to engage is a logical next step. Replacing one-size-fits-all group therapy with leading-edge approaches and teaching based on neuroscience models is a needed upgrade for the wash, rinse, and repeat approach widely in use. We can acknowledge that all effort made on behalf of someone's recovery has value, whether by the person, their loved ones, or professionals. It's time for innovation. Treatment sets the stage for recovery to follow. In general, treatment needs to look critically at its focus on abstinence and the (sometimes personal) bias of professionals toward that, while focusing on more diverse, and individualized, approaches to recovery.

Recovery should impress upon people the unlimited possibilities awaiting them in a life without addiction. Supporting people to transcend the problems they used addiction to escape from with a solution-focused programming empowers them to step into their greatness as human beings. Sure, be powerless over substances... and people and places as well if that's your thing. However, recognize that potential for change is limited only by the limitations we place on ourselves.

High end recovery is not a random outcome of showing up and hoping for the best. Recovery is a skill, which can be taught and learned. Like treatment, recovery should be individualized in an inclusive continuum that supports each person to establish the approach best suited to their needs.

In the public sector, people are holding on to old ideas and stigma. People living with addiction are among the most marginalized and misunderstood in our society. For decades now, we have seen incarceration, legislation, and more recently medication, fail to impact substance use and its collateral damage. A recovery friendly culture can only start with better understanding of the problem.

Addiction and substance use are not the same thing. The principles of harm reduction made the already murky picture even more blurry. I'm here to explain how this works and why it's a good thing.

What was old is new again. Psychedelics are back, both in the culture and in the research lab. Once demonized, hallucinogenic substances are now realizing the hope originally attributed to them five decades ago. In similar fashion, cannabis is now part of mainstream culture. Medicinal or recreational, weed never left, and there is a lot to know.

And speaking of what's new, gas stations have become your one-stop shopping destination where you can fill up your tank, then grab a donut and a mind-altering substance. Kratom has been flying under the radar for a few years now. While some see benefit to its use as an opioid alternative, many are falling under its spell, much to their detriment. This is something people should know about.

As we reexamine relationships with substances, tobacco and vaping can no longer be ignored as addictive and dangerous substances. Part of both history and culture, the checkered past of the tobacco industry has laid the foundation for a checkered present. I make the case for seeing these legal yet addictive substances in a new light, along with modifying our approach to smoking/vaping in the treatment setting.

Today, I have the recovery and life of my dreams. I wish there were more hours in the day for meaningful work, supportive and gratifying relationships, and enriching peak experiences. I created this—believing in it and actually feeling it—before I could see it. Now I'm living it. My sobriety is effortless. While life can be challenging, that makes it more interesting. Most days I actually well up in gratitude when I stop to think about all my gifts. Based on my knowledge base, skill set, and lived experience, I provide the highest caliber addiction treatment available. I'm on a mission to change the way people recover from addiction, and I bring decades of experience to that cause.

I once viewed the world through the lens of the open bottle of vodka kept under the seat of my car. Today, I see unlimited possibilities for helping people and enacting positive change.

I'm here to share my hard-learned insight with you. Let's go!

# Chapter 1
# My Story: Addiction

"At some point, the goal of becoming unconscious became the unconscious goal."

~ Keith Keller

## Best Drink Ever

It wasn't my first drink, but it was my best drink ever.

It was 50 years ago, but I can still remember it vividly: a Friday afternoon in November when I was 13. School was closed for Veteran's Day. I was hanging out with a couple of older friends from the next town.

Because my friends were older, I paid close attention to them. I thought they were cool and edgy as they postured and debated one another. We hung out at one fellow's place listening to the latest Allman Brothers Band record. Eventually, we decided that we would walk to the other guy's house.

Once we were out of sight of his house, my friend opened his jacket to bring out a bottle. "Thanks, Dad," he said. It was an open fifth or quart of his dad's rum with about a third remaining in the bottle. He took a big gulp and handed it over to my other friend who did the same, then handed it to me. I looked at the bottle's owner, hesitant. "Come on, Keller, don't be a pussy." I took a swig.

Yikes! Hard liquor assaulted my 13-year-old senses. I somehow managed not to gag. I had several more swigs probably totaling three or four shots worth. And soon came the effect—a profoundly relaxing and completely liberating sense of euphoria. Anxiety—gone. Inhibitions—gone. Cares and concerns over being the youngest present—gone.

So, why do I remember this drink 50 years later? The resulting euphoria felt like the warm hug I had been waiting all of my short life to receive, a fusion of relief, inner peace, and total freedom. My early adolescent angst was put on time-out. I felt comfortable in my own skin, having had no realization that my typical state was one of relative discomfort.

After returning home, I called a girl! Not just any girl but (insert made up name). She was a competitive swimmer and blond, beautiful, and smart. I had a massive crush on her. This brazen behavior was not my norm; I have no idea what I said, but she actually talked with me—reinforcement. The following Monday, when I saw her on the bus, I could barely look at her; that was me back to normal.

Without knowing or understanding why, or even realizing what I was doing, I spent most of the next two decades unsuccessfully trying to duplicate that best ever drink, the pursuit of the perfect buzz.

## Predisposition

If there was a day when my substance use disorder was born, it was that day, but why? What exactly made me into dry tinder waiting to be sparked that day by that perfect alcohol buzz?

Someone who drinks at age 15 or younger has a 50 percent chance of developing alcohol use disorder; the odds are 10 percent for someone who starts at age 21 or older.[1]

Circumstances in my early life likely created a predisposition to my alcohol and substance addictions. Based on my three decades of recovery-related work, it seems likely that my brain was conditioned by the effects of negative events to use alcohol to self-soothe.

I don't blame my deceased parents. I have tremendous gratitude for the many gifts and blessings they gave to me. They got so much right. I understand their circumstances, their stressors, their tough decisions... along with the realities of their influences and environment, and the times they lived in. For a long time, I could not accept my therapist's assessment that my early life was laden with "horrific" trauma. What? No! How could that be?

I had parents but markedly lacked parenting.

My parents separated twice—first when I was five, and again over many months when I was between ages eight and nine. When I was five, one day I woke from a nap after a terrible bad dream. I'd dreamt that my father was leaving. In her attempt to comfort me, my mother somehow decided that was the right moment to tell me that my father was, in fact, leaving.

My father became the once-a-week divorced dad; he'd already been emotionally distant, the likely result of his own childhood ordeal. I most likely never resolved the five-year-old's false perception that my father's departure was all about me.

My mother, meanwhile, struggled across the board. My father left her twice, and the stigma of divorce was more significant in the late 1960s than it is now. She also lived with the weight of her new single-parent responsibilities and intense financial insecurity. She developed a drinking habit that would eventually end her life.

In the kitchen, there would typically be a tumbler glass of gin or cheap Scotch placed discreetly behind some implement, or on the low shelves of the cupboards. Hidden, but not well, and even more poorly later in the day. Sometimes, I'd see it first thing in the morning.

I developed a peculiar sensitivity, like a form of radar, to my mother's intoxication. I could tell from the tone and timbre of her voice if she was intoxicated; this was particularly anxiety-inducing when I needed a ride somewhere.

I was just trying to be a kid. Mom and I had battles too numerous to recall. Sometimes I would get so frustrated I would just leave the house. Then she would call the cops to round me up.

I couldn't escape the feelings, a helpless frustration—powerlessness as I understand it today. Nor could I make them stop. To endure these things, I would shut down and detach, checking out emotionally, resulting in a flat affect, the absence of expression or emotion.

The brain regulates emotion neurochemically. Over time, this could favor negative emotion and pain over pleasure and well-being. The result was a downward recalibration of certain neurotransmitters, given time and reinforcement, depressing brain chemicals like dopamine and serotonin.

Checking out emotionally raises the threshold of discomfort tolerance by lowering the baseline of the happiness/pleasure chemicals. That's why the artificial boost of using alcohol or other substances feels amazing. The dry tinder ignited, and I spent the next decades of my life trying to reproduce that warm hug.

## Being Cool

Growing up, I wanted to be athletic, popular, and smart. In reality, I couldn't hit a baseball, dribble a basketball, or catch a football. I was shy and socially awkward, not to mention average in school. I saw a serious gap between the way I was and the way I wanted to be. Thus, I sought to reinvent myself as a cool dude. This was largely about the perception of my peer group and others.

I was fascinated with drums and drumming. I blame it on Ringo, the underrated Beatle, who gained so much attention while seemingly having so much fun. I wanted that.

My elementary school had a robust music program, and I took drum lessons in fourth grade. The payoff for this was a little starter drum set—orange sparkle, small, and well used—and set up in my bedroom. I do not know how my mother and sisters tolerated the noise. The volume level increased when I discovered I could play along with records, jamming for hours every day with the Beatles, Stones, and Jimi Hendrix. As a fringe benefit, beating those drums was good for venting frustration.

I absorbed every bit of musical knowledge. My goal was to play in rock bands, but I understood the path to that was through studying, practice, and other musical experiences. I was invited to perform with various school performing groups as well as a community orchestra.

Sometime during middle school, I became obsessed with the idea of image and persona. I desperately wanted to be cool, to be the cool kid. At its core, this was a statement that the real me was not okay and required fixing. Like a cry for attention, a pretentious one at that, I adopted this affectation until I sold it to myself.

Somewhere about the time of my best drink ever I discovered the game room at the local bowling alley. The bowling alley was across from the town park, next to the Community House, and within sight of the town library and police station. This community landmark led a double life. The candle pin, small ball, bowling lanes were wholesome, family recreation at its finest. The game room off the entryway, with its pool table, pinball machines, and riffraff occupants was anything but. The game room's denizens were older kids, some who did not complete high school. While I did not aspire to follow their example to the dead end, this seemed like the place where an aspiring cool kid should hang out. I could make a few quarters and a couple of Winstons lifted from Mom into an evening out.

With a few more dollars, I could often find someone of drinking age to procure beer, which we drank clandestinely inside the game room. The going rate for a joint was one dollar. When we found someone who would sell one, we would go out around the side along the railroad tracks to get high.

Deep down, I knew that the business of real life wasn't about getting drunk and high all the time, but at the time I was fixated on my cool kid shtick, informed partly by Cheech & Chong. I got a hold of *Big Bambú*, their 1972 iconic comedy album, which was designed to resemble an oversized pack of Bambú rolling papers, and even famously included one that was giant and functional.

Completing the persona was the look: long hair, snug-fitting pants, tops that strategically minimized my chubbiness, and wireframe glasses.

If nothing else, I dared to be different.

One episode that illustrates this involved vodka, bad judgment, and a school dance. I thought it was a well-crafted plan to eat dinner, pound down 10 to 12 ounces of Smirnoff, then head to the dance. I was later told that I was dancing by myself, having a great time—until I wasn't. A couple of my buddies became concerned; it wasn't too hard for them to predict my future. I was passed out as they took me into the men's room, and I began vomiting spectacularly. The chaperones descended. I was told there was legitimate concern for my well-being, but I was pumping my own stomach quite effectively. My mother was called, and one of the chaperones carried me to my bed.

I woke up in the middle of the night. As I slowly realized what had occurred, my mental and emotional state soon aligned with the wretched way my body felt. I was mostly scared of the consequences and what would happen when I returned to school. I languished through the weekend while the weight of my actions continued to sink in. Prepared for suspension on Monday morning in the office of the school principal, I received only a serious talking to and banishment from all dances to follow that year. I was dismissed and sent to homeroom. As I entered through the door at the front of the room, the silence was deafening. Those who hadn't observed my debacle on Friday night had surely heard about it. My cool kid act had taken a decidedly bad-boy turn.

Experiences such as the vodka vomiting rampage and others served to define me in the perception of others. Later introspection revealed I was keenly aware of this and went with it in a kind of total commitment. I was all in with the phony persona. It wasn't the kind of attention I really wanted, but it was attention. At a high school reunion, a one-time childhood acquaintance told me, "Like you or hate you, everyone wanted to be you." I never realized any such thing back in the day.

For years I lived with my choices, felt the stigma, and tried to drink it away.

## The Quest for the Ultimate Note

My drumming abilities were steadily improving. My first year in high school, on a school night, I could be found jamming in some area bar with older musicians and being paid in drinks. By the end of that year, I played my first professional gig. The name of the band was Stolen Silver, lifted from an episode of the TV series *Kung Fu.* Despite months of rehearsal, we had to repeat a couple of songs to make the three hours. I don't think there was time for a sound check, and there was lots of that deafening feedback. We played old Top 40 songs like The Stones, Jimi Hendrix, and David Bowie. We made a hundred dollars, though that also had to cover the U-Haul trailer and gas money.

Steady gigs followed through sophomore and junior year, and I traded up through a succession of local bands, each one more accomplished than the previous. The partying was also becoming progressively more intense.

By the second half of my junior year, I was drumming in a band of twentysomethings called Wood Sorrel, playing at area schools and clubs. This band was distinguished by virtue of playing 10 Led Zeppelin covers. We drank and got high at practice, and I was dating the gorgeous 21-year-old sister of the rhythm guitarist. I was 17.

Eventually Wood Sorrel broke up over the usual nonsense—egos, girlfriends, and musical preferences. This freed me to actually work on becoming a better musician. I had set my sights on Berklee College of Music. I transferred to a new school that offered different music courses and returned to lessons after a few years away. In the new school, I found a small but dedicated group of jazz players who broadened my horizons. The music department offered a jazz improvisation credit elective that had immense vocational value.

My time at Berklee was highly influential and valuable but hampered by my substance use. My ability to absorb valuable information in courses such as listening/analysis, harmony and arranging was significantly compromised. I was too immature and shortsighted to understand the opportunity going there presented, and my time there was squandered. I had no support, felt overwhelmed, and drank every night when I should have been studying.

The following summer, I had an opportunity to play with a traveling show band, touring the northeast US and the Caribbean. The restraints were off, or so I thought. All I had to do was be alert and professional for four hours a night, yet I was immature and unable to grasp the basic reality of adult responsibility. I thought the extra sink in the hotel rooms was to ice beer. I was fired in four months.

Next, I drank myself out of my first opportunity to play in a cool original band that also did TV soundtracking. My perception of these playing situations was somehow rooted in a belief that excessive alcohol use was acceptable. Twenty-year-old me did not realize that I was no longer in high school and had much growing up to do. I could have made so much of these opportunities and grown as a musician and person. People tried to talk sense into me to no avail due to my substance use, which was completely married to my music.

I think this is a notion common to some who are artistically inclined—that altering consciousness improves the work. I loved music and I loved playing the drums. I loved the experience of creating music with other musicians. In terms of being in the moment, few things surpass musical improvisation. Substance use affected this in two ways. Not only were my creativity and my playing influenced but also my perception of the quality of my performance was altered. Sadly, my quest for the ultimate note had involved being drunk or high from the start.

One night on stage with the show band playing in Curaçao, I had an experience that was as close as I ever came to the ultimate note. It came during the climax of a song that was the climax of the set. All seven band members were wailing away, and the energy had built to a level of intensity that felt different, just more, much more, than usual. This was not about the song so much as my perception of the passion in the moment. While I was physically there, playing and interacting with the other musicians and the audience, I felt swept up into something elemental that was beyond physical reality. The sensation I experienced was like an orgasm from the neck up. The Kundalini experience described in yoga culture sounds remarkably similar. It was amazing. It left me questioning what had happened but also wondering how to make it happen again.

I tried to repeat that peak experience for the rest of my musical career, convinced that substance use was key. That thing that was so in the moment did not repeat, but my music's marriage to substance use cemented. The quest for the ultimate note and the pursuit of the perfect buzz fused. While it elevated the quest for the perfect buzz, it rendered my experience of music into a lesser version, effectively corrupting the part of me that held such creative promise.

## Addiction

The feeling of the warm hug was long gone.

At the end of my active substance use, I could not go a day without drinking. I smoked weed every day as well as about half a pack of Marlboros. When an opportunity to use other drugs came my way, I never declined. Cocaine and hallucinogens made the short list, along with various stimulants. The goal of becoming unconscious became the unconscious goal. I have described that time frame as a cycle of a pleasure center-driven obsession with the acquisition and use of mind-altering substances leading to a fleeting instant of euphoria, then oblivion—followed by a sense of profound loss, emptiness, and lack that would drive me right back to the beginning of the cycle in ceaseless repetition. My life was a grotesque nightmarish version of *Groundhog Day*. Every day, the car seemed to drive itself to the same little family-owned liquor store after work where I bought the same bottle of vodka, which I opened moments after driving away.

The physical effects of daily substance use slowly but markedly insinuated themselves. I was working as a surgical tech in the operating room of a major Boston medical center when I was only 23. There had been some mishap, a needlestick, and I needed to be seen by employee health. A routine check of my vital signs showed alarmingly high blood pressure. "This is very high. Are you on medication for this? You need to see your primary care doctor if you're not," said the attending doctor. I did not have a primary care doctor. I was there getting the third degree instead of catching my train home, and all I could think about was how I needed to get the fuck out of there and get a drink.

Through my 20s, my health was poor. I had the overactive gag reflex and cranky digestive system that accompanies regular heavy drinking. My body was no longer recovering as well in the mornings.

My relationships suffered.

Mary was a nurse I'd met while I was going to surgical tech school. She was five years older. She was smart and fun and supported my goal of getting into healthcare as well as my musical endeavors. She enjoyed a beer after work and seemed to tolerate my drinking, although she was not aware of much of it. We were together five years through my mid-20s. Eventually I left the relationship because it limited my drinking and partying.

Patricia and I were introduced by people I'd gone to school and grown up with. We eventually moved in together and had a loose engagement, having impulsively agreed in the midst of a drunken weekend that we would marry. She was smart, assertive, and liked Scotch.

The natural evolution of both those relationships could have easily been marriage, family, and the pursuit of happiness. Neither one of these beautiful, healthy women fully realized that they were in open or triangular relationships. Alcohol was the other partner, and that's where my real fidelity lay.

In my mind, my primary vocation was music, but this required a supporting source of livelihood, the proverbial day job. I needed to pay the rent. I had entered a program and trained to become a surgical technologist. After a year working at the major medical center, I secured a position in a community hospital and moved nearby. My Monday-through-Friday responsibilities were setting up and participating in routine surgeries. Additionally, this required me to be on call, available to respond to urgently scheduled surgery in response to emergencies.

The entire proposition of this day job had elements of responsibility and respectability that were foreign to me.

As I settled into the surgical tech role, I began pushing the boundaries of working after hours while intoxicated. Those boundaries were stretched to their limit one night when I was called in for an emergency caesarean section in the obstetrics department. Rudely yanked out of the trancelike state that masquerades as sleep when I'd been drinking, I attended to my duties of setting up for the procedure. I brought the Mayo stand, a sterile instrument tray on rollers, to the surgical field. Unfortunately, the stand was not what I was accustomed to, and it spun and toppled as I moved it. This was a total showstopper, necessitating new sterile instruments, which needed to be counted. Ugh. The surgeon, a true gentleman, commented, "Okay then, we'll have to wait for Keith to pick up the tools." †

A dark haze descended. There was an inescapable, big-picture feeling that I had irrevocably mishandled the cards I was dealt. I felt like I had screwed up my educational experiences and job prospects. Not only did I feel like I had done things wrong but also that there was no way back. Everything felt like quicksand; the more I struggled, the deeper I sank. And there was the central question—was it all due to drinking?

In AA parlance, this is referred to as the gift of desperation. Having experienced this so poignantly and personally, I understand what others are experiencing as they come up against their personal limitations. For me, it wasn't an ordeal; it was a gift.

As my 20s wound down, no longer sure whether I was a musician or a surgical technician, I knew I was a drinker. My quest for the ultimate note started with that one best drink ever, but that drink had strings attached. There followed many thousands of decidedly not best drinks ever over the next two decades. I thought I was playing percussion in some grand cosmic orchestra. In reality, like Don Quixote

† As a little addendum to the anecdote about the dropped surgical instruments... I crossed paths with the surgeon years later. He was indeed a gentleman and had served the women and families of the community for years as a dedicated OB/GYN practitioner. About 20 years later, I was again working in a major medical center operating room, but this time as a registered nurse and 15 years in recovery. One afternoon, as I went to the preop area to check on my next patient, I found there the surgeon and his wife, who was the patient. We immediately recognized each other. However, the roles were different, and so was I. I was now a man in sobriety who had advanced his career and grown up, and no longer the instrument-dropping tech who showed up buzzed for emergency surgery. I was able to atone for the past by rendering compassionate and competent care. Maybe it was just me, and nothing was said directly, but it felt like a circle had been completed.

chasing windmills, I was half a beat behind and unable to sense the tempo of my reality. The bitter end of my drinking had me pacing the floor, thinking about ending my life, but first I needed to reach my breaking point. My pursuit of the perfect buzz was taking me to my rock bottom.

# Chapter 2
# My Story: Rock Bottom

"Thank God the elevator's broken."
~ Stevie Ray Vaughan

## Spiraling

One Saturday afternoon in late April 1990, Patricia answered the phone. "Hey, some doctor wants to talk to you."

This was strange, because I wasn't on call. The doctor introduced himself and told me my mother was in grave condition. Her time was short, he said, insistently encouraging me to inform my sisters.

My mother had been on a mission since her divorce nearly 20 years prior. She had basically set out to drink herself to death, planning to accomplish this when my youngest sister came of age. She had openly verbalized this at various times. During my early 20s, I'd lost patience with her drama and detached. We went a couple of years without speaking; Mom's drinking was like a mirror for my own, showing me what I swore I wouldn't become.

I felt slammed, overwhelmed. My relationship with Patricia had become more serious, and, with that as motivation, I took the initiative to mend things with my mother. While I hadn't become a doting son by any stretch, I had been in touch a few weeks prior, and she seemed fine. This call came out of nowhere.

Although somewhat intoxicated, I made it to her bedside within an hour.

Though no stranger to gravely ill people because of my job working in surgery, I was still completely unprepared for my mother's condition when I arrived. My mother bore scant resemblance to the version of her I had last seen. She was emaciated. She was void of normal color; there was a grayish quality with a hint of liver-problem yellow. She was semiconscious. I don't know if she knew I was there.

My mother had some serious alcohol-related health issues in the past. I'd ridden the roller coaster of preparing for the worst before, hence my hesitancy to climb aboard again without personally assessing the situation. Caught completely off guard with this, I considered the ramifications. Rather than contact my sisters, I really just wanted to drink. It felt like my mother's drama was once again bulldozing over my life.

I had a dilemma. This was not as simple as just following the doctor's direction that I make the rest of my family aware of my mother's condition. My youngest sister was in the middle of her senior year of college finals. The other was vacationing on a Caribbean island, emotional recovery from a miscarriage a few months prior. The experiences of the past wore heavily on me, and I wanted to avoid alarming my sisters unnecessarily. I was frozen with anxiety.

Drinking on it the rest of the weekend, I had a moment of clarity on Monday, sobering up for work. I spoke with my manager (tearfully) and returned to the hospital. I needed to see my mother and her condition one more time. She had continued to decline, and I accepted that her time was short.

I contacted my sisters. I supported my youngest sister's decision to stay at college and complete her examinations. There was nothing she could do, after all, and she and Mom had recently spent quality time together. My sister in the Caribbean was more challenging to reach—all I knew was the name of the island. I started by dialing zero (literally dialing, that's how it worked then), starting with a local operator connecting me to an island operator who connected me to a hotel where I left an urgent message. After we spoke, my sister and her husband were just able to book passage on the once-daily puddle jumper to the main airport and flew home the following day. She made it to the hospital at 7:30. My mother passed minutes later.

Somehow, I had made the right decisions in the right time frame, although nothing felt right. That the rudimentary problem-solving of connecting with my sister in the Caribbean felt like a Herculean task speaks to how compromised I was. I was absolutely dysfunctional.

The decision to inform my sisters was emotionally charged, but it was overwhelming to me only because I was so self-absorbed.

My mother's death was caused by drinking. Cancer that started in her liver metastasized to her lungs and brain. Her death triggered the final spiral of my drinking. Aside from the loss of a parent, there was subconscious existential terror that alcohol would do the same to me. I did not envision life in my 30s… and I was 30.

My mother had wished to be cremated. Meetings with the attorney who was executor of her estate and subsequently the funeral director were an alcohol-distorted blur. I do remember sorting her belongings at her small apartment and chugging vodka as I pulled out of the parking lot. My sisters, a family friend, and I spread her ashes at a forest reservation next to our childhood home with awkward ceremony. I recall this happened within a day or two of Mother's Day. That's when everything started to unravel.

Perhaps most impacted was my music. The consensus was summed up by a bandmate when he came to my house to fire me in person: "Good drummer, bad drinker." This was about my personality much more than my playing. Argumentative would be an understatement; I didn't know how to take no for an answer. In the collaborative, give-and-take of ideas that form the basis of most musical endeavors, this was the equivalent of pointing, aiming, and shooting myself in the foot. In fact, I was fired two times in the same week.

The first firing had been building. A few weeks after Mom passed, the proverbial camel's back was broken. I charged at the soundman over his perceived incompetence after the final night of a three-night stand at the prestigious Beach Club. Whether he was screwing around with the volume level of my bass drum to intentionally mess with me was moot due to my level of intoxication and uncivilized reaction.

The second dismissal came in the form of a phone call. The leader of Blind Owl, the original music band I'd been affiliated with for the last year, let me know they'd no longer be focusing on live performances. In other words, they were going in a different direction, and it didn't include a drummer who couldn't get through a rehearsal without a trip to his van for a few swigs of vodka.

Band rehearsals and performances had structured my time. Drinking took its place. I became more depressed.

At work, my manager pulled me aside. She said there was concern that I smelled like alcohol, particularly when called in at night. This was warranted. She was visibly uncomfortable with the conversation. No action was taken, as if the message was to simply get breath mints.

I continued downhill. One morning, a police officer observed me swerve out of my lane. Because the officer was coming from the other direction, however, I had a chance to throw out the open beer can between my legs. Probably because it was morning, he didn't question my sobriety and only wrote me a ticket. About a week later, I had a car accident while drunk, swerving and hitting a parked car at a curving intersection. Miraculously, I avoided arrest for driving while intoxicated. I knew I had caught some breaks, but the big picture was lost on me.

My relationship with Patricia would be next.

Patricia came from a family of drinkers, including her father, her stepfather, and her brother. However, as my issues became her issues, she consciously stopped facilitating. I soon found myself sitting in the office of a psychologist for the purpose of sorting out our issues as a couple. I was none too keen on being told that our problems centered on my drinking.

The picture I'm painting here, these examples are the classic areas where substance use blows up people's lives. Relationships, livelihood, legal issues, social interactions, and, as previously mentioned, health are typically made worse, damaged, or even destroyed by addiction. This was how my life circled the drain; now I recognize the signs when I see them. I was a live-action example of substance use despite negative consequences—a diagnostic criteria. I saw my drinking as substance use when it met the definition of substance use disorder. We want to think that we're just people who enjoy drinking or using substances; the reality is that we are living with addiction.

By summer's end, I was losing my grip. My anxiety was so intense that it took a tremendous act of will to get out of the car and go into work in the morning. I'd been seeing a counselor for most of the summer. About mid-September, I had an emotional meltdown and could no longer function. I left work because I was incapable of the necessary focus. I was constantly on the verge of tears with no idea exactly why. The therapist suggested a local psychiatric facility, and I went in on a Monday evening. I was admitted to a brief treatment unit. Although they offered a 28-day addiction treatment program, I wanted no part of that. In my mind, I was there because I had other issues. I just needed some help solving my problems... and in subconscious parentheses—so I could resume *normal* drinking. I wanted crisis intervention, not a life of sobriety. They were offering me serious treatment. Because I wasn't ready to handle the diagnosis, I opted instead for a Band-Aid.

Somewhere in this process, a seed was planted. It began with the admission assessment, with its many questions regarding use of alcohol and substances. There was a counselor who sent me to AA meetings and kept trying to shove a Big Book (the primary text of Alcoholics Anonymous) in my hand. The subject of alcohol was constantly thrust upon my attention. I was there for depression, not for my alcohol consumption. The thought that I had a problem like that was, well, depressing. In reality, I wasn't yet able to face my alcohol use disorder, because I still denied its existence. I clung tenaciously to the idea that I could drink socially, casually, normally.

I attended my first AA meeting on-site. The details are blurry, and other than hearing people talk about losing their driver's licenses, nothing stood out. My defenses were up, my skepticism set to 11 on a 10 dial and nothing stuck.

During the course of the week I spent in the hospital, I was able to acknowledge that my drinking was out of my control. My feelings of depression and inability to cope with life had overwhelmed me. Therefore, I clung to the notion that I drank too much as a result of my problems and rationalized that I could manage drinking. I thought this would require ongoing support, so I decided to attend AA meetings, believing I could gain insight that would allow me to control my drinking. On discharge, I began what I look back on as an orientation period.

## Orientation

I attended AA meetings and stayed sober for close to two weeks… until I drank. It was neither planned nor unplanned. Patricia and I attended a concert. I went to get her a drink, ordered it, and it was as though someone else had said, "And a Heineken, please."

This single beer, consumed at a concert, did not cause the planet to go off its axis. So began my personal experiment with controlled drinking.

A day or two later, as I thought about the results of that first experiment, I remembered that an important part of any experiment includes duplicating the results. I set about "controlling" a six-pack. Fast-forward to a couple of days later, and an open bottle of vodka was once again under the seat of the car. This had been accomplished in a matter of days and started with a single beer. The experiment in controlled drinking was a spectacular failure.

At some level, I knew I was in trouble and at risk of getting back to the ugly place that had put me in the hospital for a week. I desperately wanted to drink normally, but once I started, I couldn't seem to stop.

In hopes of controlling my drinking and keeping my life from going off kilter again, I attended more AA meetings. There must be some wisdom, I believed, some secret knowledge about alcohol that I could analyze and abstract for my own purposes. In Alcoholics Anonymous, I hoped to find the secret to dialing back my drinking to manageable levels. Uncomfortable with going to meetings in my hometown, I went to nearby communities. One day I might go to a meeting, the next I might drink. Some days I drank and went to meetings. On weekends, I tended to drink. Over time, the drinking became heavier. I was not finding any secret to catching that perfect buzz without overdoing it.

One evening, as I went up to get coffee before the meeting, the guy in front of me in line turned around and said hello. This was one of those classic awkward moments; he looked familiar, and I felt panic as I struggled to place him. He was someone from another compartment of my life, and his presence in my secret AA thing sent a wave of horrible anxiety through me. Then I figured it out. He was Michael, the hospital's director of human resources. This was tremendously unsettling, and exactly why I didn't go to meetings in my hometown. Worsening matters, I was drunk. The whole thing was starting to feel like a sham. It was.

This situation would later come to a head, but for now, as 1990 moved into its final months, drinking no longer felt right. At the same time, the idea of being sober felt completely foreign. I couldn't drink, and I couldn't not drink.

The problem was that I saw something in the Alcoholics Anonymous meetings. In the words and ideas of the people I encountered at the meetings, there seemed to be something that I couldn't quite grasp. It was as if they had insight into some aspect of life about which I was clueless. Witnessing people with this level of wholeness that was decidedly lacking in my life made me feel as though I'd been absent the day the human being owner's manuals were given out. I'd always felt that way, it was just more obvious now. Here were people who talked about getting along with one another, handling life's problems, and just being happy in general. I wanted this something that I saw but could not yet grasp that if I wanted what they had, I needed to do what they did.

On a Saturday afternoon between Christmas and New Year's, I decided to build a snowman. Sculpting out the snowman's features, I jammed the long finger of my right hand, snapping off the tendon on the back of the finger that enables it to straighten. While not even painful, this seemingly minor injury affected not just my drumming but also my job.

I was able to have my finger seen by a hand surgeon the following Monday at work. Operating room work had certain perks. He needed no X-rays to know what was wrong and explained that the finger needed to remain straight for weeks. The best way of ensuring success was by inserting a pin through the bones to prevent bending.

Forced to take off work for 10 days, I spent most of that time in a drunken stupor. In the face of even this minor adversity, I had no capacity for resisting the urge to drink to oblivion. All bets were off. I would drink the way I really wanted to while injured and out of work and sort things out later.

One day blurred into the next. I sat around, drank, and wasted the hours away. My days consisted of early trips out to get vodka and perhaps a rental movie. I scheduled doctor's office visits for early in the day, so as not to interfere much with the day's drinking. Patricia didn't say much about my state, although she had to be noticing that I was semicomatose when she came home from work.

I had worrisome thoughts about the effects of my finger's injury on drumming and, looming larger, the issue of my drinking. I knew that this binge was merely postponing the inevitable. This *alcoholic* monster I'd been wrestling with for three months was only asleep. It hadn't gone away.

A second visit to the doctor cleared me to return to work, and my anxiety mounted. On the day before my scheduled return, I went to an AA meeting, the one a couple of towns away. I was barely able to drive. I remember finding no solace there, no relief from the gnawing feeling that my life was hopelessly screwed up. When I got home, I drank again—the last of the vodka in the basement. Rather than falling asleep, I passed out.

I overslept the next morning. Reporting to work after a 10-day absence, I looked like something a cat coughed up. Much worse than merely being hung over, I was still intoxicated.

Horrified after seeing my compromised condition, my manager had some strong words. In the midst of her usual morning managerial chaos, she now had to cope with an impaired worker in her operating room. She told me to stay out of the way, and we would be talking. This was real trouble.

I panicked. I went to the relative refuge of the changing room and contemplated where I stood. My mind quickly raced from immediate concerns through short-term consequences to the bigger picture. I was a pitiful, helpless drunk. I was powerless over alcohol. The last 10 days were proof that my life was unmanageable.

I changed into my street clothes and snuck out the back door.

I was despondent and overwhelmed. I drove home and had an anxiety attack. I paced the floor. I felt as if my life was over.

I felt massive guilt about my actions and choices. The self-loathing ran deeper than my behavior. This rock bottom was defined by despising what I had become, my identity. This was true shame. Hating what I was felt somehow worse than hating what I did.

Denial and rationalization are the layers of protection we wrap ourselves with. This is unconscious, a bad coping skill that buffers us from guilt and shame. Unfortunately, there was no current-day version of myself present to explain that I had a chronic medical condition that affected my behavior and ability to make decisions. While we need not wait for crisis to take action, most of us keep going until our lives are blown up. Sometimes it's just a matter of timing and the right support presenting when the crack in the walls of addiction forms.

I stepped fully into the darkness for a few minutes. I felt irrevocably fucked, no hope. Because I've been to that dark place and made it back out, I can understand what others are experiencing.

The weight of the consequences of my choices and actions crashed down on me. I could not go on as I had been. My whole way of life no longer worked; it hadn't in a long time. I couldn't continue living as I had been living, and as I paced the floor, I thought about ending my life. This scared me so much that I called Samaritans, the suicide hotline, and spoke with someone for a long time. I did not want to live as I had been, but I did not want to die either. A realization came to me. I had overwhelming problems. I had desperately clung to the idea that I drank as a result of these troubles. The truth was not that I drank over my problems; I had problems because I drank. This realization, so simple yet so profound, represented the moving of a mountain in my way of looking at my life.

The easiest thing in the moment would have been to drink. The hardest thing to do was reach out and ask for help. I called the hospital and asked for the human resources department. Holding the 800-pound receiver, I waited for the man from the AA meeting coffee line to pick up the call.

Unsurprisingly, he was well aware of my brief appearance at work earlier that morning. Michael's routine duty as human resources director was to be aware of the unroutine, and I had not merely broken, but fully trampled the hospital code of conduct.

My call to another AA, who also happened to be a human resources director, simultaneously solved and created problems. There had been concern for me, in addition to concern about me. Michael was addressing the hospital's problem by being in contact with me; he knew I was home and safe. That I'd had a personal crisis and reached the point of surrender to my alcohol problem presented a complicated dilemma. He was pulled in two directions. On one hand, he was ethically duty bound to serve the interests of the hospital. He wanted the other hand to be that of AA, extended to a suffering person who needed and sincerely wanted help. Whether he could do both was clearly up to me.

Sincere I was. I had come to a powerful realization about my drinking and my life in my most desperate moment. All the bits and pieces of information I'd heard at meetings had filtered into my awareness, as if by osmosis, crystalizing into vivid understanding: I am an *alcoholic*. In that moment, I had taken the first step. I am powerless over alcohol. I made a decision with an intensity and level of energy and conviction that was as powerful as any thought I've ever had. For the first time, I truly decided to stop drinking.

Michael agreed to be my temporary sponsor. He made it clear that he would not compromise his principles or his job; my fate was absolutely in my hands. He told me to not drink and to go to a meeting that night.

I didn't drink and I went to two meetings.

While this orientation period was an experience in abject misery at the time, it yielded valuable lessons. I came to understand how that first drink had set me back in motion; I came to understand the benefits of supports, and that cravings and my drinking habit of years were more powerful than my resolve, as evidenced by drinking against my own will.

When I was able to integrate my feelings with my experiences and circumstances, it was like a switch flipped, and I realized I had everything backward. The realization that I wasn't a man who drank because he had problems, but instead I was a man who had problems because he drank, was game-changing. Simple, yet so powerful. My slow, painful journey toward readiness and the recovery that followed are typical of what I observe many experiencing as they face their own substance use.

At rock bottom comes a turning point. The elevator ride down was over. I'd be taking the steps back up.

# Chapter 3
# The Problem with Addiction

"The greatest cruelty is our casual blindness
to the despair of others."
~ Unknown

Addiction is a lot like sex. Am I right?

Sex is something you must experience to fully comprehend. You can hear about it, read about it, talk about it, even watch it, but until you experience it for yourself, you won't understand what all the fuss is about.

Addiction is the same way. For someone who has not experienced it for themselves, understanding addiction is nearly impossible.

Referring to addiction as a problem is trite.

"According to the 2022 National Survey on Drug Use and Health, 48.7 million people (or 17.3 percent) aged 12 or older had a past-year substance use disorder." [2]

Meanwhile, more than 93 percent of Americans who need treatment for substance use do not receive it.[3]

"More than 106,000 persons in the US died from drug-involved overdose in 2021, including illicit drugs and prescription opioids." [4]

"The Alcohol-Related Disease Impact application estimates that each year there are more than 178,000 deaths (approximately 120,000 male deaths and 59,000 female deaths) attributable to excessive alcohol use." [5]

The addiction problem has been a constant for decades, but has markedly intensified through the 2010s. Driven by the trend in the illicit drug trade toward using fentanyl, first as an additive, then as the primary product, the spike in unintentional opioid overdoses garnered attention and became known as the opioid crisis. Smuggling heroin across borders literally became obsolete when drug cartels realized they could manufacture the significantly more concentrated fentanyl anywhere—and from chemical components they could easily import, often legally. The issues are twofold. Demand for and addiction to opioids of all types have gone up steadily since the late 1990s/early 2000s. Meeting that demand is a supply that is dangerously unpredictable in terms of potency and lethality. Many of the victims of this opioid crisis were young people across the socioeconomic spectrum, cut down in their prime, or worse—before their prime—as though by an insidious and invisible grim reaper. As America's sons and daughters died in numbers much too great to ignore, the attention of the nation was captured in jarring fashion.

The case I'm making here, supported by the numbers shown previously, is that the opioid phenomenon is part of a larger overall problem. As horrible as it is, the opioid crisis is a symptom of the addiction problem. It's a highly significant part, but it is just that, a part of this issue. Just as significant, even more so in terms of fatality numbers, is alcohol use disorder. Legal, widely available, and socially acceptable, alcohol is every bit as much a drug of abuse as opioids are. While the two could be likened to apples and oranges, they're both fruit. While these two substances have the starring roles in this tragedy, cannabis, cocaine, methamphetamine, and benzodiazepines, with a special guest appearance by tobacco, round out the supporting cast of addictive substances.

Opioids got everyone's attention, but addiction is much more than that. It makes perfect sense that things turned out as they did with fentanyl, but no one saw it coming. The word addiction comes from the Latin word addicere, which means *enslaved by* or *bound to*, and originally referred to alcohol dependence. While paying attention is a necessary first step, what really matters is what we do about it.

The addiction problem has many moving parts. Dedicated scientists are working diligently to gain better understanding. Medicine and healthcare are scrambling to put treatment systems in place. The detox and rehabilitation business is working hard to meet demand. The self-help movement continues to grow. The US Department of Homeland Security, the US Drug Enforcement Administration, and the US Border Patrol work to prevent drugs from entering the country, although

US Attorney's Offices and Border Patrol sources estimate that between 1 and 10 percent of drugs are actually prevented from crossing our borders.[6] The criminal justice system apprehends, prosecutes, and incarcerates thousands each year, but 80 percent of all incarcerated offenders use alcohol and drugs, with 50 percent clinically addicted.[7]

The collateral problems continue to intensify. The worsening plight of the unhoused has a two-way relationship; addiction is both a cause and a result. The same could be said for mental illness. Co-occurring disorders, a chronic persistent mental illness coupled with a harmful substance use, have become the rule rather than the exception. And what could be more confusing than medicine and healthcare classifying addiction as a disease while the criminal justice system holds the addicted responsible? The one constant has been stigma. Many people still believe addiction is a choice, but those dedicated scientists I mentioned have proven that it's not.

While the statistics should be enough for us to consider the addiction problem one of the most critical things we face, for some reason we're just not taking it that seriously. Try reframing it this way... What if a terrorist organization or a foreign power was doing to the children, families, and communities of this nation what addiction is doing? We would come together and declare war, bringing every necessary resource, both human and economic, to bear on the problem. Instead, we seem to be waiting for it to get better by itself.

In 2018, I wrote the following in my last book.

> "If something like the viral infection causing severe acute respiratory syndrome (SARS) came along and started killing a thousand people a week, what do you think would happen? The Office of the Surgeon General, the Centers for Disease Control and Prevention (CDC), and state, regional and local agencies would immediately mobilize, as would all required resources and expertise necessary to respond to the threat."

Then came the COVID pandemic. I didn't have a crystal ball and took no satisfaction in being right. Okay, maybe a little. The point is that too often we wait for crisis before we act. Sometimes we just fail to act. The building is burning and people are yelling "Fire," but we don't recognize the addiction problem as a threat to our way of life that we could be fixing.

The addiction problem is killing thousands weekly, impacting countless lives collaterally, and costing us billions annually. Somehow, people don't recognize substance use as a problem. Dynamic Gallup polling placed drugs 23rd on a list of noneconomic problems facing the US in November 2023; it wasn't on the list of noneconomic problems in February 2026.[8] Whether this collective national blind spot is the result of fear or old-fashioned shame, this is denial on a titanic scale.

### Recovery Nerd

I'm a recovery nerd. I subscribe to weekly and monthly newsletters from organizations like the National Institute on Drug Abuse, NIDA, and the Recovery Research Institute. I dive into the linked studies to track new trends in medicine and science. I haven't read fiction in years, preferring subjects like harm reduction, trauma, family therapy approaches, and new therapeutic approaches. I listen to podcasts on neuroscience and addiction/recovery, lead an online support community—Infinite Recovery Support and Discussion—with a thousand people from a dozen countries, and regularly connect with other recovery professionals, on and off social media.

Talking and learning about addiction, recovery, and the related medicine and science truly fascinates me. For this reason, I'm happy to be your personal recovery nerd. As someone who attempts to keep my finger on the proverbial pulse of the recovery world, I'm amazed at how fast things are changing now. A good friend, now retired from a long career training other recovery professionals, and with decades of personal abstinence-based recovery, summed it up by saying, "The recovery field is like watching a teenager in a growth spurt." It's a different world than it was just a few years ago.

Like a proportion of those who work in the treatment field, I am in recovery myself. Most would characterize my recovery as successful. It began in Alcoholics Anonymous, AA, and evolved from there to incorporate elements of science, psychology, and alternative healing. I've written about this in two previous books. Happy and content in my own life, I have long since shifted my focus to helping others who live the way I once did in active addiction. At this stage of my nursing career there are many areas and specialties I could engage in, but my heart's desire is to work in the substance use disorder treatment and recovery field.

My standard identification these days is that I am a person in long-term, abstinence-based recovery from substance use disorder. By standard identification, I refer to how I describe my recovery status in most settings. A notable exception is at some type of peer-support recovery meetings, such as AA, where self-identifying as an *alcoholic* remains the norm. Another exception would be in the context of a therapeutic relationship, where self-disclosure should only occur under special circumstances. I do tend to self-identify in a variety of situations where others might not, such as most job interviews and certain public forums. My rationale for outing myself is that I think people should know. I'm a registered nurse, productive citizen, and member of the community. I have rendered competent medical care and service to others in a variety of healthcare settings and being in recovery has made that possible. Every time I do that, I'm basically kicking stigma where it hurts.

Being a person in recovery can have challenges in the workplace. For example, working in the restaurant, bar, and hospitality industry, i.e., where people are engaging in recreational substance use (alcohol), might be *triggering*, recovery jargon for something that causes a craving or temptation to use. Being a person in recovery who works in the recovery field has both liabilities and assets, pros and cons. The most obvious upside is the empathy I bring, understanding firsthand what people are experiencing. The most obvious liability can also be the empathy... to survive and thrive, one must clearly define the gray area between working in the field of recovery and working on personal recovery. The other significant challenge, and equally double-edged, is the constant challenging of my own ideas caused by the aforementioned growth spurt in the field of recovery.

Being a recovery nerd comes with a price. Many things that I believed to be true for years are either no longer valid or were just wrong to begin with. The recovery world is turning. I cannot ignore things I have learned about and observed directly. I have the choice of admitting and confronting my bias or succumbing to what psychologists call cognitive dissonance—that is, the state of emotional discomfort created by the discrepancy between my beliefs and reality that is often accompanied by denial.

A lot of what I *knew* to be true 10 years ago is wrong.

### A New World

I'm a hybrid. My worlds collide at the intersection of personal recovery, initiated at least, in the AA traditional model (12 Step) and working in the science-based medical and behavioral health recovery model.

When I entered recovery over three decades ago, there weren't any other viable options; AA had a plan and I did not. AA is organic and folksy. It has elements of fundamentalism and encourages members to find their own belief system somewhere between agnosticism and religious spirituality. It has a body of knowledge based in practical experience of alcohol addiction and recovery. The core belief, based on that experience, is that recovery from alcohol dependence works best with complete abstinence. While the average AA member has little or no working relationship with the word abstinence—they don't think about it—their goal is complete sobriety as a fundamental value.

The medical/behavioral model, in most instances, now embraces many pathways to recovery and harm reduction. As the term implies, many pathways are approaches to recovery besides the pathway of rigid abstinence. Harm reduction focuses on the very, very gray areas and stages a person with substance use disorder passes through as they start to change. Support, establishing rapport and trust, and meeting people where they are define the approach of harm reduction.

These two approaches take starkly differing positions on both addiction and recovery. My exposure to new (to me) ideas and experiences working with people over the last decade slowly changed my mind. I found myself operating in those gray areas almost daily. My bias in favor of abstinence has slowly shifted to a neutral and mindful stance.

Calvin and Julie are a married couple I worked with. They are a success story, both of them stable in their opioid use disorder recoveries. To work their own recoveries, they scheduled their follow-up appointments on different days. They have a daughter who is a competitive cheerleader, and I would get updates on her squad's successes. Calvin and Julie are regular users of cannabis. "We always wait until the kids go to bed; we want to be good examples," said Calvin. "We know what some people say—that it will lead us back to opioids. We don't think so."

Julie said they rarely drink alcohol but had not formally decided to abstain. "The weed is just our end-of-the-day grownup thing that we do, sort of like a ritual. We do it as a couple. It helps us unwind and relax."

On the other end of the spectrum, Rob is a patient who began receiving Vivitrol injections when he was under stress during a divorce and felt his recovery was threatened. He has been sober since his early 20s. Rob has maintained complete abstinence from alcohol and other mind-altering substances for 17 years as of this writing.

"I've thought about it," he said. "A little weed or microdosing psilocybin might have benefits; it's hard to say." However, he continued, "I've always heard about it ending badly for people who try to do that. It's just simpler this way. For me, I think it would just be opening the floodgates. But I knew that the first drink would destroy me."

Real life is messy when working in the field of addictions. Philosophy and policies are nice and easy, often reducing things to neat, well-defined basics. Then a real person steps into your office, and all the clear, easy-to-define elements are out the window. The goal becomes supporting the highest interest of each individual. Are they stable in their opioid therapy but using cannabis? Drinking? A situation like that invites a conversation about whether the other substances might represent a threat to recovery versus being a random occurrence. Are they struggling with something, and if so, are they at risk for resuming use of the opioids? Open-ended questions to get the person thinking about their recovery goals benefit them more than projecting some external ideal of recovery onto them.

Each individual situation was unique to that person in a Suboxone program, to that week, etc. The cannabis situation was common, but the best practice of doing routine urine drug screens could reveal fentanyl or other opioids in patients' systems. The harm reduction approach to this is support. We've learned the hard way that a rigid or punitive approach fails, and when failure means someone gets kicked out of their program, their alternative is returning to street substances with all the risks that entails. Navigating these types of situations became my routine in my nursing work.

Jeannie, another office treatment patient, faced ongoing challenges with her nonabstinence approach. She took prescribed Suboxone and was stable in her recovery from opioids. She did continue drinking alcohol, however. This was evidenced by her routine urine drug screens; she was consistently positive for metabolites that indicated alcohol consumption in previous days, even up to a week prior. She had a history of being hospitalized for pancreatitis, a serious indicator of unhealthy alcohol use. One day at a routine appointment, I suspected she had been drinking prior to coming in. Because that was against a specific rule of the program, we had one of those difficult conversations like the one at the start of the book. Happily, and though that was a difficult day for her, she was able to move past that and stay in the program. "I guess alcohol just became a substitute for my other drugs. It's weird because it's legal and everything. I thought it would be okay."

In the meantime, my personal approach was abstinence. Sobriety, and abstaining from all mind-altering substances—except caffeine—was and is my way of life. This is not blind obedience to AA and its dictums. Believe me when I say I was never the poster boy. I was always the one asking pesky questions and testing the limits.

I am the poster boy in one significant way though. I am absolutely neutral about alcohol, substances, and other people's choices about alcohol and substances. This neutral attitude is akin to a Holy Grail in AA. This is my unique gift I guess, and I received it early in my recovery journey. I go where alcohol is served. If there is a lengthy wait for a table in a restaurant but seating is available at the bar, we sit at the bar. I meet people for drinks; it's a given that I will order club soda and lime. I serve alcoholic beverages to company in my home, which I go to a liquor or wine store to purchase. I can hold another person's glass and appreciate the nose on the wine they are sipping and hand it back. I find the occasional aroma of cannabis to be pleasant but can't stand cigarette smoke. I never experience temptation or craving. It also bears mentioning that I'm responsible for a fair number of controlled substances. I stopped thinking about it long ago but occasionally notice the consternation of others who do not understand how this can be. It is a level of recovery that I do not see widely attained by others.

I eventually realized that I brought some bias, completely unintentionally, into my work. This took the form of passing my thoughts through the filter of the harm reduction approach, then realizing that the correct clinical intervention differed from my personal instinct.

Hmmm. What's right for someone else isn't right for me. Interesting concept. Ethically, I had no problem with this, as I was able to clearly process the difference between the two layers, clinical and personal concepts. However, it raised some questions.

The language was the first thing I thought about. Recovery vernacular, the everyday language that we used to talk about ourselves, our addictions and our recoveries, was different from the way medical and clinical people spoke. In healthcare, awareness of stigma was driving a new form of politically correct language based in a person first, strength-based approach. Operating in both worlds, I saw that the gap between the way folks in recovery and their caregivers spoke was rapidly widening.

Also, looking back at my previous writings, I can see a progression as my language moved from more focus on alcohol use disorder, AUD, in my first book to the all-addiction focus of my second book. Articles and blog posts I wrote years ago are partial toward an abstinence-based recovery approach. Sometimes it was not subtle. I am waking up to the fact that my early recovery, with the foundation I worked hard to build, has strongly colored my disposition in ways that are both understated and obvious. I am fortunate to have a network of professional colleagues and trusted friends who appreciate me for the recovery nerd I am. We talk about these things. That's how I recognized it in the first place. We all need some kind of mirror, a way of grounding our thinking.

That more objective thought process, taking hold and building slowly over the last couple of years, became an itch that was increasingly more difficult to ignore. Writing this book is my way of scratching that itch. Recovery genuinely excites me, and I don't think a week goes by when I don't learn something that modifies, if even just slightly, my position and thought process. And there have been times when I realized that I was just wrong in my opinion or incorrect in my approach. We're constantly learning more about addiction and constantly applying that to recovery. The best thing we can strive for is remaining teachable during the growth spurt.

As the expression goes, *we need to fetch ourselves up*. My experience of bias toward abstinence, conscious and unconscious, certainly cannot be unique among recovery professionals, whether themselves in recovery or not. Also, the underlying basis of the treatment movement as a whole is skewed toward the abstinence perspective. Rather than continue a trend moving toward two distinct and separate categories of recovery, abstinence versus harm reduction, we should find accommodation for both perspectives in the interest of dealing with the addiction problem. We need to all get along.

Where my last book attempted to be a how-to guide based on my personal recovery and clinical experience, this is my humble effort at reporting new developments. It represents a commitment to set my bias aside and explore some areas and ideas that might be the fringe of recovery today but could be the mainstream of tomorrow. Unlike the tech world, where the focus on "the next big thing" means personal gain, the next big thing in the recovery field is about changing lives for the better. New ideas and innovation have been the basis of radical shifts in life as we know (or knew) it—the industrial age, the advent of electricity, radio, television, computing, and smartphones as examples. Solutions to the addiction *problem* might come from unexpected sources.

However, if we are going to solve, or even mitigate, the addiction problem, a logical first step might be a clear and honest admission that we have the problem, as well as acknowledging the bias we all bring. Next, we need to make a decision that we are going to do something about it. Hmmm, those actionable steps toward solving the addiction problem sound remarkably like the same actions an individual takes to solve their own addiction problem. Funny how that works. The next two chapters sketch a rough overview of treatment and illustrate how it misses the mark.

# Chapter 4
# Treatment

"The most difficult thing is the decision to act. The rest is merely tenacity. The fears are paper tigers. You can do anything you decide to do. You can act to change and control your life; and the procedure, the process is its own reward."

~ Amelia Earhart

My experience with treatment, described a little way back, was brief and generic. Detox, groups, AA meetings. My real bottom, my rock bottom, came a couple of months later. I wish I had known more about treatment options at the time. People often ask about treatment. What is it? What happens there? How does it work?

## History

Historically, society associated addiction with moral failing. The approach was often punishment or social ostracism for those living with substance use. During the Middle Ages and Renaissance periods, addiction was often viewed through a religious lens, and individuals who used alcohol or drugs were considered morally weak or possessed by evil spirits. Treatment often involved religious rituals, exorcisms, or punishment rather than medical intervention.

In 16th–17th century England, the drunkard's cloak was used to punish drunkenness, especially repeat offenders. This consisted of a wooden barrel with holes cut out for the head and arms and worn like a crude garment. The offender then had to walk around in public. This shaming and humiliation might have been deterrence for some, but nothing about this was therapeutic.

The 19th century saw the emergence of early medical and scientific understanding of addiction. However, this period also saw the rise of the temperance movement, which advocated for abstinence as a solution to alcohol-related problems.

In the early 20th century, problematic alcohol use was treated with mechanical manipulation, natural therapies (water, air, sunlight), and chemical and electroconvulsive therapies. Then there was involuntary sterilization, an outgrowth of the eugenics movement, to which more than 60,000 Americans were subjected in the first half of the 20th century. This was proposed as one solution to alcohol and narcotic addiction. In the 1920s, Harry H. Laughlin of the Eugenics Record Office identified "inebriates" among "socially inadequate" persons—also including the "feebleminded, insane, criminalistic, epileptic, blind, deaf, deformed, and dependent"—as targets for sterilization. [9]

*Alcoholism* was recognized as a national problem in the late 1800s and early 20th century. Individual states sought to implement taxes on alcohol and saloons for the purpose of establishing treatment institutions. These initiatives met staunch resistance. Either state hospitals or private sanitariums were the options for addiction treatment.

In the late 1940s, the administrators of the Division of Public Assistance of the Board of Welfare of the City of Minneapolis, Minnesota, recognized the relationship between alcohol use and welfare recipients. Heads of households who drank to excess often failed to provide for their families. They closed one family's case after 10 years when the husband sobered up and began supporting his family. The welfare department saw potential in this possibility and initiated a one-year experiment providing social services to other such families. The welfare board concluded that they could get people off welfare if they could help stop excessive alcohol use. This led to the creation of a dedicated facility for the treatment of *alcoholics*.

What followed was an early example of stigma and pushback against a recovery program. "City Buys Dormitory for Drunks," screamed a local newspaper; the neighbors were up in arms. A new residential treatment initiative, the first of its kind, was nevertheless launched.

According to addiction historian William White, Minneapolis enlisted a member of AA, Pat C., to run the program, which was called Pioneer House. Pat felt compelled to consult with AA's New York foundation, where he received encouragement directly from founder Bill Wilson. He would not function in the capacity of a member of Alcoholics Anonymous, but rather as a "social worker." With no real model to follow, they based the two-to-three-week residential treatment program on AA philosophy.

At the time, this was radical.

The Minnesota Model, as it came to be known, is possibly the most recognized and influential approach to addiction treatment and has had significant impact both within the United States and internationally. A farm called Hazelden and Wilmar State Hospital adapted similar approaches. By the early 1950s, the Minnesota Model was gaining recognition, and Hazelden in particular grew into a facility of renown. Word began to filter out across the country through professional conferences and alumni. Professionals came en masse to observe the techniques and receive training. Prior to this, addiction treatment was where a professional career went to die. No one wanted to treat substance use disorder, and this began to shift as a result of the Minnesota Model.

They defined *alcoholism* as an involuntary, chronic, and progressive disease that was not curable but could be arrested, which was also radical for the day. Treatment included physical, psychological, social, and spiritual dimensions. The treatment viewed alcohol and drug use as a problem of chemical dependency, and abstinence was the solution. The model utilized *alcoholism* counselors, themselves recovering, and encouraged to use self-disclosure for therapeutic discussion. The multidisciplinary team engaged clients in psychoeducation and orientation to AA's 12 Steps. The aftercare plan was for graduates to go to AA.[10]

In the early days, the Minnesota Model treatment was strictly post-detox. Clients had to arrive after completing detox in hospitals, state facilities, or the medical wards of jails. Detox prior to admission was required. By the 1960s, Hazelden and others began to recognize the importance of medically supervised withdrawal. Detox came to be seen as the first phase of treatment, along with a growth in nursing and physician involvement in treatment. By the late 1970s, Hazelden incorporated a structured medical detoxification unit as part of the admission process. As pharmacology advanced, withdrawal management progressed from hourly shots of whiskey, belladonna, and phenobarbital to benzodiazepines as the medical standard.

The Minnesota Model was the treatment I received in 1990 and remains essentially the treatment model in use today. Librium, the benzodiazepine I received 35 years ago during my detox, is still used. People with lived experience in abstinence-based recovery working in direct care and counseling roles faded out, then returned. Today's recovery coaches and peer specialists have assumed the former role of *alcoholism* counselors.

When I admitted myself to a treatment facility in 1990, I was in a contained situation with no alcohol or other substances available. I received medication to manage my withdrawal, psychoeducation to support my coping skills, and introduction to 12-Step peer recovery support in the form of AA meetings. My discharge plan consisted of an invitation to weekly Wednesday evening alumni support meetings and suggestion to attend AA on the outside.

Today, a typical treatment facility will provide the exact same treatment. In fact, the basis of our treatment system, psychoeducation and a not-so-warm handoff to the nonprofessional, peer-support movement hasn't really changed since it began decades ago.

I have worked at and observed numerous inpatient substance use disorder treatment and psychiatric facilities in the decades following my single, week-long inpatient treatment experience. They have ranged from a state hospital to moderately high-end facilities. People have shared details of their experiences at many others, and I refer clients to and interface with still more. From a therapeutic perspective, they all basically operate the same way.

In my case, as I was not yet motivated to change, the most effective and influential elements were (1) being taken out of my normal environment with no availability of mind-altering substances and (2) exposure to the idea that alcohol use disorder (totally referred to as *alcoholism* in the day) is a chronic, progressive condition. I had the choice to address it or allow it to worsen. Also, the introduction to Alcoholics Anonymous proved highly significant in the big picture.

The problem was that I just wasn't ready for that. The people treating me put me in the "hot seat" in a therapeutic group, in front of my peers, and told me that alcohol was my problem. Then they tried to stick a Big Book in my hand. Based on my past history, recent history, ambivalence regarding alcohol, and my stated reason for seeking help, these interventions only made me defensive. Based on what they felt I needed, their approach sought to break down my resistance. It was obvious to everyone that I needed to stop drinking and go to AA, so why couldn't I see it?

The cookie-cutter approach wasn't working, and it was my fault.

Admittedly, quantifying successful treatment is complicated, but since I resumed drinking in under two weeks, it's fair to say my experience was unsuccessful. My anxiety level had reached critical mass and therefore benefited from the downtime. It was like a reset. However, nothing in the treatment regimen directly addressed my ambivalence toward my substance use. To me, it wasn't the problem, the anxiety was.

They did not ask me about my history and relationship with alcohol. They did not ask me to ponder what alcohol did for me versus what it did to me. They didn't ask what problems alcohol had caused or been part of to bring me to the crisis point. They didn't ask where I saw my relationship with alcohol and my life in five years. They never even asked me why I drank!

Instead, they projected an ideal of what recovery should be according to the treatment establishment—abstinence-based in the 12-Step model.

"They" were well-qualified people trying to do their best, but they were stuck in the box, following a script that hadn't changed in years, and, in fact, still hasn't changed.

It's entirely possible that I might have entered recovery months before I eventually did. Had the people treating me understood my motivation and level of readiness to change, and acted accordingly, my response might have been quite different. Instead of doubling down on my resistance, I might have directed that same energy toward questioning my relationship with alcohol. Of course, I ultimately did, but this was despite my treatment, not because of it.

Substance use disorder treatment is often described by the term rehab, short for rehabilitation. The stereotype is that to go from active substance use to recovery entails and requires an inpatient hospital or facility stay where they somehow transform you. Substance use disorder can't be reduced to anything remotely that predictable. Here's how the treatment is designed.

## Detox and Clinical Stabilization Services

When someone uses a substance like alcohol or opioids on a regular and continuous basis, they may become dependent on that substance physically. Dependence means that their bodies have adjusted to consistent intake of a substance by reregulating how certain systems work. The human body is always working to maintain a state of equilibrium referred to as homeostasis. In my case, my body was trying to maintain homeostasis by compensating for the effects of a liter of vodka, multiple beers, and cannabis daily. Symptoms referred to as withdrawal are the consequences of abruptly stopping, or withdrawing, the intoxicating substances. The first goal in treatment is allowing the body to detoxify residual toxins from the substances remaining in the system while managing the potentially dangerous withdrawal symptoms. This is where the term detox comes from. The body will work to restore equilibrium of the systems in a matter of days.

Detoxification/withdrawal is managed medically. Untreated, the process is often uncomfortable, and in the case of alcohol withdrawal potentially dangerous. Therefore, the inpatient detox, where someone stays in a facility, has become the norm. Depending on the substances used, duration of use, baseline physical condition, and other factors, the process of detoxing can take a few days to as long as a few weeks. On average, people generally feel better between three and five days.

Withdrawal symptoms might include, but are not limited to, elevated blood pressure and pulse, abdominal/digestive issues, including nausea, vomiting, cramping and diarrhea, temperature dysregulation with chills and sweating, sleep disturbance, appetite disturbance, mood disturbance, anxiety ranging to severe agitation, impaired cognition, cravings, muscle and joint aches, and painful, restless legs (giving literal meaning to the term kicking the habit).

I experienced two versions of this. The first time was in a facility and mitigated with Librium; it consisted of a headache and people seeming super-annoying. The second one, ridden out over three to four days on a couch, was considerably worse. I had the same headache but on steroids and shakes that amounted to an ongoing five on the Richter scale. My brain couldn't decide if I was hot or cold, and my skin alternated between sweaty or just clammy. If I slept, it was for no longer than 15 minutes before I would jolt awake, my body seeming to abruptly levitate off the couch. I don't think I've ever observed anyone that bad; my job, my purpose for observing them, is to prevent that.

Important to note is that alcohol withdrawal can result in a combination of dangerous psychiatric and neurological symptoms referred to as delirium tremens. Symptoms are significant confusion and disorientation, restlessness, agitation ranging to possible aggression, along with visual and auditory hallucinations. The autonomic branch of the central nervous system responsible for regulating vital functions, such as heart rate, blood pressure, and temperature, becomes overactive. Heart rate and blood pressure are elevated. Severe tremors, sweating, and insomnia are common. Because of the neurological and cardiovascular risks, this complication of withdrawal is a medical emergency.

Medical staff administer medications to ease symptoms, typically following an established, one-size-fits-all protocol of dosages and schedules. For uncomplicated alcohol withdrawal, medications from the drug class of benzodiazepines are often utilized in a schedule and dosage that tapers down over several days. The other discomforts are treated symptomatically, i.e., antiemetics for nausea, analgesics for pain, etc.

Buprenorphine is the medication treatment standard for people withdrawing from opioid dependence. Buprenorphine, often in the form of a combination product with naloxone called Suboxone, is classified as a partial opioid agonist. The medication replaces opioids in the central nervous system's receptor sites, thereby decreasing or eliminating cravings. The medication may be used in tapering dosages to manage withdrawal but is also utilized as an ongoing therapy, referred to as medications for addiction treatment, MAT.

The goal of medical withdrawal management is to keep someone as comfortable as possible while their body works to restore itself to a state of equilibrium. Given a chance, the remarkable human body will work to heal itself.

Outpatient or at-home alcohol detox is a more recent development. Addiction medicine specialists, sometimes primary care office-based, have newer protocols and approaches for this. This approach is appropriate for people who meet specific criteria, and the severity of their withdrawal symptoms is mild to moderate. The protocols typically take four to five days, so a possible limitation might be initiating the protocol late in the week in a practice with a Monday-through-Friday schedule. The patient comes for an initial assessment and receives the necessary education on alcohol use disorder and managing the withdrawal symptoms. They will agree to come daily for monitoring of vital signs and withdrawal severity assessment and receive daily prescriptions for benzodiazepine medications previously mentioned, as well as other comfort medications. For the right people, this is a great option. The right person is generally motivated to change and open to lifestyle modification and utilizing ongoing recovery supports.

There are several advantages to inpatient detox or treatment in general. The period in someone's life when they enter treatment (or get sober, make significant lifestyle changes) can be intense on numerous levels. There is often anxiety associated with events precipitating treatment. Putting that on time-out, a few days away from everyday problems and stressors, can be like hitting the reset button. It allows a person to focus. And, of course, zero availability of mind-altering substances reinforces the changes that the individual originally set as their intention.

Alice is a divorced single mother of two young children and had achieved a fragile sobriety. She is a nurse and was enrolled in a graduate program part-time. She is highly intelligent. Her mother is overbearing, and her ex-husband still has the proverbial hooks in her, frequently treading on her boundaries. It's possible she has an undiagnosed, untreated, attention deficit condition. Along with the other stressors, school seemed to be what triggered her drinking bouts, which would quickly escalate to the need for hospitalization. After detox, she finally wound up in a residential program in one of the region's premier facilities. I would go visit her, and though she didn't like being away from her children, it was obvious that being removed from her stressors made a huge difference. There was noticeable improvement almost on a daily basis, even in the previous hospitalizations. Despite the availability of supports, she needed inpatient care to arrest the drinking cycle.

In my situation back in 1990, inpatient containment was indicated due to my anxiety level as well as alcohol dependence. Managing my withdrawal was medically indicated, obviously necessary although I had not directly sought treatment for alcohol use. I needed the time-out.

## The Bigger Picture

Richard is a middle-aged businessman. He resides in Texas with his lovely wife. He is a kind, generous individual who is loved by his family and his employees, his work family. He has good friends. He runs a large building-and-development company that he owns along with a partner. He has worked hard to build a good life, and he is successful by anyone's measure—he has it all, as they say. In addition to his beautiful home in Texas, he has another in the Florida Keys; he flies between them in his own jet. "I'm very blessed," he acknowledges.

Richard is the perfect example of someone who should be free to enjoy his life… except for his drinking.

He has been to numerous inpatient detoxes and clinical stabilization settings, tried residential treatment, went to AA where he attended meetings and had a sponsor. He would resume drinking and quickly lose control until he would be drinking around the clock.

"It's like I'd get it in my head that I could just have a break. I'll just have one, but then there's the rest of the bottle… and then I can't stop myself. And I know I'm in trouble."

After he arranged for a successful private detox for his adult son, he decided to try that himself. That's how we met. His detox was uneventful. We attended AA meetings together and he reconnected with his sponsor. We enrolled him in an aftercare program with medication management, counseling, and remote intensive outpatient program, IOP, meetings. I spoke with him daily for weeks after I departed and he remained alcohol-free. The sequence of detoxing and connection to concrete supports was the indicated standard of care.

The average length of stay in a detox facility is five to seven days. During this time, staff will collaborate with the individual on a plan for discharge, including options on how to best continue in recovery. Continuing treatment on an inpatient basis, as withdrawal symptoms resolve and the acute detox winds up, is one option. This has different names in different areas and facilities, but is often referred to as clinical stabilization services, CSS, or short-term residential treatment. This can mean transferring to another facility, to a different unit of the same facility, or simply staying where they are with a status change. Typically, CSS patients have successfully met criteria for completing the detox process and are medically stable. Some medications may be continued, but the detoxification protocols are discontinued. Education is the focus of CSS, and therapeutic groups are the means. The goal is to prepare someone for independent recovery out in the world.

They likely kept me a few days over what could have been a reasonable discharge date, hoping I would have some kind of breakthrough. Given my certainty, lack of readiness really, that alcohol wasn't my problem, the breakthrough never came. I had no interest in further treatment.

While treatment in the detox phase is focused on more immediate and medical concerns, treatment in CSS will address a broader range of issues. Specialty therapies and services will be tailored for specific needs of each person in an individualized treatment plan designed toward desired outcomes. Goals will be formulated, and the treatment will work toward meeting these.

Co-occurring disorders are a significant issue for many entering recovery. Whether that be chronic, persistent mental illness in forms like schizophrenia or major depression, or conditions that are often substance-use related, like anxiety, these need to be addressed. Trauma, attention-related disorders, eating disorders... left untreated will hamper recovery. Whether by specialized treatment or medication, or both, mental health interventions should be initiated or at least arranged during clinical stabilization. According to a 2020 report, 58 percent of all facilities provide comprehensive mental health assessment or diagnosis while 71 percent of all facilities provide mental health services.[11]

Clinical stabilization is also an appropriate time frame for decisions regarding ongoing addiction treatment in the form of opioid replacement therapy. The American Society of Addiction Medicine, ASAM, considers medications for addiction treatment, MAT, the best practice and an appropriate approach in many cases of substance use disorder. As mentioned earlier, buprenorphine, used to block the action of opioids, can be used as an ongoing therapy to support people, essentially taking cravings for nonprescribed substances out of the proverbial equation. Several different medication options are commonly utilized in routine clinical practice. Depending on location, this might also be referred to as medications for opioid use disorder, MOUD.

Chronic pain can be a significant contributing factor or even the primary cause of addiction. A Substance Abuse and Mental Health

Services Administration, SAMSHA, survey found that 22 percent of facilities address co-occurring pain and substance use through education or referrals to pain management specialists who will treat individuals and follow their progress.[12] Teaching on alternatives to narcotic pain medications, counseling on pain psychology, and therapeutic approaches for coping with pain help minimize the risk of resuming nonprescribed substance use.

Finally, case management is oversight and coordination of treatment and also entails discharge planning. Recovery progress is assessed and monitored, with attention to high-risk circumstances, troubleshooting, and advocacy. Clinicians will focus on preventing symptom recurrence, both on the level of personal sobriety and life circumstances. For the individual, obstacles and issues need to be identified and addressed. For example, if someone is unhoused, this is a barrier to sobriety maintenance, post-discharge. Referrals and applications for housing or residential treatment would be facilitated. Therapeutic scaffolding—temporary supports designed to build independence—is provided with the goal of sustaining sobriety beyond the safety of the treatment setting. Sobriety maintenance and coping strategies, outpatient treatment referrals, possibly recovery coaching, even job-training programs are the types of supports case managers and discharge planners provide.

## Residential Treatment

Another post-detox option is transferring to a residential program. Sometimes the terminology overlaps; CSS-type treatment might also be termed residential treatment and continue up to 28 days or even beyond. Residential, or sober living, programs can range from a few months to a year, and are post-acute, a step down from the inpatient level of care. There are a wide range of these, from sober residences—housing for people in recovery—to highly structured programs. Also known as sober living or transitional housing, they serve as a bridge between the intensive structure of inpatient care and the return to independent living.

"I want to get this right the first time, so I don't have to keep doing it over again," said Melanie, a 45-year-old, in her initial interview with the intake coordinator of the residential program she was interested in. She had remained in CSS post-detox and was contemplating her next step. She felt she needed more structure than a basic sober living environment.

"Residential options were a confusing landscape, and I was grateful to have a case manager to explain the options and what might be right for me." She went to a program that was structured with daily groups, activities, and case management, "All in a home environment instead of a facility feel." The home environment part was poignant because Melanie was experiencing homelessness before she decided to stop drinking.

Sober living environments strive to balance structure and autonomy in a supportive setting. Residents share the living space where accountability, cooperation, and a sense of community are the principal goals and benefits. Each facility or organization has its own policies regarding monitoring. The expectation is a drug-and-alcohol-free environment, and regular drug testing is performed, usually randomly. Each residence has its own rules and guidelines for curfews, mandatory or voluntary house meetings, outside support meetings, and expectations for fulfilling the necessary chores needed to support the household. Kitchens and bathrooms with multiple people using them don't clean themselves!

Treatment will continue, assuming the residential program has a therapeutic component. Ideally, the therapies and initiatives begun during inpatient treatment will be sustained. Individual counseling addresses ongoing challenges and helps an individual to set goals and solidify relapse prevention skills. The new element in the residential setting is people building longer-lasting peer relationships than in the more transient inpatient setting. In the short weeks of an inpatient stay, people tend to come and go. In residential, people are able to form relationships, give and receive support, and improve healthy socialization and interpersonal dynamics. In reality, this is not without drama, but that too is part of growing up in recovery, and navigating these things substance-free supports emotional growth and coping skills.

Therapeutic groups offer further opportunities for personal growth and the sharing of experiences and challenges. Where indicated, involving family members in the therapy process enhances an individual's support system. Improving communication and addressing family-related issues strengthens recovery; the family of the person in recovery has likely faced stressors and challenges as well.

I had the opportunity to work in a nursing role in a residential setting. I oversaw all medication administration and worked directly with the other staff to support them in that part of resident care. All medical matters and concerns, appointments, etc., were part of my responsibilities. I provided education in the form of therapeutic groups on topics ranging from substance use, tobacco use, sexually transmitted diseases and MAT. I also participated in staff development.

As the person in recovery moves beyond physical dependence on a substance and the day-to-day lifestyle issues of substance use disorder, focus naturally shifts outward and ahead. The logical next steps are reintegration into the community and workforce. An individual might receive employment assistance in the form of job-search support, vocational training, or support to consider and pursue further education. The goal is employability. Jobs outside the residence are encouraged and sometimes a requirement.

Finally, reengaging in the outside community, and the recovery community specifically, will support an individual's capacity to live independently and continue the recovery process on their own. Peer-support recovery in the form of meetings of AA, NA, Self-Management and Recovery Training, SMART, Recovery, or others, is encouraged and often required. The meetings provide additional support, offer a sense of belonging, and assist someone to establish connections and relationships that will sustain them later in their recovery process. By the time someone is winding up their time in a residential program, they've worked on the necessary skills to be comfortable in recovery and the community at large.

Richard's wife reached out seeking assistance six months after I treated him initially. He had resumed drinking after disengaging with the therapist and IOP. He described drifting away from meetings, losing touch with his sponsor.

"I don't know what comes over me, but I have the thought that I can sneak one and it will work this time." His subsequent detox was more difficult than the previous treatment; his withdrawal symptoms were more severe.

"We need to learn from past experience," I said. "How can we do better?"

Richard's motivation was strong and he signed up for a six-week stint at a high-intensity residential program. He shared with me that he didn't like it initially. Then, after they completed his assessment phase, they set up his treatment based on the 12-Step program that Richard had wanted. He finished the program and continued with the new organization's remote IOP.

"Research suggests that most people need at least three months in treatment to significantly reduce or stop their drug use and that the best outcomes occur with longer durations of treatment," according to NIDA.[13]

The level of treatment described herein is sadly not the standard of care that most people receive. Longer treatment and ongoing support equate to better outcomes. Doctors[14] and pilots[15] have to spend months in treatment and have access to continued monitoring and support. Doctors have an 80 percent abstinence rate at five years, 90 percent for pilots. The success rate for everyone else is less than half of the half who complete treatment. Residential treatment offers the environment that people experiencing the slow physiological and cognitive changes of recovery need to ensure success.

Eight months later, Richard's wife again contacted us: he needed another detox treatment. He planned to return to the residential treatment center where he had been previously. After a longer stint of residential treatment and some neuropsychological testing, Richard entered an outpatient phase with the same organization but stepped up from the previous time. He would spend a week at home alternating with a week of Monday-through-Friday attendance at the organization's in-person outpatient program.

## Outpatient Treatment

ASAM has established criteria that is the most widely used and comprehensive set of standards for placement, continued service, and transfer of patients with addiction and co-occurring conditions. ASAM criteria includes a detailed assessment of the person seeking treatment across six "dimensions," including their biological, emotional, and social needs. Levels of care are indicated based on the outcome of the assessment. These levels of care are scaled ranging from 0.5 to 4, with 4 being the most intensive. Level 4 corresponds to intensive medical management, i.e., detox treatment previously described. The descending levels and intensity of care are intended as a continuum, through outpatient care, and finally transitioning to independent living. Unfortunately, the majority of people are not receiving this type of formal assessment. The options to continue with professional recovery support on an outpatient basis are most frequently dictated by what's available and what is acceptable to a given individual.

In 2020, 94 percent of all treatment for substance use disorder was rendered on an outpatient basis.[16]

The most rigorous nonresidential version is a high-intensity outpatient program, HIOP, (formerly partial hospitalization program). This can be as structured as inpatient hospitalization in terms of clinical care and supervision. Attendance is typically daily for several hours, five days a week. Medical and psychiatric services may be available on-site, and a HIOP offers a substantial level of therapeutic support, including individual and group counseling.

The next step down is intensive outpatient program, IOP. Similar, but less demanding than the high intensity counterpart, IOP also offers a structured approach, but typically meets several times per week for a few hours each day. There is often a remote option. IOP offers a higher level of therapeutic intensity than standard outpatient programs, making it suitable for individuals who require more support but do not need 24-hour supervision. Also incorporated can be individual and group therapies and educational components. One advantage is that individuals can maintain commitments like work or school. A similar approach is called structured outpatient addiction program, SOAP.

The outpatient formats as well as individual and group counseling and other services might be offered by outpatient divisions of facilities or organizations that provide inpatient treatment as well. Sometimes the outpatient divisions grew out of recognition of the need for continuity of care, and referrals for outpatient treatment go across the hall instead of across town. New treatment providers are starting up, and established organizations are expanding.

## Medications for Addiction Treatment

Medications for addiction treatment, MAT, is an evidence-based medical approach that supports individuals to reduce or discontinue substance use. One of a variety of medication therapies is utilized in conjunction with behavioral health therapies in keeping with best practice. The medications act to eliminate or minimize cravings. MAT ideally treats an individual holistically, encompassing the range of recovery global health needs, including primary healthcare and psychosocial supports, i.e., counseling. Medications are utilized primarily according to the specific addiction being treated—opioid use disorder, OUD, or alcohol use disorder, AUD.

OUD may be treated with several medications. Methadone was first developed as a pain reliever (analgesic) with a milder and longer-lasting effect than morphine. As the first treatment for opioid dependence, methadone was stigmatized, and programs often encountered opposition due to misconceptions about the medication. In reality, methadone maintenance treatment has been associated with improved health outcomes, reduced criminal activity, and increased social functioning.[17] The downside is that, as a full opioid agonist that activates opiate receptors in the brain, it's as difficult to discontinue as street opioids—an individual will be dependent on methadone the same way. SAMHSA reported that approximately 400,000 people were utilizing outpatient methadone treatment in 2024.

Methadone for OUD is dispensed at clinics and facilities that follow stringent Drug Enforcement Administration, DEA, guidelines. It is a Schedule II controlled substance. People come daily and receive their medication under direct observation. After an individual meets certain criteria, they may become eligible for take-home doses of medication. The criteria include length of time in treatment, negative urine drug screens, and overall stability.

Buprenorphine is prescribed in various settings, including primary care offices and dedicated clinics. It's a partial opioid agonist that binds to opiate receptors but does not fully activate them. It is administered alone or in combination with naloxone, as Suboxone, to deter nonmedical use. Buprenorphine treatment can be initiated in an office setting, a procedure sometimes referred to as induction. This can render inpatient detox unnecessary.

When initiating buprenorphine, it has been considered necessary for the patient to abstain from opioid use until they are in moderate withdrawal. This is because the partial agonist effect and the naloxone component of Suboxone can cause a reaction known as precipitated withdrawal, when remaining opioids are abruptly dislodged from central nervous system receptor sites. This is extremely uncomfortable.

Buprenorphine maintenance is similar to methadone in that the person utilizing the medication will be dependent on it, as they were with opioids. Once treatment is initiated, the patient will meet with the provider regularly with the goal of achieving stability. As stability is attained, the visits will become less frequent, i.e., starting weekly, then to biweekly, every three weeks, and finally to every 28 days, which is the maximum number of days prescriptions can be written for in most locations. Following the visit with the medication provider, the patient will obtain medication from a retail pharmacy. Best practice is for wraparound services, such as behavioral health, primary medical care, and any indicated social services. Also, part of best practice is routine urine drug screening to verify the presence of the prescribed buprenorphine, as well as any nonprescribed or street substances. Stability could be defined as attaining the optimal dosage of medication, regular attendance at scheduled appointments and urine drug screen results as anticipated.

Sublocade is a brand-name prescription medication used to treat moderate-to-severe OUD. It is a long-acting, extended-release injection of buprenorphine. The medication is administered every 26 to 28 days by a trained healthcare professional such as a registered nurse.

Another element in the medical provision of MAT is participation in the prescription drug monitoring program (PDMP), or the individual state's equivalent. The PDMP is a secure online system that tracks prescriptions of controlled substances for all patients. This was originally conceived as a remedy for people "doctor shopping" for multiple opioid prescriptions. Today, it is an integral part of MAT prescribing. Prior to all new prescriptions, the provider is able to verify that the previous prescription was picked up, and equally as important, when the prescription was picked up. Regular and prompt picking up of prescriptions is another element of patient stability.

Naltrexone rounds out three main medications utilized for OUD. It is an opioid antagonist that blocks the effects of opioids by binding to receptor sites, preventing the euphoric effects. It comes as a tablet taken daily or as an extended-release injection called Vivitrol, intended to be administered every 28 days. The patient must be completely detoxed from opioids to initiate naltrexone treatment. If there is any question of residual opioids in someone's system, a small test dose of naltrexone is administered under observation. The medication has some advantages. It's not a controlled substance, and patients can receive a 30-day prescription with refills or even receive 90-day prescriptions for the oral medication. The injection must be administered by a trained healthcare professional; the advantage of the long-acting injection is that patients don't need to take the tablet daily, which can act as a safety measure during a temporary lapse in someone's resolve to recover. Another significant advantage of naltrexone is that the patient utilizing it has no dependence on the medication.

Naltrexone is approved for treatment of both opioids and alcohol. By blocking opiate receptors, it interferes with the brain's reward system, making alcohol less reinforcing. It is particularly useful in preventing resumption of active drinking in individuals who have successfully stopped. Studies have shown that naltrexone can lead to a reduction in the quantity and frequency of alcohol consumption and is associated with a decrease in the number of drinking days and a decrease in the total amount of alcohol consumed on drinking days.[18]

Naltrexone is often prescribed in combination with behavioral therapies to address both the physiological and psychological aspects of alcohol use for a more comprehensive approach to treatment.

Another medication utilized as therapy for alcohol use disorder is acamprosate, which works at the neurotransmitter level to stabilize the brain's chemical balance. Taken in oral form, it reduces cravings and supports abstinence from alcohol.

Disulfiram, commonly known as Antabuse, is also used for alcohol use disorder. It is taken in oral form. It works by creating an unpleasant reaction in the body when alcohol is consumed and relies on patient adherence and commitment to maintaining abstinence from alcohol. A recent client told me that the daily ritual of taking the medication serves as a reminder that they have "a new lease on life!"

Detractors argue that MAT is just substituting one drug for another, especially in the cases of methadone and buprenorphine, where the individual utilizing the medications is still dependent on them. Proponents point out that people are receiving an appropriate dose of unadulterated, legal medication, paid for by insurance, under the supervision of a qualified prescriber, along with associated medical and behavioral healthcare. Furthermore, a person living with substance use disorder, while still subject to persisting stigma unfortunately, is no longer a *criminal* in the eyes of society.

MAT significantly supports individuals in recovery, addressing physiological and psychological aspects of substance use disorder.

The specific substance use disorder, individual needs and preferences, and medical considerations are the elements in selecting which type of MAT is best for each person. And finally, the best outcomes are achieved by combining MAT with counseling and behavioral therapies.

## New Approaches

Internationally trained neuroscientist Henrietta Szutorisz, PhD, is working on a new approach to match recovering individuals with the most appropriate available addiction treatment. Dr. Szutorisz is a biomedical scientist based in New York. She is the founder and CEO of Objective Recovery, a new startup that uses neurobiology and modern technology to address the lack of effective personalized solutions to substance use disorders.

"Recovery is not a moment," she said. "People's condition moves across time, and rigid adherence to one model limits flexibility. The question isn't which philosophy is right, but which strategy matches a person's state and goals," she said in an interview earlier this year.

Dr. Szutorisz has resolved a serious addiction, hence her dedication to working on the leading edge of various health conditions, with special focus on addictions and associated mental health. In a short time span, her concept has evolved to incorporate both a human element and artificial intelligence, AI, to model optimal forms of available individualized treatments. The goal is a "precision assessment and individualized recovery strategy."

Something that Objective Recovery might recommend to an individual seeking detoxification from opioids is a new technology for treating opioid withdrawal. The concept is called transcutaneous auricular neurostimulation. The US Food and Drug Administration, FDA, has granted approval for a couple of these devices that work by stimulating specific cranial nerves via small electrodes planted on and around the ear. The electrodes are connected to a small control unit, and the entire system is noninvasive. The Speranza Therapeutics Genesis and the Sparrow Ascent are available for home use with a prescription. Though presently not covered by insurance, and rather pricey ($4500 for the Ascent), this technology should become more accessible after research and development is recouped. The dreaded opioid withdrawal symptoms are the primary existential fear of anyone living with opioid use disorder, OUD. To many, the detox process feels like a Herculean task, an obstacle standing between them and recovery. Transcutaneous neurostimulation could be the game changer that is sorely needed. This nonpharmacological approach to managing opioid withdrawal symptoms represents a quantum leap forward.

The standard approach for opioid detox has been switching an individual from their nonprescribed substances (fentanyl or pharmaceutical opioids—heroin is almost nonexistent these days) to buprenorphine, methadone, or naltrexone. For those desiring buprenorphine, the challenge has always been the necessity of waiting the requisite amount of time for opioids to start leaving an individual's central nervous system. Initiating buprenorphine, or the combination product Suboxone, requires an individual to be in moderate withdrawal, as assessed by the Clinical Opiate Withdrawal Scale, COWS. This is further complicated by fentanyl being lipophilic; it binds to fat and stays in the system much longer. Making the switch is often unpredictable and uncomfortable. If the buprenorphine initiation is attempted too soon, the extremely unpleasant precipitated withdrawal reaction might occur. The buprenorphine abruptly dislodges the opioids from the receptor sites, but without activating the receptor sites—no euphoric effect.

A new approach to this utilizes microdosing buprenorphine, sometimes with a transdermal (through the skin) patch. Buprenorphine is gradually introduced in small increments, even while the opioids are continued but tapered. The effect is that the new medication comes in *under the radar*, and the uncomfortable waiting period is bypassed. This method is being trialed successfully in both facilities and home settings. Macrodosing is essentially the opposite. Large doses are introduced in an expedited time frame, steamrolling over the opioid occupation of the receptor sites. Numerous studies have been undertaken for both approaches, and there are established protocols. Both of these new approaches require a fair amount of supervision, but they basically eliminate the discomfort associated with starting these medications. The perception of an uncomfortable ordeal has been an obstacle for many.

Finally, what if a substance disordered brain could be literally repaired? Skip right past selecting the right treatment and more comfortable ways to initiate it. How about just correcting the substance-craving part of the brain? Ultrasound treatment for addiction, also known as transcranial focused ultrasound, is an emerging therapeutic approach that involves the use of focused ultrasound waves to modulate neural activity in brain regions associated with reward processing, craving, impulsivity, and decision-making. Some of the notable organizations and researchers engaged in this area include Harvard Medical School, Stanford University School of Medicine, Johns Hopkins University School of Medicine and the National Institutes of Health (NIH). While this technology is still in the experimental stages and undergoing research, it holds potential as a noninvasive and targeted treatment option for addiction.

## Summary

If the 30-year-old version of me, as described in the beginning of the second chapter, was in treatment today, there are a range of possibilities for the outcome. It might have been different. Today, there are solid approaches that might have worked better for me. The problem, even today, is that they are not consistently or correctly used. Most of the programs and settings out there today are remarkably similar to what I experienced 35 years ago. Had I received individualized, evidence-based treatment, free from foregone conclusions, judgment and stigma, I might have skipped my orientation period or at least shortened it. The injury, the epic 10-day bender, the job jeopardy... all of it might have been different.

Substance use treatment is frozen in amber. It's like an unlucky insect that was trapped and preserved in hardened tree resin ages ago, a glimpse into a bygone era. Treatment hasn't changed much in the 70-ish years since it started. The current interdisciplinary model originated as a means to get people off social welfare rather than a focused initiative to treat substance use. One result of using mid-20th century approaches is failure to implement and leverage leading-edge, evidence-based approaches.

Treatment is a weak link between active substance use and stable recovery. Less than half of people complete treatment, and over half of those who finish resume active substance use.[19] Only 14 percent of the 48.7 million people in the US who meet criteria for substance use disorder received any form of treatment at all in 2022.[20]

The current system fails to treat people as individuals. Cookie-cutter, one-size-fits-all, treatment plans administered in conveyor belt fashion fail because of the sheer diversity of addiction. This approach works randomly for a proportion of people the same way a broken clock is right twice a day.

The current system also fails to treat people holistically, instead reducing them to their condition or diagnosis or worse. Addiction is the only chronic medical condition where the patient is held responsible for poor outcomes. As with any serious disease, such as cancer, diabetes, kidney failure, etc., bad outcomes happen. In the case of addiction, the assumption of blame lies with the patient. They didn't engage in their treatment. They weren't motivated for treatment. They didn't follow through with treatment. Literal blame is ascribed to the person with the condition.

Richard reached out to me a fourth time, again seeking a detox treatment and guidance. We (the national treatment company I partner with) recommended a different aftercare approach this time. He was able to go directly from his longer and more difficult detox to a new residential program that was both intensive and comprehensive. He received evaluation from a multidisciplinary team who provided him with education and big-picture direction for the range of life elements, including history of head injuries and emotional trauma, driving his alcohol use. He transitioned home with a sober companion who assisted him to integrate back into his everyday life. He goes to AA and utilizes monthly Vivitrol injections and daily breathalyzer checks for accountability. He is sober as of this writing.

How is it that someone who has the means to access any and every treatment out there still struggles? And how can we bring those processes and treatments to everyone?

The accountability found in the treatment of any other chronic medical condition is not present in addiction treatment. Quality assurance, a standard of mainstream healthcare, is conspicuously absent. Whether rendering evidence-based techniques or alternative and complementary approaches, treatment organizations do little or nothing to track their services' effectiveness beyond exit surveys. We need to incentivize a higher standard of care and innovative ways to deliver it.

A major reason addiction is winning is because treatment is losing.

# Chapter 5
# The Trouble with Treatment

"There is no education like adversity."
~ Benjamin Disraeli

## The Cookie-Cutter Problem

The vast majority of treatment facilities and organizations trace their lineage from the Minnesota Model; an interdisciplinary team of medical and clinical professionals provide support and education with goals based on a treatment plan. On the one hand, I'm glad we use it instead of sterilization.

On the other hand, this approach is not working.

Recall that less than half of people complete treatment. Of those who do, 40 to 60 percent resume using substances after treatment.[21]

The first problem is that they are doing it the same way for everyone. If they were hairstylists, clothing or car manufacturers, or restaurants, how would that work out?

People from different cultures, different backgrounds, different circumstances, with different personal histories use different substances in different ways for different lengths of time with varying intensity. The Midwestern woman in her late 20s who drinks three glasses of wine daily and gets a little shaky when she stops is different than the woman in her late 30s from Florida who takes large quantities of dextromethorphan (the active ingredient in over-the-counter cough medicine), even though she has the same symptoms. Two men in their late 50s both use cocaine. One has been snorting a couple of grams a month for the last three years, primarily on weekends. The other has been smoking $1500 of crack weekly for most of the last year.

Why would the same treatment work for everyone?

Let's start with the detox protocol, which I already mentioned. The reality of a one-size-fits-all approach is that it only fits a minority and probably not that well. Anyone from the clothing industry can tell you that. The comfort level during detox sets the tone for the rest of treatment. Withdrawal symptoms and the anxiety they generate are completely counterproductive to a positive experience.

In my work directly managing detox treatments over the last three years, we are using a technique we refer to as frontloading. On day one of an alcohol treatment, I assess history, substance use patterns, and, most important, the presentation of symptoms in the moment. I medicate generously. Proactive symptom management trumps playing catch-up any day. Once symptoms break through, blood pressure and pulse elevate, anxiety level goes up, and along with that adrenaline and cortisol, chemicals of stress, and it takes more medication in the long run to get that horse back in the barn.

I stay on top of the assessments, using the indicated scale for the substance, and just go where the symptoms take us in terms of the medication total for the first day. The second day is variable. We can usually start tapering down to between 60 and 80 percent of the previous day's total. However, sometimes the withdrawal symptoms will peak higher on day two; as much or more medication is indicated on the second day than the first. This is where many protocols go wrong, because they typically lower the dose on day two irrespective of the patient's presentation. Regardless of whether we taper the second day, we see the need for medication, again based on assessment, drop precipitously in the subsequent days. I am often giving 50 percent of the prior day's medication on days four and five.

The same general guiding principles apply to both alcohol and opioid detox.

Customized withdrawal management based on individual symptoms and other factors provides a superior experience both physically and psychologically. A comfortable detox puts an individual on the best possible footing for the treatment to follow, which should be equally individualized.

The next thing to consider is the interdisciplinary treatment plan. In every setting I've worked in that utilized the Minnesota Model team approach, the admitting registered nurse, RN, generated a treatment plan as part of the admission assessment.

The interdisciplinary treatment plan for substance use disorder is a collaborative care approach integrating input from the range of professionals on the team. The plan is derived from a problem list and incorporates goals addressing those problems, along with interventions, who is responsible, and target time frames.

When I say the plan is generated, I mean literally. Facilities and organizations are using electronic health records. These are software programs supplied by vendors. The various platforms are HIPAA compliant to protect sensitive health information and usually cloud-based. Organizations must frequently choose between user-friendliness/customization and affordability. Affordability usually wins. In terms of treatment plans, this means that the user is starting with something generic, inputting a little data and selecting from drop-down menus. This unwieldy approach to something that should be uniquely personalized often results in basic or generic treatment plans. Years ago, I wrote better treatment plans at a facility that hadn't yet gone electronic.

Patients typically do not have much input into this process. Treatment plans would be more effective if they were prepared collaboratively by the team along with the patient. Goals and timelines should be set according to the individual's readiness and unique circumstances.

Different settings and organizations have different workflow and admission procedures. The best-case scenario would have both nursing and clinical staff perform the six assessment dimensions endorsed by ASAM. Dimensions 1 and 2 cover intoxication and medical considerations while the remaining dimensions are concerned with psychosocial elements and, significantly, readiness to change. This occasion, with the in-depth conversation of the assessment, would be a logical continuation point for a collaborative dialogue on goals, priorities, and other considerations the client may have. In an ideal workflow, this assessment would occur during the first 48 hours of treatment. It should be deferred until physical symptoms of withdrawal have been assessed and managed.

According to Dr. John Kelly, "One of the best ways we can improve treatment is to use measurement much better to drive care. What I call recovery vital signs, a bit like what we would do in hypertension or diabetes, having some standardized metric is key. We may need more than one metric for addiction or other complex psychiatric illnesses." [22] The best source of information about the patient is the patient.

Treatment teams generally convene at the convenience of the admitting physician or medical director. The procedure has the patients paraded through, conveyor belt style, while their plans are reviewed and progress is updated. This format does not lend itself to a longer, more in-depth exploration of the client's problems or goals or collaboration toward their resolution. Again, some people will have basic, cookie-cutter type situations. Others, likely the majority, will not, simply based on the wide range of presentations of substance use disorder, SUD, and the unlimited psychosocial possibilities.

If the treatment plan is a road map, it makes sense to start the trip with the best possible set of directions. That means a more individualized approach to both the navigation of treatment and desired destination. Organizations need to review their procedures and protocols to make them person-centered.

## The Assembly-Line Problem

Henry Ford pioneered the assembly line as a way to maximize efficiency in the automobile industry. The use of conveyor belt techniques and specialized assemblers repeating the same task over and over effectively contained costs. Treatment facilities seem to be emulating this approach.

This is usually a top-down phenomenon, as ownership/management usually signs off on, if not overtly dictates, how things are done. So, who owns these places? The four inpatient detox and short-term residential treatment facilities located closest to me are all private for-profit organizations. One of them is owned by a woman who married the last owner who is now deceased. They met years ago when she was a housekeeper at the facility (sounds a little spicy). One of them is owned by a guy from Pennsylvania who started his chain with a quarter billion dollars in venture capital investment money. Another has its third corporate owner in the 10 years since it opened, plus a holding LLC and a real estate trust or two. The other was started by four guys who met in rehab. Common to these facilities and organizations is a goal of running at 95 percent capacity. Except for the widow... she wanted hers running at 100 percent, at least when I worked there.

Private for-profit organizations are 43 percent of the total, whereas nonprofits are 50 percent. However, that 43 percent of for-profit organizations provides care for 56 percent of people receiving treatment.[23] The facilities I mentioned are literally the closest to me geographically. I have either worked for them or, at a minimum, toured them.

At the beginning of the assembly line is an admissions department, office, or equivalent. This is the first point of contact for a prospective patient, usually the result of calling an 800 number. The prospective patient might also be represented by a referring organization. The job of the admissions department, usually the only job, is to arrange admissions. These sections of the organization are often located remotely because their work is telephonic. In two of the four organizations I mentioned, they were on-site; however, they were completely separate from the patient care areas, in a separate building in one instance.

This amounts to the admission machine pumping as hard as it can, often while simultaneously disconnected from whatever might be going on at the patient care side. Meanwhile, farther down the assembly line on the detox unit, nursing and support staff must perform the numerous tasks required to admit someone. This includes, but is not limited to, meeting and greeting, explaining the admission procedure to follow, explaining numerous documents and obtaining signatures, obtaining vital signs and performing a physical assessment, obtaining a urine drug screen, possibly drawing blood for labs, a body search, a belonging search, performing the admission assessment, reconciling and counting all medications brought by the patient, providing an orientation to the unit, and settling them into a room. Then, all of the above is documented in the electronic health record... along with the new treatment plan generated somewhere in the process.

As the assembly line of substance use disorder treatment progresses, the imperative mandate of filling 19 out of every 20 beds, the overarching goal in many situations, literally and figuratively chokes the system farther down the conveyor belt. Overlooked is the fact that the same staff responsible for receiving and settling in those new patients must simultaneously care for the ones who are already there.

Depending on the acuity of the unit, i.e., the collective severity of the patients' conditions, this may present challenges. Each nurse has time-sensitive tasks, such as administering medications, treatments, and documenting for all the other patients in their assigned caseload. Naturally, these people will have questions and needs both physical and emotional. Nursing and patient care in substance use treatment has devolved to this type of assembly line. But the admissions team keep chugging along and the phone keeps ringing on the unit.

Now, I know this sounds like an old nurse grousing about doing a little hard work. Every time I pointed this out to a manager, the response was something to the effect of, "It can't be helped," or "That's part of the job." Hard work is part of the job, and the goal of most nurses is to work smart, as well as hard. It's the "can't be helped" part that I'm disputing. Yes, it can be helped. It can be helped by adequate staff and better communication. If the manager who told me it can't be helped had their finger to the pulse of the facility, they would know the level of engagement and attention needed by the current group of patients, referred to as the tenor of the unit. They would know, as an example, that the third of three admissions arriving minutes apart, the woman with chronic persistent mental illness in addition to substance use disorder, who was living in a tent by some river, is going to be a difficult and time-consuming admission after she arrives with every item she owns.

There is a difference between busy spells and life on the unit just being one long emergency with substandard care. Most facility staff identify with the latter. When a facility's staff is overwhelmed, everyone suffers, but, most of all, it's the quality of care that takes the real hit. This is not an acute care medical facility where we set broken bones, bandage folks up, and run the IVs while leaving people to heal as they watch TV in their rooms and relatives provide support. These are people in the midst of an intense physical and psychological shift. Yes, we are medicating them while their withdrawal process runs its course. While that is going on, their hearts and minds need support. When someone comes and says, "I'm anxious," what they really need is a conversation. The current system, the assembly line, wants me to give them a pill instead.

The experience of a client I worked with in the last year illustrates issues with disconnection between the admissions end of the assembly line and the actual care received. In past experiences with this client, a gentleman in his mid-60s, he was consistently not receptive to post-detox follow-up. When I treated him, he was starting to experience several alcohol-related health problems. He was receptive to our conversations with education and encouragement for aftercare but did not agree to any options presented while I was still treating him. The following week, his wife reached out to inform me that the client had agreed to go to one of the residential programs I'd recommended. They would be traveling there the following Friday. She described how the admission agent, located in Pennsylvania, had provided assurances that there would be therapeutic groups and care provided over the weekend when he was admitted at the Florida facility.

His experience went sideways almost immediately after being admitted. When his urine drug screen was positive for the benzodiazepines I had personally administered over the course of his seven-day detox, an on-call doctor ordered him to be on a lockdown protocol. His movements and freedom to even go outside were restricted. Worsening the situation, there were absolutely no groups or activities to engage him for the entire weekend, his first two days there. His comprehensive admission assessment was deferred until Monday, by which time he'd soured on the whole process. He signed himself out. After the investment of so much energy and encouragement, and this man finally opened himself up to the possibility of getting more help, his entire process was sabotaged by aggressive admissions staff promising anything to get him to sign on the dotted line.

Half of people aren't even completing treatment.

What's the latest trend with assembly lines? Automation. Even robotics. Yes, we need to be efficient. We need to be organized. Any organization or system benefits from good management. The thing that is getting lost in assembly-line style substance treatment is the human element.

We need to emphasize compassion, empathy, and the concept of the therapeutic alliance. To reach the point of seeking treatment, people wrestle with more than substance use. For many, the biggest obstacle to change has been themselves. They have moved from feelings of denial and ambivalence about their condition to a readiness to take action. To anyone who hasn't been in this position, hasn't experienced this, it might be difficult to fully comprehend the magnitude of seeking treatment. Seeking help feels risky; in reality, it is courageous. What people encounter on the other side of this scary leap of faith matters. If people find warm human connection and unconditional positive regard, they are likely to feel their turmoil was validated and move forward. If they land in an assembly line masquerading as compassionate treatment, with chintzy, structured interactions by a staff that is too busy to be authentically human with them, they're probably going to be discouraged. They're going to question why they took that leap and leave treatment.

### Evidenced-Based Connection

The most vivid recollection of my inpatient treatment experience years ago was a unit counselor named David. He stands out more than the groups, my roommate, my first AA meetings, the psychiatrist, the food... when I think about my rehab experience, he's what I remember most. The first time I met him, he was standing behind the unit desk with a cup of coffee in his hand. I was envious. I was returning from breakfast where the patient coffee was a sad decaffeinated brownish liquid. We talked about that, and he explained the hospital policy, the caffeine was a stimulant, etc. We had numerous conversations while I was there… He was the one who gave me the hot seat treatment in one of my last groups. He later said he was sorry for that, and that he knew it was hard. He truly believed he was helping me, and he put the effort in. In a more basic and essential way, he was.

David was indeed helping me—not by grilling me or shoving a Big Book in my hand, both of which he did—but by having genuine empathy and putting a human face on my experience in treatment.

So, why is that human connection so important in SUD treatment?

Substance use typically confers some sort of benefit in the beginning. It might solve a problem like anxiety or alleviate pain. When people enter a relationship with a substance it feels new, exciting, and fresh. Fresh could also describe the central nervous system receptor sites that maximize the effect of a substance… before they start to adapt. Over time, whether rapidly or gradually, the effect of a substance will diminish. Tolerance will occur, and it will take more of the substance to get the same effect. The substance, like a friend who stops caring, starts to turn on the user.

It's not just the lack of effect. The relationship with the substance often changes dynamics with others in the user's life, even to the point of driving a wedge between the user and other relationships, be they family, social, or livelihood related. If someone comes into your life, changes everything, then stops doing whatever they did in the first place, you'd be like WTF? You might be confused or conflicted. When a friend betrays us, we can be angry while still caring about that person.

As people enter treatment, these conflicted feelings represent the subtext of their relationship with substances. They don't want to break up, but, at some level, they know there's no possible future in which it works out. The substance will always take them back, but there's no getting back to the wonderful early stage.

The need for human connection is foremost in the beginning of treatment. This is where the therapeutic alliance comes in. It fills the vacuum left in the wake of the betrayal by the false friend, the substance. The therapeutic alliance traces its lineage back to giants of psychiatry and psychology like Sigmund Freud and Carl Rogers.

In my current role, working one-to-one with a client, rapport based on unconditional positive regard is essential. In the first minutes of the working relationship, I strive to form a connection that will sustain us through an entire treatment, five or more days. I can only make one first impression, and I do this by being authentic, demonstrating genuine empathy, and bringing a confident "we got this" vibe. Anyone who has committed to undergoing treatment, starting with detox, is surrendering to the process, but also more. They have come to terms with that friend, the substance, that doesn't care about them anymore, that turned on them, betrayed them. Talk about a loaded situation!

Sometimes this does not unfold right away or spontaneously. Sometimes the layers need to be gently peeled back. Recall my client John, who was not ready to surrender his medication. Self-preservation is the strongest motivator and taps into our primal survival instincts. The therapeutic alliance, the empathetic rapport, is the key, the way to free someone to move forward. After we resolved John's impasse with the Xanax medication he withheld, he shared how much better he felt, that a weight had been lifted. The strengthening of our alliance reinforced all of John's treatment that followed.

This therapeutic alliance is one of the fundamental tenets of the evidence-based therapeutic communication style, motivational interviewing, MI. MI is a collaborative, person-centered counseling style intended to elicit and strengthen an individual's motivation for change. It applies to both individual and group settings. MI recognizes the nature of the complicated relationship with a substance that can have both pros and cons and the resulting ambivalence toward change. MI rolls with resistance rather than challenging it. The benefit is all the energy that might otherwise be channeled to resistance is now freed up to resolve that ambivalence.

Rather than seeking to project an ideal of treatment and recovery onto an individual, MI elicits the individual's own ideal, which will continue to evolve.

Empathy embodies the "spirit" of MI. Simply put, empathy is understanding and connecting with another person's experience. Sharing perspective, being nonjudgmental, recognizing the emotion in others, and communication are the elements. Therapeutic empathy can be learned and improved through practice.

Motivational interviewing ranked as the fourth most commonly used clinical approach among all addiction treatment facilities. Although widely used in SUD treatment, implementation rates and quality vary by region, program type, and workforce training. Only 54.8 percent reported having had at least one day of training in MI. And only 64.3 percent of the trained professionals felt sufficiently trained for their area of responsibility.[24]

MI has been around since the 1980s, but this is a case of older is better. Evidence and studies support the efficacy of motivational interviewing. I'll be the first to say it's not easy to learn. MI is not standard training for RNs. The various trainings and home study modules and books I've absorbed over the years probably add up to less than a week's worth of training. I'll also be among the first to say that it's hard to sit through when someone who's just learning applies the approach on you. However, genuine empathy is never hard to sit through. It's the secret sauce.

MI should be more widely implemented, and the spirit of MI should be universally adopted. Empathy needs to be stressed, if for no other reason than it correlates to retention in treatment and better outcomes.[25] [26] [27] The value of therapeutic alliance needs recognition that it's not receiving. It may be the least tangible and softest of sciences, but human connection is a sorely missing piece and potential game changer in substance use disorder treatment.

## Group Therapy

A few years ago, I worked at a nearby detox facility (briefly) where I observed a tendency for clients to roam the halls but not aimlessly. They would make frequent stops at the nurse's station to inquire, "When can I get something?" The something they were asking for was essentially any "as needed" medication. This facility offered only one group daily. I asked why and was told that because the patients were there strictly for the detox phase, management felt it wasn't warranted. This constituted a significant failure of this organization to support their patients in the first phase of their recovery. By default, these people were left to focus on chemical mood modification, a mindset that does not bode well for long-term recovery.

I visited another nearby treatment organization and had opportunity to shadow one of the RNs. Part of her duties was running a group that day. She gave the participants the choice of reading from the AA Step book or playing Jenga. The patients played Jenga.

Not too long after the Jenga experience, I participated in a week-long training on group therapy at an area outpatient program. The owner/operator of the organization, a personal friend, graciously invited me to attend daily classes facilitated by a national trainer of addiction and mental health organizations. As a registered nurse, I'd received no formal training in leading groups. Although I had run some groups over the years, I was basically emulating what I had seen other facilitators do. The week of classes was highly enlightening but leaned on behavioral health concepts that were a little outside my training and experience. The class culminated in each participant leading a group incorporating the elements of the training. For mine, I borrowed some learning concepts from my personal development and neuroscience training. Mine was a group session on how to get more out of a group session. I hit it out of the park, and they asked for my notes.

Group therapy is the delivery system for education, information, and practical skills that is widely utilized in the treatment setting. Group therapy seeks to build a community of support by emphasizing peer relationships, goal setting, and managing stressors and challenges to recovery. Maximum engagement and actual practice of skills are defining characteristics of high-quality group therapy.

Unfortunately, high-quality group therapy is the exception rather than the rule.

Little or no group therapy is the first problem. In the facility with the patients roaming the halls, failing to engage people's thought process is problematic. The idea is for people to learn better living without chemistry, not double down on the mindset of chemical mood modification. Playing games or watching videos is only a slight step up. People hoping to change their relationships with substances need more than custodial care while their withdrawal is medically managed. Failing to offer constructive engagement that supports lasting change is a failure of treatment.

A brief perusal of random recovery organization mission statements demonstrates some remarkable commonalities. Here are some abridged examples.

*Strives to raise the standard in comprehensive holistic addiction treatment.*

*Provides an unsurpassed treatment experience for our clients.*

*Provides the highest-level Drug and Alcohol Recovery Treatment.*

*Provides high-quality care that addresses the complex nature of addiction.*

*Provides the highest quality of services to individuals seeking treatment for substance use.*

Andrew was the trainer of the course I was privileged to take. He holds a graduate degree in education, has extensive organizational training experience, and points out that every organization has something like the above on their websites. "They don't live by their mission statements because they are not willing to invest in staff development," he said.[28] In other words, they're committed to high quality until it costs more than words on their website.

Andrew endorses that good therapy should be 20 percent therapist, 80 percent participant in terms of who is talking. This is accomplished by breakout discussion groups or simply having participants take turns explaining things to the person next to them.

Total engagement means pulling in those people who want to sit quietly in the back. They may be more comfortable sharing their thoughts with two of their peers in a small breakout group, but the effect is cumulative. Practicing skills repeatedly develops the kind of *muscle memory* (Andrew's term) it takes to apply a skill in the real world. For example, repeated role-playing of a job interview exponentially increases the confidence level someone will take into a real job interview. If someone stands in the front of the room reciting information, clients might be able to repeat the information back, at best. If participants can be assisted to connect the topic to their lives and experience, that has so much more traction. Talking is good, processing is better.

What about when people decline to participate or get involved? Facilitator: "Okay, we're going to write out a list of..." Participant: "No, I'm not, and you can't make me." Andrew said his response to this would be something along the lines of asking the participant, "How would you act as if... ?" or "How would you do that for someone else?" Always seek some level of engagement.

Each group should have stated outcome goals and some form of measuring whether those were accomplished. Example: "After you have participated in this group on recovery skills, you will have identified your three strongest skills and the situations where using them will support you." The outcome is measured by whether the participant can, at a minimum, state the goals and the situations. Ideally, a client will return demonstrate the skill. Goals should be attainable and reinforced through role-play. In many situations, the therapist won't have the answers, but the group will. The therapist is there to facilitate. When the group mind is properly channeled, it can meet the needs of the participants.

## Evidence and Accountability

Ken was an AA friend who owned a lawn company. One summer, he told me he needed to have surgery on both hands for carpal tunnel. He was unhappy about this because his surgeon advised him that he would be healing for the entire summer. This was highly inconvenient given his livelihood. I knew from my surgical experience that this meant the surgeon planned the standard, open-technique, carpal tunnel repair. I explained to my friend that most carpal tunnel repair was done with a tiny incision and a little endoscope (camera), with much faster healing time. However, the technique was newer and not all surgeons had learned it. I suggested he get a second opinion, which he did. He had the endoscopic procedure and healed in just a couple of weeks instead of the whole summer.

Leading-edge, evidence-based therapy approaches are not always utilized in substance treatment. My friend's experience is a stark example of how people don't exactly advertise the fact when they use older techniques that are not state-of-the-art. Unfortunately, this is also the case in substance treatment.

As with the example of group therapy, treatment approaches and the quality of those approaches vary greatly from organization to organization and practitioner to practitioner. Motivational interviewing is an example, with only a proportion of clinicians trained and practicing the approach.

Evidence-based interventions are prescribed psychological treatments that have been proven to change behavior among those seeking treatment for substance use disorder. They have undergone testing. They've been utilized and investigated with control protocols in different population groups in different settings. Then they are retested by different scientists who observe the same results before concluding that these interventions are effective.

Three specific approaches have been demonstrated as particularly useful in supporting behavior change in substance treatment. They are the previously mentioned motivational interviewing, cognitive behavioral therapy, and 12-Step facilitation.

The cognitive behavioral model explains the emotional response to a situation. Cognitive behavioral therapy seeks to change and improve unhealthy emotional responses. The 12-Step facilitation originated from the same principles as the 12 Steps of AA, however, it is based more on science and less on religion/spirituality.

According to the National Institute on Drug Abuse report, *Adoption of NIDA's Evidence-Based Treatments in Real World Settings*, practitioner attitudes toward evidence-based therapies can vary, with some providers expressing skepticism about their applicability in "real world" settings.

According to therapist and author David Patterson, "The problem is not a lack of effective interventions; it is their insufficient deployment. The majority of treatment centers do not use the big three in a concerted, focused, organized way, yet at the same time many of these treatment facilities and therapists mistakenly believe they are providing high quality, state-of-the-art care. They are not. They are flying by the seat of their pants." [29]

NIDA refers to this as the "research-practice gap," and bridging it is the focus of NIDA's research portfolio, including its *2022–2026 NIDA Strategic Plan,* which highlights implementation science as a priority area.

Go on any treatment organization's website and you will see claims that they're using these approaches, but that could mean they have a single person on staff who is trained in the modality. They don't have to use evidence-based treatment and we just don't know.

If providers were using the best approaches, would treatment be failing this badly? That's rhetorical because we don't know if providers are using evidence-based approaches. The reason we don't know is because they don't have to tell anyone what they're doing. Unlike any other care sector, substance use treatment has scant accountability. They have a better deal than weathercasters—they can get it completely wrong and nobody will even know.

Accountability in substance use disorder treatment suffers from fragmented oversight. Federal regulation is limited to opioid treatment programs and anything federally funded. For the rest, state regulatory agencies have variable standards. Some are licensed by state "*substance abuse*" agencies; some are licensed by state departments of health. Some are licensed by both. And 6 percent have no license, accreditation, or certification of any kind.[30]

According to Dr. John Kelly of the Recovery Research Institute, who has consulted for the National Association of Addiction Treatment Providers, "There's more pressure on programs now to have some kind of external validation or accreditation like CARF or JCAHO. So, they have to be open to audit so that the people can come in and view what they're doing to make sure they're meeting certain standards."

The Commission on Accreditation of Rehabilitation Facilities, CARF, has accredited 30 percent of substance treatment facilities. The Joint Commission (formerly the Joint Commission on Accreditation of Healthcare Organizations, JCAHO) has granted accreditation to 23 percent.[31] Just over half of facilities have sought and received accreditation, which is voluntary.

Drilling down to assess the differences is helpful. CARF focuses strongly on person-centered care, rehabilitation, and community-based programs. The Joint Commission focus is hospital-oriented and emphasizes medical standards, patient safety, and risk management. The CARF survey requires organizations to track outcomes for treatment completion rates, *relapse* or readmission, abstinence/reduction in use, along with client satisfaction and functional improvement—

the good stuff! It also requires ongoing quality assurance with measurable improvement goals. All of that criteria represents accountability, but again, that's only 30 percent.

Unfortunately, even that 30 percent isn't searchable beyond the voluntary response to the annual SAMHSA survey. We can't see it. For comparison, cancer statistics are found on websites like the National Cancer Institute's Surveillance, Epidemiology, and End Results Program, the Centers for Disease Control and Prevention, CDC, and in publications such as the *Annual Report to the Nation on the Status of Cancer.* These sources provide official US federal data and offer interactive tools to explore statistics by cancer type, demographics, and geographic area. The number of annual deaths and new cases, 1.8 million people, was available with a single click from the CDC. The CDC had no similar result for new cases of substance use disorder. The closest result is SAMHSA's report on "prevalence," 48.7 million people having a past-year SUD.

In the 2000s, I worked for a hospice. After a year as a case manager, I transitioned to an administrative role, becoming the quality assessment and performance improvement coordinator. The organization became my patient. The job consisted of auditing charts for compliance, compiling statistics, and writing reports. I could tell you how many admissions and discharges the organization had, provide a breakdown by diagnosis, and I could tell you how many patients the social worker saw in a month, as examples. Monthly information was compiled into quarterly reports, which were submitted to the director. The director submitted them to the Centers for Medicare and Medicaid Services, CMS.

Quality assurance is a concept in both business and healthcare that seeks to ensure products, services, and processes meet predefined standards. It involves continuous improvement, regulatory compliance, and efficiency through activities like planning, monitoring, auditing, and data analysis. It's a fairly common concept... except in substance use disorder treatment.

I asked some people I know in the treatment industry about this. First, I asked friends and acquaintances. Then I put a post on LinkedIn, "Treatment professionals, does your organization have a dedicated quality assurance role?" I received a response from someone on a board of directors who was proud of his organization's exit surveys. Nobody I spoke with in the treatment industry knew what I was talking about. In truth, neither did the exit survey guy.

Before we can have an Annual Report to the Nation on the Status of SUD, we need treatment facilities to track and report their statistics as a requirement, not a voluntary response to a survey from an overworked, underfunded, government agency with 85 percent compliance. Substance treatment needs accountability.

# Chapter 6
# Better Treatment

"The future is already here—it's just not evenly distributed."
~ William Gibson

## How

How to individualize treatment in a system geared toward mass production?

I'm fortunate to operate in a format that allows me to work one-to-one with people. This individual approach has advantages that translate to better outcomes for people. The detox is tailored to the person's specific symptoms. The treatment plan is also individualized. How can we modify basic inpatient treatment to leverage these advantages for everyone?

Let's start with detox and protocols. The basis of protocols is that they are a set of standardized orders. The system of provider orders is how care is administered in any hospital, facility, or treatment setting. The orders have been designed in advance, and a doctor, physician assistant, or nurse practitioner, NP, signs off on their implementation for each individual. Nurses then follow these orders and administer medications according to a predetermined schedule.

We could do away with that. There are numerous possible approaches to providing individualized management of withdrawal symptoms.

Restructuring the care team is one approach. Nurse practitioners could be embedded or have their roles redefined. Procedures for assessment, medication, and documentation could be refined and customized to meet a facility's needs. Unit rounds could be conducted every two, three, or even four hours, leaving plenty of time for other duties for the prescriber, such as admissions and treatment team meetings. Lapses in nurse practitioner coverage, such as overnights or off shifts could be managed with as needed, PRN, protocols, as could the need for extra medication doses, although such need would be greatly decreased with individualized medicating.

This kind of rounding procedure, with its individualized assessment and medication administration, could be expedited with templates. An NP and an RN could work in tandem with a medication cart and mobile documentation platform.

This redefining of the established role of the nurse practitioner, whose scope of practice includes diagnosing and prescribing, does defy the existing care model somewhat. Obviously, there are many possible variations on this that would not defy established practice norms as blatantly. One such approach would be broader use of PRN medications while implementing procedures where the RNs perform the assessments in addition to administering the medications. PRN medications utilize a set of instructions known as parameters, the means by which registered nurses follow specific instructions when giving the meds. This would be a facility-acceptable version of what I do when I am in a client's home. The availability of a prescriber for guidance or the occasional question would further enhance this approach.

The assessment tools are currently in use almost universally or should be. The Clinical Institute Withdrawal Assessment of Alcohol Scale—Revised (CIWA-Ar), measures alcohol withdrawal across 10 symptoms. The Clinical Opiate Withdrawal Scale (COWS) is an 11-item scale to assess opioid withdrawal. By scoring patients across the specific symptoms of their respective substance withdrawal, an objective numerical assessment is provided for purposes of administering medication.

I use phone apps for these assessments, which take literally only seconds.

To a nonmedical person, this probably reads with the visceral intensity and entertainment value of assembly instructions for a piece of furniture. Sorry, but this is how the sausage is made. While it sounds procedural, the goal is for withdrawal medication to be administered based on the way someone is feeling as opposed to a set of generic instructions.

We need to look at the person in front of us, not the generic, system-generated instructions.

I'm advocating for the mindset utilized in effective pain management. Just as preventing pain is easier than controlling established pain, the same is true for managing withdrawal symptoms. Keeping people comfortable ahead of withdrawal symptoms—frontloading—works better in the long run for a couple of reasons. It's been documented that the detox portion takes less time and less medication overall. [32] Going big on the front end decreases need for medication on the back end.

The other consideration is psychological value. People typically feel considerable anxiety related to treatment, especially the detox portion. Concern over the discomfort, the perception of discomfort, and the anticipation of discomfort are principal reasons people don't finish treatment or choose not to have treatment in the first place. Remember my client John, who came close to pulling the plug on the whole treatment over his fear of discomfort. The value of a few extra milligrams of medication in these situations is considerable. The mere fact that people believe they will be comfortable enhances their comfort.

While medicating for comfort is always the goal, this bears a little further discussion and clarification. Previously, I said I medicate generously. While this sounds like a euphemism for overmedicating, that's not the intention. Bearing in mind that this is not an exact science, that human beings are not machines, there is a target range, a sweet spot. People will feel medicated. This is not an occasion where people need fine motor coordination; they won't be using heavy machinery. The goal is more than merely masking withdrawal symptoms; it's complete physical comfort. Error should be on the side of sedation rather than awareness of withdrawal symptoms. Remember that we're only talking about a day or two of the most intense withdrawal symptoms.

This raises a couple of issues. First, safety is paramount. Equilibrium, balance, and gait can be impacted by this level of medication. Risk of falling and injury needs to be mitigated. Patients need to be made fully aware that their coordination might be affected. Safety checks and even direct observation should be utilized as indicated.

The other issue raised by emphasis on effective use of medication is central to the proposition of treatment itself. Using mind-altering medications to treat people for the use of mind-altering substances has ramifications. This is the true intersection of addiction and treatment. Some people are going to like it too much, and it touches on an individual's motivation and their very intention behind seeking treatment. Chemical mood modification is counterintuitive to recovery from substance use disorder. The problem is that these wagon wheels have left some deep grooves. Sometimes it's just not easy to move in a different direction.

Most nursing staff in the treatment field have observed patients and clients who are preoccupied with their medication. Years ago, I had a client at a treatment facility who emerged from her room nightly to request a specific PRN medication, by its more difficult brand name, at precisely the time that it became available. She knew the medication, the schedule, and the parameters for administration. This stands out because it was 2 AM, and she set her alarm to wake her up to make the request. When patients are more focused on the medication than the symptom it is intended to alleviate, this is sometimes referred to as medication-seeking behavior. While that should not be used as a label, the behavior appropriately warrants acknowledgment by the treatment team.

The first objective of providers, nursing staff, and the treatment team should be evaluation to make sure that patients exhibiting this behavior are indeed adequately medicated. As an example, if people are asking for extra pain medication consistently, the medication could be scheduled or dosages modified, etc.

After that, we find ourselves in a challenging gray area. Reducing this behavior to a label used by treatment staff everywhere, "med seeker" is not only marginalizing but also ignorant of the fact that this is a manifestation of substance use disorder. This is addiction running on autopilot. Like zombie ants serving the needs of the invasive fungus controlling their brains, people become drug-taking machines. Their prime directive is feeding the beast. They have forgotten who they are. Again, the example of my client John hiding medication out of fear of being undermedicated indicates that there are multiple layers to this.

In this gray area, critics will likely point out that some people will continue to use substances to the point of oblivion or worse.

This is where we could consider the portion of the comprehensive assessment and treatment plan that assesses readiness and motivation for recovery.

## Treatment Plans

The transtheoretical model, commonly known as the stages of change model, was developed in the early 1980s by psychologists James Prochaska and Carlo DiClemente. It's a framework for better understanding how people change problem behaviors or adopt new healthy behaviors. By analyzing how people change addictive behaviors, the model recognizes that behavior change is a process, as opposed to an event, and that people are at varying levels of motivation and readiness to change. Individuals move through distinct stages at their own pace. I experienced this during what I termed my orientation period, and I recognize this process in my clients.

The stages are as follows.

1. Precontemplation—The person is not considering change and may be unaware or in denial of the problem.
2. Contemplation—The person acknowledges the problem and is thinking about change, weighing the pros and cons. They are prone to ambivalence.
3. Preparation—The person intends to take action soon, developing a plan.
4. Action—The person actively modifies their behavior, experiences, or environment to overcome the problem, requiring considerable commitment and energy.
5. Maintenance—The person works to sustain the change and prevent repeating or returning to the behavior.

Looking at these stages, it's easy to see how they apply to people as they come to terms with problematic substance use. What's not easy is moving from one stage to the next without fully processing the change and thoroughly integrating it into one's understanding and behavior. It's an inside job and cannot be forced by external factors or influence. I learned this from my own experience, and I see it frequently in my work. Recognizing that I can't move someone up the scale, but rather that I can only support them in their process is absolutely fundamental.

This is not any revolutionary concept, and yet… treatment continues to hammer away at the only nail it recognizes—abstinence.

Dimension 4 of the ASAM assessment criteria for treatment placement measures motivation for treatment and recovery. It assesses awareness of problems and willingness to change while evaluating resistance or ambivalence.

What does treatment or recovery look like for the individual who brings a "gimme-drugs" mindset? Is the mindset addiction autopilot, possibly based in deep-seated, previously unrecognized trauma? Is it a deep-rooted fear of discomfort? Does it reflect a lack of readiness for the action stage? Identifying what underlies this behavior and treating accordingly does the greatest service to this individual. The first and most fundamental element of a treatment plan would be an accurate read on whether someone is ready and motivated for recovery; second, what are the goals of that recovery? There is no cookie cutter for this. There are infinite approaches. However, if an initial period of abstinence is unacceptable, an individual may not be fully invested in the action stage, i.e., not ready for treatment as it has traditionally been rendered.

The concept of readiness for treatment needs to be reevaluated. The treatment field, as well as the traditional model of recovery, clings to the notion that some people just aren't ready for treatment and consigns them to some corresponding secondary status where they don't get help. And they're not ready for treatment, conventional treatment that is, as our cookie-cutter system continues to apply it. The treatment machine wants to keep jamming people it considers to be square pegs into the round holes of abstinence-based treatment and recovery.

There needs to be a middle ground. We have the tools to assess and evaluate this, and we have tools to support patient ambivalence. When someone shows up bouncing between the stages of preparation and contemplation, or even shades of precontemplation, they need a treatment plan that reflects this. People who are stuck that way, and find themselves in treatment for whatever reason, need motivational interviewing and therapeutic alliance. They need unconditional positive regard. Treatment needs to accommodate this. When part of the chronic medical condition is resistance to treatment, treatment needs to adapt instead of expecting the patient to somehow come to their senses and conform. We still have the same mindset and approach that was applied in my situation 35 years ago.

More therapeutic alliance needs to be built into treatment in general, and treatment plans specifically, listed directly as an intervention. The question is how to provide something as intangible as relationship as a treatment measure. It can't be quantified or dosed like medication.

The first step in building therapeutic alliance into treatment is recognizing its value and prioritizing it as both an intervention and a goal. The second step, implementation, requires dedicated staffing. This function would not need to be performed by licensed staff such as counselors or registered nurses, although the more challenging cases would benefit from the skill level brought by those professionals. Recovery coaches and peer-support specialists are ideally suited to this role. In fact, it is the basis of their training and mandate. The issue is usually one of a caseload that proves contrary to establishing the necessary level of rapport. Facilities would have to dedicate resources toward this goal. Staff need both the time and directive to work with people on this level. They need training. It requires more specialized training and support from management. As well as being in treatment plans, it needs to be in the staff's job descriptions. This would necessitate not only a cultural shift but also an actual paradigm shift in the way our treatment system currently operates.

## Paradigm Shift

Private interests, operating with profit as the sole motivation, have entered SUD treatment in a big way. The problems inherent in the treatment industry are the same things that make it attractive to aggressive business interests. Unfortunately, it's viewed as a growth industry. The presence and prevalence of substance use disorder is a given. Policy changes are also driving the perception of treatment as a growth area. The Affordable Care Act and the Mental Health Parity and Addiction Equity Act have expanded and mandated insurance coverage for behavioral health conditions. The industry is fragmented; standalone facilities or small organizations are like helpless sheep separated from the protection of the flock, vulnerable to the wolf that is private equity. Standards are flexible, and there is no requirement for accountability.

As previously mentioned, private for-profit organizations are 43 percent compared to about 50 percent nonprofit. However, the 43 percent of organizations provide 56 percent of the care when the numbers are broken down.

Private equity firms acquire businesses with the intention of selling them quickly, a practice called flipping. The typical timeline for this is between three and seven years,[33] during which time the facility is essentially stripped down to the bare bones to make it more profitable. The private equity standard is to double or triple their initial investment.[34] This practice is obviously in direct conflict with quality of care and the highest interest of the population seeking treatment from substance use disorder.

The current paradigm, flawed treatment in a system destined to get worse as it continues to cannibalize itself, is not sustainable. Addiction treatment cannot continue to be the playground of dispassionate investors.

Dr. John Kelly said, "I think the question has partially to do with the kind of bad actors, quote-unquote, out there in terms of exploiting vulnerable populations for profit. There is always that element, I think, in every area of medicine, and probably every area of life among human beings being exploited for profit. And one of them is treatment, sadly."

In 2008, when my hospice organization moved me to a quality assessment coordinator position, they were anticipating industry-wide regulatory changes. In the years prior, hospice had become its own type of Wild West. Suffering from loose regulation and loopholes, the hospice industry became populated by opportunists. Long-term care organizations and facilities saw opportunities to mine reimbursement from Medicare and private insurance. Everybody and his uncle opened a hospice, and patients were on hospice for years (six months is a reasonable time frame for terminal patients in hospice).

CMS rolled out new Conditions of Participation, i.e., sweeping, industry-wide regulatory changes. Failure to meet these conditions would result in organizations having to return reimbursement for the entire quarter in which they were not in compliance. The typical hospice downsized its census by 30 percent. The hospice I worked for was up for sale in a matter of months.

Substance use disorder treatment needs sweeping, industry-wide regulatory changes. It needs standards for accountability. It needs mandatory best practice treatment approaches. Someone living with substance use disorder who wants treatment needs to be able to get individualized treatment that works. TREATMENT THAT WORKS.

Recently, a billionaire whom I was treating pointed out to me that hospice and substance use treatment are not the same thing. He didn't think the same thing could happen with treatment.

He made the point on the heels of a conversation about the failings of the treatment industry. Robert is both a consumer and a savvy businessman. He is one of the smartest people I've ever met, and it's relative, but that might be saying something. Not only is he successful but he's also just a good human being, and he has a charisma to him.

"It felt like they were getting ready to sell the place," he said, referring to the treatment facility where he spent only a few days before signing himself out over legitimate issues.

"I've been in private equity long enough to know what that looks like, and I really got that feeling." He cited lack of help (employees), services, and the high-quality clinical people he had met previously who were no longer there. "That's a major sign, when they get rid of people who have been at a place for a long time, earning higher salaries."

The mere fact that we were having the conversation was because even being a billionaire couldn't get him treatment that worked in the mainstream treatment industry. I know how Pollyanna I sound, but I suspect the Pure Food and Drug Act sounded the same way 120 years ago. That's what I've been saying anyway. Substance use disorder, addiction, cannot be reduced to a chronic medical condition. It defies treatment. Until we recognize what addiction is doing to us as a nation and realize that the current cost (both in dollars and human suffering) far exceeds the cost of better treatment, nothing is going to get better.

# Chapter 7
# My Story: Recovery

"New beginnings are often disguised as painful endings."
~Lao Tzu

## The Day after Rock Bottom

My job was in jeopardy.

I had an ugly blast of anxiety, which hit me as I drew my first breath of the day. I was in trouble. I'd been out of work with a legitimate injury before, but now I was in some vague unexcused-absence situation, with drunkenness on the job involved. I did not exactly wake up with a new lease on life on the next day following the events of my first real day in recovery.

The other reason I didn't wake up to greet a new day full of promise was because I was detoxing. Thursday morning, January 10, 1991, I was about 36 hours removed from my last drink of vodka. My body was panicking.

I managed to go to two meetings that first Wednesday evening, though I shook so intensely that I couldn't hold a cup of coffee. The withdrawal was peaking by the next day.

Withdrawal is discussed in some detail in the chapter on treatment. The short version is that, instead of snapping back to normal, the central nervous system takes a few days to recalibrate. My sleep was fitful that first night. The tremors continued, soon to be joined by a headache and sweats that alternated with chills. I had no appetite. My anxiety was substantial, and that was just baseline. When I thought about my situation, it went off the chart. My skin felt like it was crawling. I stayed on the couch all day, occasionally dozing only to jolt awake as though I'd levitated and suddenly fallen. Sleep was scant the following nights as the symptoms continued. In ranking this second detox among the unpleasant experiences of my life, this withdrawal felt like my prostate biopsy and root canal had a grotesque love child, and the labor lasted four days.

I was stupid to do this alone. While not anticipating a pleasant experience by any stretch, I didn't take into account that my previous detox had been significantly assisted by close supervision and medication as was indicated. They'd given me some little capsules, which didn't seem to do anything, or so I thought at the time. I realize now that they had done a lot for me during that previous detox. I had minimized the benefit of hospitalization, and though I did not know it at the time, detoxing myself at home was dangerous.[‡]

Thursday and Friday were the same. The couch. Feeling like crap. Two meetings. Fitful sleep. While I knew that a drink would fix everything, I never questioned my powerful decision.

By Saturday, the worst was over. I dug out of a significant snowfall, a couple of feet, to get to a meeting on Saturday. Daily meetings became my task. Even though the literal physical need for alcohol was rapidly fading, I still had a mental and emotional compulsion to drink. It was my daily habit, my constant companion, and pruning out that hardwired behavior would take time. Meetings were the first step in that process.

I had left a bad mess at work. I had presented myself for duty in an unfit state, been called right out on it, and had fled the scene. However, I had several things going for me at this point. First and foremost, I had done the hardest thing I could do—I sobered up. Not only that but I had also taken serious action toward working on my underlying problem. Though the details were not something that could be openly discussed at a disciplinary meeting, HR director Michael knew this.

The situation was not black and white. As a human resources director, Michael had a duty to the hospital. As a member of the AA

[‡] Please do not do this yourself. I did not understand this over 30 years ago, but significant withdrawal, especially from alcohol, should be medically supervised. The process is potentially life-threatening. The short list of the potential hazards are stroke, seizure, or cardiac problems. Please seek qualified medical supervision.

fellowship, he saw a bigger picture, and I knew this posed a dilemma for him. He carefully explained to me that he was bound by his obligation as the administrator who made decisions on such matters, and that things had to be done by the book. That he was privy to all the details of my situation actually made his job simpler in one way, but he was ethically bound to do things a certain way. That certain way entailed my facing the consequences of my actions. There would be no free pass from another AA member.

A meeting at work took place the following week, giving my anxiety plenty of time to build. In attendance were Michael and the operating room manager who had called me out on my drunkenness the previous Wednesday morning. This was eerily reminiscent of the meeting with the principal at the junior high school, following my drunken vomit rampage in eighth grade.

I admitted everything, my drinking problem, my bingeing while being out on injury, and my intoxication on return. I took responsibility and apologized. I meant it. I accepted and signed some sort of written discipline measure, which I'm sure spelled out that I was a cat with no more lives. There would be no other chances, no further tolerance.

I returned to work the next day. It was awkward. The reception was not warm, but not hostile. I don't know what my coworkers had been told, but it was a small department with few secrets. This episode that caused me to contemplate ending my life at the time would eventually be water under the bridge.

After returning to work, I immediately noticed that being home alone in the afternoon was brutally difficult. The temptation to drink, a craving sensation, was constant. Persistent, unwanted thoughts about drinking seemed to occur at the time of day when I would start consuming alcohol. Nothing felt right.

The thing that got me through had been the next domino, the next pivotal event. Five days into my fledgling recovery, barely beyond withdrawal, I had a full-on mystical experience.

I was thinking in real terms of getting sober, thinking about what I needed to do and what the obstacles were. I didn't know how to stay sober. My fevered brain never stopped analyzing, and it became increasingly obvious that there would have to be some reckoning with "the God thing." God or a higher power is a mainstay in AA. The concept is woven all through the steps and the literature. I noticed that the people who were succeeding at sobriety, and life for that matter, had worked out this higher power thing. I kept hearing people say that they got on their knees and prayed to God. They asked for help to not drink on that given day. I also heard people say it worked.

This was a huge stumbling block. Growing up, there had been no religion, no spirituality, no God. When I was a little boy one Sunday morning, I had asked my parents if I could play with a neighborhood friend. "No," I was told, "his family is at church." I asked why we didn't go to church. "That's something you'll make your own mind up about someday," they said. I had no real ideas about spirituality.

The "someday" my parents told me about had arrived. It was Sunday morning, and I planned to attend a local speaker meeting for the first time. I had been thinking hard about the spirituality question and resolved that I would try something new and different. After getting dressed, I went in the bathroom and closed the door.

I got on my knees. Out loud, I said something close to the following: "I don't know if there is anything or anyone there, but if there is, could you please give me some kind of sign so I know you are there?" I said this solemnly, but not too loudly, as my girlfriend was around.

Lightning didn't strike and the world again stayed on its axis. I got up and left the bathroom. Patricia did give me a look. I went to the meeting as planned. This was the largest meeting I had attended up to that time; there were more than 200 people in a school cafeteria. The format is known as open speaker, where a series of 10- to 20-minute talks are given by members of a visiting group. The meeting is open to anyone, as opposed to just AA members.

For the uninitiated, Alcoholics Anonymous, AA, is everywhere; they just aren't putting marquees out front saying "AA meeting today." If you had driven down Main Street in Bradford on a Sunday morning, you might have noticed people congregating in front of the Sacred Hearts School, most likely smoking. You might have noticed that lots of the cars parked along the street, slightly more clunker-ish than average, had bumper stickers with sayings like "Easy Does It," and "One Day at a Time." These would be the only external indications that the Sunday morning Wide Awake Group was meeting inside. Had you ventured inside the short distance to the cafeteria, you would have observed people moving around and seated at the cafeteria tables. The aisle down the middle of the large room was the demarcation between smoking and nonsmoking areas.[§] At the back of the room, there was ample coffee and an assortment of doughnuts rivaling the Dunkin' Donuts down the street where they came from. The considerable cacophony from hundreds of conversations would immediately cease when the group secretary banged the gavel at 10 AM.

The third person who spoke looked familiar. She was a twentysomething, nondescript woman. As she introduced herself and began speaking, I distinctly remembered having heard her tell the same story on a previous occasion. In fact, I was so sure of recently hearing her speak that I almost stepped out for a cigarette but decided not to as I was trying to be dedicated. I would sit and listen to this "rerun." I remembered details of her story vividly: she was painfully shy until she drank, then became the life of the party; teaching ballet to the football team; having her friend ring a neighbor's doorbell as a decoy, while she snuck in his back door and stole his booze when he answered the front door; horror stories of fights with her mother; drinking at the laundromat; her general self-loathing; her alcohol bottom; and the gift of her finding recovery. I remembered these significant and specific details from some previous occasion as she told them again that morning. I remember them to this day. Then the meeting adjourned to the break.

I was glad I had stayed and listened. On my way outside, I crossed paths with the woman who had just spoken. She was with another young woman. I said hello and thanked her for speaking. I mentioned that I had recently heard her speak elsewhere, but liked it even more this morning, or something like that. She looked at her friend and then looked at me strangely. She asked when I had heard her speak. This was a little fuzzy to me; I could not pinpoint exactly where and when this had been. I told her where/when I thought it might have been, obviously during the previous few months when I had been going to meetings. She looked at her friend again and at me even more strangely and said that this morning was the first time she had spoken in over six months.

[§] Yes, in the early 1990s in a school cafeteria, you could have a section where smoking was allowed and a section for nonsmokers. I have a swimming pool analogy where there is a buoy line down the middle of the pool, with urinating allowed on one side of the buoys while the other side is non-urinating. Those were different times. The expectation was that the smoke would disregard the fundamental chemical process of diffusion and remain on the smoking side of the room.

About that moment I was wishing I could turn invisible. Something weird was happening. Awkwardly excusing myself, I continued outside. I pondered what happened for the rest of the meeting and then for the rest of the day.

My experience of listening to the young woman at the meeting, secure in the knowledge that I had heard her before, only to find out that was not possible was profoundly moving. In truth, it was earth-shattering. As the significance of my morning began to settle in on me, it was almost like the world slowed, then stopped. Something in the gray area between paranormal and mystical experience had taken place. And I could not stop thinking that I had asked for it.

Behind my first-ever prayer was a genuine desire to be shown something. What followed was so unexpected, so out of the ordinary, that my ideas about reality were shaken. Not only did the next domino fall but this was also a glimpse of light at the end of the tunnel. My powerful decision was taking me somewhere I hadn't believed existed. As I assimilated this event slowly, and over a long time, this became the basis of my spirituality and belief system.

In the short term, this new belief in light at the end of the tunnel bolstered me against those afternoon cravings.

From that point on, my recovery and my life became a series of daily meetings. I was on a mission. My objective was changing my routine, changing my behaviors... changing my mind. Sometimes those meetings were just routine gatherings, but sometimes there were lessons, even peak experiences. And I was hungry for knowledge. I wanted to learn. The whole thing was a bit mysterious, like there was some body of secret wisdom that I would eventually acquire. I observed the people with established recovery and saw that many of them shared desirable qualities. They spoke of meeting life's challenges; they still faced adversity but had somehow acquired the ability to do so. Most of all, some of these people radiated a sense of calm that was something I truly desired.

## Assimilation

I assimilated into the recovery community. I acquired the AA version of a mentor, referred to as a sponsor. The sponsor relationship is a two-sided equation. The sponsor shares experience and guidance, while I become accountable.

My first sponsor was Chris. He was five years sober when we met and took recovery seriously. He attended meetings daily and was well-versed in the culture and objectives of AA. There is no Policy and Procedures Manual in AA, so the sponsor becomes a walking, talking version of this. Chris showed me the basics and guided me through the 12 Steps.

Chris had a sponsor, Don. Don had been sponsored by a guy who AA founder Bill W. sponsored. It was fascinating to me how we traced our lineage from the origin of the program. Don was one of those old-timers who typically sounded like, "When I was just coming around, we had to walk to meetings. Uphill, both ways. In the snow. Barefoot." Not exactly, but sort of like that—old school and by the book, i.e., the Big Book (the primary AA text from whence the name of the program was also derived). Chris brought the traditional influence, just without the uphill both ways stuff. From him, I learned a code of ethics and a code of conduct. Although this old-school approach is not universally transmitted, it was part of my foundation.

Over the first few months, I adopted a recovery routine that included regular meetings, the sponsor relationship, and service-related activity. I achieved the small milestones of the first year, three months, six months, nine months... one year of continuous sobriety. The suggested AA program of recovery was working well for me.

My life was not drama free by any stretch. Patricia and I had gone our separate ways, and I became involved in an early sobriety relationship with a woman named Lisa. Because she was sober for nine months to my three, I trusted that she had her feet planted firmly on the ground. In short order, she discarded me like a used candy wrapper. When this little romance inevitably failed, I had no capacity to withstand a bruised heart without the anesthesia of alcohol. Emotionally, I was still about the same age as when I started drinking instead of maturing. Fortunately, Chris helped me get through this tragedy.

My routine was 10 meetings weekly for the first year and a half. I worked the program and did the drill, as they say. Still, I was not the proverbial poster boy. I questioned everything. Not only did I ask questions but I also challenged ideas. At some point, I couldn't say precisely when, I became a different version of myself. Completely absent in this upgraded version of me is any inclination, thoughts, or desire to drink, use drugs, or alter my consciousness in any way. I knew at some level that I would never drink again. That kind of thinking is the equivalent of heresy in AA, where they do it "a day at a time."

In the first five years of recovery, I reinvented myself. Having taken up the bottle at a tender age, I had missed some milestones. My early recovery relationship crash-and-burn served to emphasize that I hadn't grown up emotionally. My ability to cope with emotional discomfort and accept responsibility and the consequences of my actions had never come online. Given a choice between building character or having a drink, the drink had always won out. Now the tab was coming due. I began a process of rapidly catching up for my arrested development.

I had a responsible job but hadn't advanced in eight years. Being in my 30s and unmarried felt awkward. I began to contemplate the bigger picture of my life.

Health consciousness was the first major change. After my daily cigarette consumption doubled to about a pack a day over the first year of recovery, I quit smoking early in my second year. This was more for health reasons than anything, but today I see the irony. Many people in recovery still smoke, despite being in the abstinence-based, nothing mind-altering, recovery program. Mind-altering is subjective, but it's not uncommon for people in AA to have a coffee in one hand and a cigarette in the other. Perhaps it's mind-altering because they don't think smoking is an addiction. Smoking kills more people with alcohol use disorder than alcohol does, and I discuss this topic in depth later.

I began running, cycling, and working out. I was determined to reclaim the body that I had stopped caring for. I had my first routine physical exam and dentist appointment in the better part of a decade.

Using a small inheritance as a down payment, I bought a house. The sheer audacity of this was mind-boggling. Nowhere in my upbringing had there been emphasis or even mention of the most basic of American dreams, the fulfillment of the ideals of job/home/retirement. Through my 20s, I had been rudderless, just making it up as I went along. In AA, there were role models. I heard people talk about buying houses and condos. I started to feel worthy and began to think in these terms. This was the real stuff of recovery.

I returned to school, almost as though it happened by itself.

Since getting sober, I had stepped into a new level of confidence and competence in my job as a surgical technician. The man who had once sat in the parking lot, almost paralyzed by anxiety and afraid to go inside to work, now met each day as it came. It was as if I'd had one hand tied behind my back the whole time I'd been drinking to oblivion every day. A temporary nurse anesthetist was working in our operating room. After a few days of working with us, he said, "I've been watching you. You can do this job in your sleep. Why don't you get off your ass and go to nursing school?" His unsolicited remark was purely constructive.

Something registered inside me.

As if by magic, a flyer promoting sponsored college courses for hospital employees appeared on the bulletin board. In a scant couple of weeks, I was back in school, working toward admission to the local community college's highly competitive nursing program.

A little over a year after returning to school and taking prerequisite courses, I was accepted and began the evening-option registered nursing program. Evening option meant I could work my 7 AM to 3 PM surgical tech shift, then start classes and clinical rotations at 5 PM. Evening option was by no means part-time; there was, however, a fifth semester as opposed to the day option with four.

In essence, I had three full-time jobs, the operating room, school, and, most important because it made the others possible, my recovery.

This was an intense period in my life. The courses were challenging; I challenged them back. My years of clinical experience had amounted to a significant knowledge base. In a surprisingly collegiate conversation, one of the clinical leaders shared that I made some of the other instructors nervous. Something I learned as I became more seasoned is that nursing is not meant to be competitive. Although we had to compete for our places in the program, that was supposed to be the end of it. From my years working in surgery, I held the belief that the responsibility of caring for others is a sacred trust. It's a calling, not just a job. When people entrust their care to us, they deserve nothing less than excellence.

I graduated a couple of weeks before my fifth sobriety anniversary. When I sat in front of my AA home group recounting those first five years, it seemed surreal. The amount of work had been monumental—eighty- and ninety-hour weeks were the routine. Equally intense was the amount of change I had undergone in those five years.

This was a metamorphosis. Externally, I had a healthy, muscular new body. I had a new home and a new degree, ready to embark on a new phase of my career in healthcare. Internally, I had become a man who would not alter his consciousness with substances.

The truth is that I still had a long way to go to put right the damage and arrested development of my 20-year drinking and drugging binge, but I had made a beginning. As they say, progress, not perfection.

# Chapter 8
# My Story: Transformation

"I would rather have questions that can't be answered
than answers that can't be questioned."
~ Richard Feynman

The first thing I did after finishing nursing school was take a breath.

My life had been a whirlwind of work, school, a couple of weekly visits to the gym... and a few AA meetings here and there, mostly on weekends. The school part, with evening lectures or clinical shifts, as well as the studying, studying, studying was easily the equivalent of a second full-time job. When that went away, the remaining void felt peculiar. What does one do with an extra 35 or 40 hours per week?

For the first time in several years, there was no assignment due, nothing to study, nowhere to be. I remember putting my feet up on the coffee table and thinking about how long it had been since I had just relaxed like that.

More than just completing the nursing program, I was concluding a school journey that started well over a year before my first day of nursing school. The schooling itself was an odyssey within a larger odyssey, recovery. In the true spirit of that, I was fulfilling some small part of the promise of my full potential, but in my mind, I was just making up for lost time. People who didn't squander their 20s drinking had done career training when they were 10 years younger.

In the absence of the whirlwind, I pondered my options.

I had investigated the possibility of transitioning from surgical tech to RN where I'd been working. That wasn't going to happen. The job market was not welcoming to new grads at that point in time. I made a decision to leave my job, study for the nursing boards, and start my search for a position as a registered nurse. This was a risk financially, but a calculated one that paid off when I passed the licensure exam five weeks after school finished. Somehow, I managed to crowbar my way into a per diem position and subsequently a part-time position. The per diem job was on a locked psych unit at a nearby hospital. The part-time position was in a southern New Hampshire operating room. The part-time job blossomed into more hours with benefits, but I held on to the per diem job for over a year. Inpatient psychiatric experience has served me well in the substance use disorder field.

From the outset, I wanted to work in the psychiatric nursing field, because I viewed that as the transition toward working in addiction treatment, my real goal even then. However, economic realities and job opportunities didn't support that. Because of my experience as a surgical tech, operating room work more or less pulled me back in. A thin nursing job market (unheard of nowadays) and my lack of actual nursing experience were the realities.

Most nurses work in areas that range from general nursing to dedicated specialties. Operating room nursing is one such specialty. There are two essential roles, and I had mastered one of them as a surgical tech. The other role, circulating nurse, could only be performed by an RN, although nurses could do the other role. While the knowledge bases and skill sets are different for each role, knowing the surgical tech (also referred to as the scrub nurse) role is a huge advantage. Understanding the surgery at the basic level of the patient and the actual procedure supports being a better circulating nurse. I had that going for me.

I had several operating room jobs in my first few years as a nurse. Most operating room nurses are required to have working knowledge of the different surgical subspecialties. General surgery, orthopedics, obstetrics/gynecology, vascular, neuro... and the list goes on. I gained experience, becoming proficient at a minimum, even excelling in some. Versatility became my strength as a surgical nurse. Having gained modest proficiency in the nursing role, along with my previous scrub nurse experience, a temp agency recruited me.

I began working contract assignments the same way travel nurses do, except these assignments were in my region. Instead of 13 weeks at Oshkosh General Hospital, I was parking in my own driveway every night. This opportunity reflected the changing nature of nursing demand. Area hospitals could not recruit and retain adequate permanent staff, so began relying on temporary staffing. Then, in a matter of just a couple of years, the job market pendulum swung back the other way. The temporary assignments were drying up. I applied to and was hired by the community hospital in my hometown. I looked forward to the opportunity to serve my own local community.

## Building Character

The way I've described this whole journey so far sounds pretty sweet for the most part. Except for having my heart stuffed through a hamburger machine when I was three months sober, it sounds like one long ride on a unicorn. Five years into recovery and onward through the first five years of my new career to a triumphant return to where it all started sounds almost scripted. Well... I was saving the parts where I built character—euphemistic language for debacles—for this dedicated section. As I have been known to say, what could possibly go wrong? There's a saying in operating rooms—they eat their young.

Back when I was working in the southern New Hampshire OR, I had a four-day schedule. On my call day, I might work from 7 AM until 10 PM for straight-time hourly pay, no overtime until I hit 40 hours, which seldom happened. The typical perk of most operating rooms was time-and-a-half after eight hours.

I jumped ship to an operating room job closer to home with a standard 40-hour schedule but was summarily fired within a few months. I was summoned to the office of the surgical services director and berated before being walked out by security. I was devastated. I was also mystified, as no legitimate grounds for the termination were cited. Regardless, I thought my nursing career was over at the time. Those immediate feelings of unworthiness hit me hard. They are a common theme for many in recovery. We carry the stigma, and when bad things happen, we feel that's what we deserve anyway.

My only sliver of offense was speaking to a young male patient in the actual way that two guys speak to each other. He was having a minor procedure under local anesthetic and would be awake for the procedure. I had to put little safety straps over his arms. Rather than explain how he would compromise the sterility of his surgery, I said "The straps are to remind you not to reach down to scratch your balls." I was being my authentic self. I was the one who had met and interviewed him, checked his paperwork, and assessed his level of anxiety. Support is different across the age span. Had I been in his place, it would have helped me to realize that real human beings were caring for me.

It wasn't a genius move, not my finest moment. Today I would practice a little more decorum. I was nervous. I was always nervous, always feeling like I had to prove myself. The feeling that the other shoe would drop, that I was impersonating a legitimate person and still not worthy of basic human dignity... imposter syndrome was a constant undercurrent.

But wouldn't that be where someone in authority would say, "Hey, have a little more decorum," making it a teaching moment? Wouldn't that be an investment in the development of a team member? Nope. Weeks later I got yelled at for five minutes and followed out by the security guard.

A week later, one of the nurses from that operating room reached out to me. She had been conflicted and chosen to break ranks about my firing. She explained that one of the nurse anesthetists who knew me previously from my days as a surgical tech had thoroughly assassinated my character before I even arrived. The well had been poisoned; the nurse anesthetist had said terrible, untrue things about me. Sadly, this was a small place and apparently with small people. I never learned exactly what his deal was. In the hierarchy, it was not even possible for me to be any kind of competition or threat. And yet... it remains a mystery. It's likely that the nurse anesthetist was not a happy person, but to go out of one's way to plant land mines in the path of someone working so hard to better themselves is just wrong. While it was good to have some explanation, the action seemed almost evil.

A couple of positive things came out of that episode, and that always seems to be the case. The staff nurse who reached out to me has become a dear friend since that time. She's like a surrogate older sister.

The other upside was that it forced me to pull myself out from under the bus where I'd been thrown. I needed to stand up for myself. Although weeks had passed, I applied for unemployment. So intense was my devastation that I just took on the assumption that I was to blame. No more. When the hospital contested my claim, I had the opportunity to confront a hapless HR representative and the hospital attorney. The unemployment administrator hearing the case laughed at the hospital for offering up the ball-scratching quote as justification for the termination and found in my favor.

Fast-forward about four years to the triumphant return. During my second, 13-week contract at a fine area hospital, I had decided to get out of the temp work while I was ahead. I had applied for and secured a position at the community hospital in my hometown where I had been a surgical tech. This was a done deal, agreements signed, salary and start date confirmed. I took three weeks off between positions to paint my house and visit my sister in Chicago. Life was good... until it wasn't.

I was notified by the hospital's human resources department that my position was "on hold." The explanation given was that the hospital was sold and surgery was down. *Okay,* I thought, *a little speedbump here, a couple of more weeks off.* However, when no actual start date or projection was provided, I inquired further. Now the response was, "You should just move on." WTF? This was as wrong as it sounded.

I reached out to some local connections, including one of the hospital's nursing supervisors. She told me that a surgeon had gone to HR and demanded that I not be hired. The extent of my egregious history with this man was an occasion when we were about to start a hand surgery. I was scant months sober at the time. In the last step before the incision, he made some markings on the patient's hand with a skin marker. There was a circular marking. In a marked lack of impulse control, I took the skin marker and made the circle into a smiley face. He acted like I'd drawn one of those obscene penises, and I later received a good talking to. I recall making a sincere apology.

Years before, I had been assigned when this surgeon did his very first case at the hospital. Of course, there was anticipation and high hopes for this freshly trained orthopedic surgeon who was joining our staff. He was a nervous disaster, as was the procedure. I remember exchanging concerned looks with the OR manager through the window to the room. When another orthopedic surgeon popped in to offer support, likely at the manager's prompting, he was unreceptive and it was just awkward. His career went on from there, stained with bad outcomes and the worst reputation in the community. He was arrogant and petty, disliked by colleagues and staff alike.

Likely oversensitive to disrespect, he had perceived my childish skin marker transgression as impertinence, not my intention, but not a stretch either. So, 10 years later he went out of his way to dictate that I not be hired.

As with the previous debacle years earlier, I wrestled with worthiness. This second instance of a hater sabotaging not only my career but also my progress and momentum in recovery made me ponder larger questions. What had I done to these people to elicit malice? And why couldn't I just be sober and get on with my life, rhetorically speaking? I had some shitty experiences in my formative years of nursing. Raising the stakes, this time frame was also formative in my recovery.

I share these humbling and messy episodes because the struggle is real. Years into recovery, the two steps forward, one step back effect was tangible.

While I had a hand in much of my strife, I was quite naïve as to the workings of the authority structure and the general ways of the world. In large part, I had been an immature wiseass in my drunken 20s. Introspection is an important part of the recovery process. Rooting out my defects of character, no matter how subtly shaded, was a major goal. If people were pissed at me, I needed to deal with that. Perhaps it was attributable to drinking and arrested development, but it was something I needed to own. As a believer in karma, I could accept it.

As a believer in unlimited possibilities, it's interesting to ask myself, "What if?"

What if I'd stayed in that first job? What if I'd just settled in and had one of those predictable, by-the-numbers kind of lives? I'd probably still be there, counting the days until I retire. That is, if I could retire, because I probably would've met some nice woman, married, and I'd be in debt and paying off the kids' tuition right now. I'm all right with that possibility not occurring, with apologies to my alternate universe self.

And what if Dr. MiserableSOB had minded his own business? That's an interesting question, because I don't think this book would be written. I moved forward from that fiasco to a different area of nursing. In hindsight, this changed my life in wonderful ways.

I was recruited by a family to work with their child who had special needs. Within a year, I was caring for a premature infant on a ventilator. The rewards and challenges of this work made me a better man and a better human being. Just as important, it made me a better nurse. I'd gone back to that fork in the road where the specialty of surgical nursing was more or less chosen for me by circumstance. I returned to my roots as a nurse. From there, options seemed to open. I gained a wealth of experience in areas such as dialysis, IV therapy, and hospice. Later, those experiences gave me the confidence to work in gerontology and subacute rehab. Naturally, all this experience has made me a better nurse in substance use disorder treatment, my true passion.

## Growing Up

My second five years of recovery are when I actually became an adult, during my mid and late 30s.

In adolescence, I had stopped developing when I started drinking. It's awkward, but the process resumes at some point in recovery. If the first five years of my recovery were devoted to catching up, the second five were devoted to growing up. The notion of making up for lost time careerwise was harsh but valid. The notion of making up for lost time emotionally and developmentally presented a different set of challenges.

After nursing school had finished, I found myself with time to relax. Aside from my mission to pass the nursing boards, I had time for self-care. I stepped up my attendance at AA meetings. During school, I had kept up a maintenance level of meetings, two or three weekly. That was recovery at the subsistence level. Now I found myself with a little free space on my mental hard drive, and I was observing and processing my environment in a different way, more fully.

At the meetings, I noticed that people struggled. They resumed active drinking and drugging (we used to call it relapsing in those days) with alarming frequency. No one seemed safe. I realized that my early recovery experience of degree earning, homebuying, fitness transforming, etc., was not the norm. This awareness that we still collectively struggled affected me deeply, becoming a recurring thought that I wrestled with. This was a combination of empathy and survivor guilt. My life wasn't chaotic anymore, but I knew I still needed support. They call that "spinning out of orbit." The challenge is staying grounded in recovery and staying sober when the cues suggest you're okay, you've changed. *Maybe you could handle it now.*

The career bumps and bruises described earlier naturally occupied my attention. The problems of the rest of the world went on the back burner when I struggled with my own. I had my best growth in the space between victimhood and accepting responsibility, gradually evolving toward the latter. Slowly but surely, I was gaining insight into my own motivation. The pressure cooker of nursing school had vastly increased my tolerance to stress. Negative events no longer threw me into depressive spells—at least not lengthy ones. I was beginning to display the qualities of resilience and emotional balance.

Recovery had also taught me to see things in a spiritual context. The belief system that was born on a Sunday morning at the Sacred Hearts School on my fifth day of sobriety was becoming established. As I mentioned, I had no basis for belief. Nothing in my life experience had prepared me; I was a blank canvas. The question, "Is there anything there," voiced in a prayer had been answered, but that only raised more questions. How did that happen? Was the woman at the meeting an angel, like Clarence in *It's a Wonderful Life*? Was I just delusional? Over time, I had decided that I was not delusional, but also that the event was no miracle. I could make a case for a creative intelligence of the universe but not for being singled out for special treatment. It was an extraordinary thing that happened when I needed it to, sometimes referred to as synchronicity.

I had traded up from my first sponsor, Chris. My sponsor at the five-year mark was a man named Bill who had many years of recovery. He was a mentor, a teacher, a father figure... whatever I needed in the moment. He rode through storms both minor and major with me. This was his calling, and he had similar relationships with a dozen other men. Our relationship stretched over decades. If something was going on with me, he could tell by the way I said hello on the phone. One of the best qualities of our relationship was Bill's capacity to respect, even encourage, my critical thinking. He enabled me to have both guidance and room to grow.

Bill was a dignified man with kind eyes and keen insight. He was a senior executive in a specialized industry, but like me had started life as a drummer. There are no coincidences. "What was your part in that?" "What was your real motivation, what did you really want?" "When you ask yourself the right questions, you'll get the answers, old buddy." He was wise, patient, and generous with his time. I could not have had a more wonderful mentor. No matter how badly I thought I screwed up, or actually did, his love was unconditional. Our relationship has spanned the decades, though he is now older.

My tendency to question the principles of recovery in AA remained and intensified. Why were so many people struggling? Why was I succeeding? I had continued going to meetings, working my program, and remained committed to abstinence. The transformation part was going fine, but I was chafing under the yoke of the traditional model. My recovery overflowed the container of the traditional model and AA. I needed more. I was not going to get answers to what was wrong with AA in AA.

## Outside the Box

Everything changed after I met a woman in the gym.

Up to this time, I was a solid scientific materialist in good standing. Trained as a nurse and working in surgery, it doesn't get any more Western, i.e., scientific, than that. The belief system with the creative intelligence and synchronicity was quietly and neatly compartmentalized. The student was ready and the teacher appeared.

The circumstances of our meeting were quirky. There was an elliptical machine that I preferred to use, and she was on the one next to it.

"That machine's broken, sorry. The last two people who tried to use it gave up."

"Really? I was on it yesterday, it's the one I always use. What's the problem?" I asked.

"It wouldn't come on for them. You know, the timer, the settings," she replied.

"Well, I'll give it a try anyway."

The machine was fine (hmmm, serendipity?), and we had a long conversation as we did cardio.

Vanessa was an attractive, athletic woman, a year or two younger than me (I was 40 at the time). Her face conveyed both character and calmness. She had long brown hair and beautiful arms that were impressive yet feminine. Her hands were unique in a way that compelled watching them as she made gestures ranging from expressive to elegant.

She told me she was a massage therapist and personal trainer (hence the arms and hands). She also told me about being a student of an energy healer. I was intrigued with that; the conversation was memorable and made a strong impression, as did she.

Our paths crossed several times in the weeks that followed, and we had wonderful conversations. She possessed a wealth of knowledge on alternative and holistic medicine. She had studied something called polarity therapy and was currently learning the energy healing techniques of a remarkable woman from California. This was outside my personal experience but oddly and irresistibly compelling.

We went for a walk one day. We had known each other four or five weeks; it was sometime in January. We met at the local park and walked the trails, resuming our ongoing conversation about energy, and she was describing polarity therapy. We were walking along the trail when she said it would be easier to show me rather than to describe it. We stopped. She asked me to close my eyes and just stand there. I did as she asked. A few seconds later, I felt myself first leaning forward, then being pulled forward off balance. I opened my eyes. She had her hands in front of my solar plexus, one over the other, as though she was manipulating an invisible object, four to six inches in diameter. It was as though she was tugging on something connected to me. She had moved me without touching me.

"How did… what…" I was clearly at a loss.

"I was manipulating your third chakra," she said. "It's an energy center that we all have. We have several of them located in various parts of the body, and they correspond to different functions. They can't be seen, but Eastern traditions have known about them for thousands of years. That's the short version of what polarity therapy does."

This was beyond extraordinary. I was completely dumbfounded, but this was obviously real.

As had happened on a January morning nine years earlier, the world and reality as I understood it had just changed. I had just had an actual Carlos Castaneda moment, and Vanessa was Don Juan.[**] This

[**] Carlos Castaneda was an anthropologist and author of a series of books based on his alleged apprenticeship with a shaman of the Meso-American tradition, Don Juan. Don Juan exposed Castaneda to a series of experiences that were completely

was amazing! What do you do when the world changes? You still go home and make dinner, but you're eating it in a different reality.

Polarity therapy is an alternative healing modality that is concerned with the human energetic system. It came as news to me, but apparently in addition to our physical, anatomical systems, we have a subtle energetic system. My new friend learned this at a nearby massage school. She had integrated this type of energy healing into her extremely successful massage practice. The theory behind polarity therapy is that we exist and function within a universal field of energy, and, in addition to our physical bodies, we have an energetic anatomy. When problems occur on this energetic level, they will likely manifest ultimately as physical problems. In principle, physical disease is rooted in energetic problems. I was fascinated.

My heart's desire at this point in my life was to find my romantic partner. While the universe seemed to be sending me a soulmate in Vanessa, it turns out that we don't always wind up with soulmates in the end. We were in a committed relationship for the better part of five years but eventually went our separate ways. Teaching was her calling, and her influence on me went far beyond rearranging my worldview. She was in my life teaching me and widening my perspective on things that are basic to my belief system today. After that day on the trail when my view of reality changed, my standing as a scientific materialist was in jeopardy.

Eastern cultures have long understood things that remain beyond the scope of our Western science. We have our own energetic systems, and we are subject to the effects of subtle energy. While such things still defy the specific and complete understanding of modern science, the fact that most states in the US license acupuncturists who use FDA-regulated needles, and that people can receive a Reiki treatment in Massachusetts General Hospital and other healthcare centers, suggests these things are real.

I learned polarity therapy and studied a few other healing modalities. Part of this training focuses on developing intuition, that thing we all have that no one really trusts. Understanding first that it exists, second that it will occur, and subsequently that it can be trusted and acted on, shifted my perspective on recovery. The creative intelligence

outside his perception of the way the conventional world is commonly understood, forcing Castaneda to adopt this new reality.

of the universe, with its synchronicity and serendipity, was getting all up in my business. Faith, especially in the form of intention, is real. I was bravely venturing outside the box of the familiar, my comfort zone, and the structured vessel of recovery, AA, of my early experience.

I redefined my relationship with a higher power. Formerly the generic, politically correct AA version of God, what I can only describe as the creative intelligence of the universe, was now demonstrating not only wider bandwidth but it was also the bandwidth. The relationship that was initially born out of necessity to stay sober and move forward was rapidly becoming an understanding and belief that there is much more than what we see, hear, taste, smell, and feel with our everyday senses.

However... that puts powerlessness in a different light. The traditional model bludgeons people with powerlessness; we're powerless over other people, places, things... but the reality is that people are incredibly powerful. We have the power to heal ourselves. We have the power to sense, interpret, and treat our illnesses and conditions. We have the power to cure ourselves in some situations. We have power to achieve amazing transformation in recovery. However, AA constantly tells us we are powerless, and that we had better stay in the humility zone or else! You'll drink. Or use. Or return to just being an immature wiseass that people go out of their way to shit on. By this time, I was done living with the dogma of recovery authoritarianism.

## Limitless Possibility

My studies of energy and alternative medicines changed my perspective on nursing, Western medicine, and especially on our healthcare system. I was no longer content to be a cog in the Western medical/industrial complex healthcare conveyor belt. I came to view with mild disdain our system in the US, essentially run as a business, with its focus on symptom management over definitive treatment of underlying causes. Yes, our system does some things remarkably well, and I appreciate how technology, integrative approaches, and most of all the astounding level of expertise that we've attained offer such promise. However, I've let go of the blind bias that healthcare in the US is the pinnacle that most people believe.

In 2012, 20 years into abstinence-based recovery, I began following the work of a neuroscientist and *New York Times* best-selling author who was starting to teach a form of meditation. While this might be legitimately described as pop-culture, self-help, possibly even fringe science, especially as time went on, it had a motivating element that actually worked. The approach is based in neuroscience and rides the wave of a paradigm shift in thinking on both genetics and physics. The work provided a practical approach to connecting with the unlimited possibilities that each of us holds as potential, the potential for change, growth, spiritual development, and especially recovery. Stepping into this approach was another pivot point. I became a daily meditator and applied the principles to my recovery, doing another entire level of work.

The alarm goes off at 4:45 AM every morning. I get up and go the short distance down the hall to use the bathroom. I return to the bedroom to sit in my usual meditating chair, put in my earbuds, and play one of several guided meditations. I meditate for an hour and 10 minutes. I did this practice every day for nine months.

After months of this routine, I had the opportunity to have my meditation analyzed. At a conference, I had an electroencephalogram, EEG, while meditating, although it was not my usual routine, i.e., a different time of day, nonguided, etc., it was also basically done on demand in a room with five other people doing the same thing at the same time.

A few weeks later, I had the opportunity to review the EEG study with a neuroscientist. He told me that, despite the unusual circumstances, I achieved the alpha brainwave pattern, or meditative state, in 45 seconds. Today, I can easily recognize when this is happening, and it usually takes me about 10 seconds. Practice pays.

By the middle of 2013, I made the leap from being someone who thought about writing a book to actually writing a book.

This is where my growth curve started to shoot up steeply. I started connecting to possibilities and bringing them into my reality. Synchronicity and serendipity on request (as opposed to on demand). Example: the week I was ready to send my manuscript to an editor, an author I met the week prior recommended hers. We connected, and the brilliant editor worked with me on both prior books and committed to this one. I was learning how to focus on desired outcomes while my reality organized itself to make them happen. This was exactly what I was writing about, simultaneously living the results.

I'm certainly not saying my life became enchanted. There were some tough lessons, to be sure. However, I view these in the context of the education and benefits they provided. First knowledge, then understanding, and finally came the wisdom that is earned with experience and perspective.

In 2017, I wrote my second book. Again, the details seemed to work themselves out. With the first book, I took a leap of faith and quit my job to settle into the routine of writing. With the second book, I worked full-time as an operating room nurse while writing the book about addiction recovery. As the second book neared completion, a designer and marketing coach materialized, as if by magic. Instead of a man who wrote books, I was becoming an author. Instead of someone who studied addiction and recovery, I was becoming an expert on the topic. The things I did morphed into the person I am, my identity.

I established and cultivated an online support community, Infinite Recovery Support and Discussion, which has been going for eight years now. Originally intended as marketing, I turned it into the real deal. Over time, and with lots of work, it has become a safe space for people of all addictions and all forms of recovery to support one another and focus on the issues and challenges we have in common. I provide education on addiction, recovery, motivation, and all types of related subjects. I frequently receive direct messages seeking support or with questions, often regarding urgent and serious matters. It has become a bona fide support community, where people engage as they are comfortable, but, most important, provide caring and supportive interaction. During the pandemic, we ran much-needed daily online meetings for the first few months.

Starting with the community, but reinforced by the clinical experiences I've been fortunate enough to manifest, my foundation and attitude regarding the abstinence-based traditional model has shifted, probably 180 degrees. I'm now an enthusiastic proponent of harm reduction and many pathways to recovery. It seems intuitive that relationships and rapport need to begin ahead of the actual recovery or sobriety. Sometimes recovery does not entail sobriety, but rather some gray area that represents where someone is in their unique journey. The point is, communication and support, and hopefully trust, pave the way for a person in active addiction to open their mind to the possibilities of recovery. For years, the standard has been something along the lines of *don't come to us until you're ready* in the abstinence-based traditional model. Today, the problem is that people could die before they meet some outdated, draconian standard of readiness. Unconditional acceptance finds its way through the cracks in the resistant walls of addiction much better than judgment and stigma ever will.

I ran a primary care-based addiction treatment program (Suboxone and Vivitrol/naltrexone) for two years, worked in inpatient detox, worked in community mental health, an intensive outpatient program, and a residential program for adolescents with substance use disorder. These experiences with patients/clients/residents, as well as collaboration with a range of other medical and behavioral health professionals, allowed me to develop and apply my clinical experience, my holistic experience, and my lived experience in recovery.

Recovery is subjective and just as unique to each individual as addiction is. There was nothing extraordinary about my addiction. My daily goal was escape from reality, and the long-term consequences of that were a co-opted brain and pathologically conditioned body. I think experiencing that for myself impacts the way I view everything from addiction through treatment to recovery, medically, psychologically, and, yes, spiritually.

I became an upgraded and different version of the man who could not go a day without a drink or drug. My disposition toward alcohol, drugs, and the substance-related choices of others is neutral. That, and the fact that I do not think about, romance, crave, or otherwise entertain the use of mind-altering substances—ever—is, in my experience, exceedingly rare. It shouldn't be! Recovery is a set of skills that can be learned. It should be individualized with an approach best suited to the needs and circumstances of each person. A big part of my upgrade is a drive, an obsession actually, to solve the riddle of addiction for those still living as I once did. I'm on a mission to change the way people recover. The biggest problem in my life is that we still collectively struggle.

# Chapter 9
# Recovery

"Give someone a fish and they'll eat for a day.
Teach them how to fish and you feed them for a lifetime."
~ Anne Isabella Thackeray Ritchie, adapted

"I'm Keith, I'm an *alcoholic*."

The words stuck in my throat. It was the fall of 1990, and I was still unaccustomed to identifying this way. I was at an aftercare meeting, held on Wednesday evenings at the facility where I was detoxed. Aftercare is exactly what it sounds like, care that happens after acute or intensive treatment.

Alumni from the small private psych hospital where I received substance use treatment were sitting in a circle of folding chairs, going around taking turns making introductions. A counselor named Daniel was leading the meeting. He had longish hair and a beard, both graying. He had a soothing voice and kind eyes. He was like an old hippie with an energy of legitimacy. The introductions concluded, and Daniel began to talk about recovery.

The purpose of this meeting was to support the patients after they left the facility and returned to their lives. The collective intention was that we were sober and maintaining recovery from our substance use.

I was not sober, however. I resumed drinking a short time after leaving the facility. I was in a kind of limbo, drinking one day, struggling to abstain the next. I questioned my choices and whether alcohol and substances even worked for me anymore. It was a special version of hell, and there are probably millions of people who have experienced their own unique version of it.

I didn't know or understand at the time, but this is how recovery starts.

This meeting was a long time ago, but a couple of things stand out. During the course of the meeting, facilitator Daniel encouraged the participants to look at the people on each side of them. "One out of every three people make it in recovery." I think it's actually less, but he was doing that for emphasis, of course.

The other thing that stands out in my mind was the recovery ritual of giving out chips for lengths of sobriety. This is a standard tradition in recovery fellowships and meetings. They give a little speech and then present chips for various lengths of sobriety. The first chip is for 24 hours to 30 days. People leave their seat to go receive their chip along with a handshake or hug. The chips are just small plastic poker-type chips with the numbers of days, 30, 60, 90, etc., on them to commemorate the length of recovery. I did not receive any chips at this meeting since I was not sober for even 24 hours.

I think I attended this meeting two or three times total. The last time I attended, after remaining seated and silent during the chip ceremony, Daniel called me out, saying, "Keith, perhaps you'll have some sobriety to share with us soon." Though well intended, this did not instill a heartwarming, supportive feeling. I didn't go back for more of that.

Today, I ponder how something that made me feel so ostracized, even stigmatized, could have benefit.

However, even though I didn't realize it, my recovery had begun.

Recovery is not signified by the presence of a chip or coin in my pocket. The process of recovery starts the moment my relationship with substances starts to wane. The moment I began to question whether I needed to change, I began recovery.

The experience of recovery, like the experience of addiction, is unique to each individual. For me, it is more than something I simply do; it's a way of being. For others, it might have radically different significance.

The terms recovery and sobriety are sometimes used interchangeably. In the strictest terms, sobriety is the absence of intoxication and means abstinence from mind-altering substances. Recovery encompasses sobriety but implies much more. I could best describe it as a sense of wholeness. It's a constructive force that spans the breadth of my life. I love my recovery; because of recovery, I love my life.

## The Mainstream

The Substance Abuse and Mental Health Services Administration (SAMHSA) defines recovery as follows.

> "Recovery is a process of change through which individuals improve their health and wellness, live self-directed lives, and strive to reach their full potential…
>
> This definition does not describe recovery as an end state, but rather as a process. Complete symptom remission is neither a prerequisite of recovery nor a necessary outcome of the process… recovery can have many pathways that may include 'professional clinical treatment; use of medications; support from families and in schools; faith-based approaches; peer support; and other approaches.' SAMHSA has identified four major dimensions that support a life in recovery:
>
> 1. Health—Learning to overcome, manage or more successfully live with symptoms and making healthy choices that support one's physical and emotional well-being;
>
> 2. Home—A stable and safe place to live;
>
> 3. Purpose—Meaningful daily activities, such as a job, school, volunteer work, or creative endeavors; and, increased ability to lead a self-directed life; and meaningful engagement in society; and
>
> 4. Community—Relationships and social networks that provide support, friendship, love, and hope." [35]

Please note that substances were not directly referenced. The concept of recovery applies to a broad cross section of people living with many different problems. Today, we acknowledge that there is recovery from trauma; there is recovery from mental illness; of course, there is recovery from physical illness… as well as recovery from substance use disorder. However, there is a common thread. Today, bookstores have self-help sections because of the chance meeting of two men in Ohio in 1935. If there was a moment when the self-help movement was born, it coincided with the birth of AA.

### A Stockbroker Almost Walks into a Bar...

Alcoholics Anonymous was started by a couple of professional guys, both coincidently born and raised in Vermont, who met in Akron, Ohio, in 1935. William (Bill) Wilson referred to himself as an *alcoholic* of the hopeless variety. He was experiencing a hard-earned period of remission and attempting to reassemble his alcohol-shattered career in finance. He traveled to Akron to conduct business, and with his meetings and appointments completed, he was awaiting the outcome. As the legend goes, he was tortured by thoughts of drinking and found himself in the lobby of his hotel. He almost walked into the bar but instead chose a pay phone. A call to a local clergy resulted in a chance meeting with Robert Smith, MD (Dr. Bob). The founding of AA was that random.

Bill had the conviction that speaking with another *alcoholic* would help him stay sober. He had achieved his fragile sobriety through association with a faith-based support group of sorts, the Oxford Group, and intensive work with others was a primary element. Wilson sought to reproduce this as a stopgap for his drinking. All he needed was another drinker to work with. A meeting was arranged with Smith, who agreed to spend 15 minutes listening to Wilson. They talked for six hours. Wilson stayed sober and Smith would drink one final time.

Based on their understanding of each other in a way nondrinkers would never grasp, their commitment to mutual support, and a commitment to selflessly help others in similar fashion, Wilson and Smith realized they had struck on something. Not only did they stay sober but also the premise was largely based on what eventually became known as carrying the message.

Wilson and Smith had no model to follow; their personal recoveries and their recovery group were prototypes. They first set about figuring out their approach to recovery and how to collectively stay sober. Meetings became their principal means of connection; sponsorship became their orientation procedure and the 12 Steps became their protocol. They honed their approach and published their flagship book, *Alcoholics Anonymous: The Story of How More Than One Hundred Men and Women Have Recovered from Alcoholism,* in 1939. As they began to receive national attention, they established the 12 Traditions, a set of guidelines for managing internal issues, finances, and public relations. By 1955, they held their first international convention, filling Madison Square Garden, and the founders transitioned the leadership of AA to a board of trustees.

The profound impact of the 12-Step movement remains the basis for the way addiction and recovery are understood and addressed. It has grown from two men seeking sobriety to a multitude of worldwide networks of support groups. Narcotics Anonymous, NA, was founded in 1953, adapting AA's principles to help individuals recovering from drug addiction. Al-Anon and Alateen were created to support the families and friends of *alcoholics*, providing them with their own 12-Step programs. In similar fashion, Gamblers Anonymous, GA, was founded in 1957, adapting the 12 Steps for individuals recovering from gambling addiction. Overeaters Anonymous, OA, was established in 1960 to address issues related to compulsive overeating. Numerous other 12-Step groups have formed to address various addictions and behavioral issues, including Sex Addicts Anonymous, SAA, Debtors Anonymous, DA, and many more. The 12-Step movement continues to help individuals reclaim their lives from addiction and other compulsive behaviors.

The 12-Step movement, as well as numerous other organizations, are vehicles. They are approaches to the concept of recovery that have their own unique set of directions or protocols. Recovery is a concept irrespective of how one goes about it. Most of the recovery organizations and approaches subscribe to the notion that substance use doesn't happen in a vacuum. Recovery often involves gaining understanding of the reasons for substance use and making some corresponding changes. Work on yourself is the common element.

### Many Pathways to Recovery

Over 35 years ago, I was truly motivated to change, and AA was the only show in town. I went all in, built a solid foundation in the 12-

Step, traditional model, and succeeded. Working with a diverse recovering population has widened my perspective. The Earth looks flat until you see it from space. My recovery began in AA, but I eventually realized that my view from a seat in a church basement did not lend perspective on differing recovery worldviews. My personal recovery evolved and eventually overflowed the container of the traditional model.

Everyone's substance use had a unique history and circumstances; recovery should also reflect our uniqueness as individuals. I would encourage anyone entering recovery to explore options. There are many pathways to recovery from which to choose. Today, there are numerous organizations that offer alternatives to traditional, 12-Step recovery. Each has their own unique elements and approach, while they have in common that they are not 12 Step.

**Nonspiritual.** The traditional 12-Step model has a built-in spiritual component. While intended to be nonreligious or sectarian, it's unacceptable to a proportion of people. There are many pathways to recovery from which to choose.

Self-Management and Recovery Training, SMART. Based in cognitive behavioral therapy and rational emotive therapy, SMART focuses on motivation, coping with and managing urges, as well as mindful management of thoughts, feelings, and behaviors. Meetings are led by a facilitator who helps individuals in the group focus on issues, thus benefiting the group as a whole.

LifeRing Secular Recovery. This organization emphasizes personal growth without a spiritual component. By focusing on individual empowerment, members are encouraged to create their own paths to sobriety.

Secular Organizations for Sobriety, SOS, encourages personal responsibility and rational thinking without incorporating religious or spiritual elements. Like the previous two approaches, SOS provides a secular alternative to 12-Step programs; SOS focuses on self-empowerment and rational decision-making.

Women for Sobriety, WFS. An organization of women, for women, WFS emphasizes positivity, self-esteem, and the importance of women supporting one another, and offers a program using affirmations to encourage emotional growth.

**Spiritual Focused.** Celebrate Recovery is a Christian-based recovery program that incorporates biblical principles and the teachings of Jesus Christ, appealing to those seeking a faith-based recovery path.

Refuge Recovery is a Buddhist-inspired path to recovery, incorporating meditation, mindfulness, and Buddhist philosophy. It seeks to guide individuals in overcoming addiction by focus on the Four Noble Truths of Buddhist tradition.

Recovery Dharma emphasizes meditation, self-inquiry, and the teachings and principles of the Buddha to support individuals in their recovery journey.

**Nonabstinence based.** The Sinclair Method, TSM, utilizes medication, naltrexone, to help reduce cravings and consumption of alcohol over time. This offers research-driven protocols designed toward moderation or even "extinction" of the compulsion to consume excessive amounts of alcohol.

Moderation Management, MM, supports individuals who aim to moderate their drinking rather than abstain completely by encouraging self-monitoring, goal setting, and moderation techniques to manage drinking behaviors.

Harm Reduction, Abstinence, and Moderation Support, HAMS, offers a harm-reduction approach that supports safer drinking, reduced drinking, or abstinence with a focus on the individual's personal objectives and self-defined goals.

## Abstinence Versus...

My recovery from substance use disorder is abstinence-based. I do not alter my consciousness with substances, and I go out of my way to avoid doing so—except for caffeine. Caffeine actually counts, but I don't think anyone would dispute that decades of zero alcohol (or cannabis, or any of the other so-called *recreational drugs* that comprised my routine) meet the broad definition of abstinence-based recovery. Total abstinence is the goal in peer-support, 12-Step recovery like Alcoholics Anonymous, where my recovery started. I usually refer to peer-support, 12-Step recovery as the traditional model because it has that set of guidelines known as the 12 Traditions, but it's also, well, traditional.

The two men who founded Alcoholics Anonymous, the forerunner of all self-help programs, would have easily met the criteria for severe alcohol use disorder by today's clinical standards. Their common goal was complete sobriety, absolute abstinence. The concept of moderation, dialing drinking back to some level consistent with normal consumption (whatever that is) was not even on their radar. To them, it was an impossibility. They tried. They considered themselves sober or not sober with no middle ground! Although they didn't bandy the term around, recovery in AA was, and has always been, abstinence based.

In addition to lending their approach to many other recovery fellowships, AA also influenced approaches to treatment both directly and indirectly. Founder Bill Wilson was a mere one degree of separation removed (he sponsored the principal lobbyist, Margaret "Marty" Mann) from legislative lobbying efforts to make *alcoholism* a medical illness and therefore covered by health insurance. The Minnesota Model of substance use treatment, originated in the late 1940s and 1950s and still largely utilized in most treatment facilities, is based on the goal of lifelong abstinence with 12-Step facilitation. The concept of absolute sobriety, synonymous with abstinence-based treatment and abstinence-based recovery, has been fundamental to the culture of recovery from its outset. This is especially true in Alcoholics Anonymous. In the traditional model, nonabstinence is radical, even disruptive.

However… in recent years, there has been a significant shift in a different direction from the absolute, black and white sobriety culture of abstinence-based recovery. The recovery landscape is changing. Everything from treatment approaches to recovery approaches and support organizations are becoming inclusive of nonabstinence-based recovery. What was once crystal clear has become hazy. And complicated.

Let's start with medications for addiction treatment, MAT. What the critics say is that an individual is substituting one medication for another. This is true in a literal, reductionist way. The bigger picture is that an individual with a harmful chronic medical condition is receiving supervised treatment in the form of a legal, monitored, unadulterated, insurance-covered medication. More important, the individual is sober; there is no euphoric or *high* effect from this medical treatment when administered correctly. Where it gets complicated is when the individual engages in the community of peer-support recovery meetings where the focus has always been on abstinence.

I checked in with numerous people who are regular attendees at

NA meetings. The consensus was that people utilizing MAT were not fully accepted, with some members going as far as opining that MAT people weren't "sober." People in AA feel the same way toward naltrexone and Vivitrol injections. Nothing could be further from the truth. However, in the most literal sense, where a medication is utilized to suppress cravings, this is not abstinence recovery, but it's also not substance use. Instead, it occupies some new recovery gray area.

"We know deep down in our hearts that the only way to let God in is to be completely sober. And you can't start step work until you're completely clean. So sometimes you gotta hurt people's feelings without pushing them out of the room," said a young man I've known since he started coming to meetings 10 years ago. He's sensitive about it, but this is his belief.

When I worked in MAT, we followed best practice protocols and obtained urine drug screens during each office visit. The frequent presence of tetrahydrocannabinol, THC, and its indication of cannabis use was not considered problematic. It would, however, elicit a conversation with the intention of resolving possible recovery issues. The cannabis was often used for relaxation (antianxiety), pain, or as a sleep aid. We would discuss relative advantages and disadvantages as compared to pharmaceuticals, and I would provide cautionary advice about sourcing, as the risk of adulteration in any substance is all too real nowadays. Additionally, we would reinforce the availability of support if someone decided to moderate or quit. Beyond that, cannabis use was not considered a problem in our program. A stable recovery from opioid use disorder with occasional or regular responsible use of cannabis is one pathway to recovery.

In the halls of 12-Step recovery, there's a running joke referring to the *marijuana maintenance program*. Cannabis use is heavily stigmatized by people in abstinence-based recovery. As of this writing, cannabis is legal for recreational use in 24 states and the District of Columbia, while 40 states have legalized cannabis for medical use. Still, at the end of the day—or any other time of day—THC is a psychoactive substance. It makes you *high* and fails to make the cut in the abstinence-based recovery world.

The downside for all those people in abstinence-based recovery is that real life has many shades of gray. A friend and colleague who spent years traveling the country, training recovery facility and organization staff on various topics, including harm reduction and many pathways to recovery, would tell the story of people approaching him confidentially or messaging him privately on Zoom. He said there were scarcely any trainings when someone wouldn't confide in him, "I smoke weed and I can't tell anyone." Honesty and Freedom from judgment are mutually exclusive. The community of recovery is supposed to be safe. The need for honesty—complete, scrupulous honesty—in recovery is paramount, and cannabis use would meet with harsh disapproval. The focus of traditional recovery programs like AA and NA remains on abstinence. This is unforgiving reality for those who don't fit neatly in the box, effectively marginalizing their best source of support, weakening it at best.

Here's the irony. As acknowledged by my previous caffeine reference, abstinence in the purest meaning of the word is a challenging concept. It's exceedingly rare, even in that black and white traditional model. That all-American stimulant, caffeine, is found in many soft drinks, as well as tea and the staple beverage of AA meetings, coffee. We can also disqualify from pure abstinence anyone recovering in the traditional model who chooses to smoke, vape, or use any tobacco product. And, if you take the occasional over-the-counter pain reliever like acetaminophen or ibuprofen (Tylenol and Motrin, respectively), you have a relationship with substances. For the most part, those who believe themselves to be abstinent might be observing the spirit as opposed to the letter of the concept.

## Moderation

As a person in long-term, abstinence-based recovery, this is admittedly foreign to my direct personal experience. As previously outlined, the traditional model emphasizes abstinence in the *caffeine doesn't count* kind of way. That was my foundation and conditioning for three-plus decades of recovery.

Like the founders of AA, the idea of drinking moderately never crossed my mind once I was established in recovery. So entrenched was I in my conviction that any form of moderate, stable, or controlled drinking or substance use was impossible that I failed to see that some people were actually doing it. I, who had once been in on the *marijuana maintenance program* joke, came to recognize the therapeutic value of cannabis. My reality has widened to not only incorporate but also to accept that people could have stable, successful recoveries on terms other than rigid abstinence.

A good starting point was the intuitive notion that there are many presentations of alcohol use disorder. In plain old traditional model jargon, there are different types of *alcoholics*. This made perfect sense when I thought about how some people went through decades of life before drinking became an issue. Furthermore, and as severely problematic as my alcohol use was, I've encountered people whose drinking was so destructive that it made me seem like an innocent frat boy, a lightweight in comparison. Alcohol use disorder is unique to each individual. Part of my recovery story is that I spent months trying to control or moderate my drinking. I've proven to myself that this won't work for me, but my failed experiment does not mean that it's that way for everyone.

There is a moderation pathway in alcohol use. Part of the philosophy is that it doesn't work for everyone, but conversely, abstinence is not the right pathway for everyone. Moderation proponents do not recommend that those who are physically dependent on alcohol or experiencing serious health problems attempt moderation. Moderation Management, a 20-year-old peer-support group, encourages individuals to honestly examine their relationship with alcohol, i.e., reasons for drinking and triggers, and endorses specific tools. These include abstaining for an initial 30 days, and then periodically abstaining for single days; drinking one drink for a day or one less drink than normal are other suggestions. Other recommendations are keeping track of the amount and how often you drink, monitoring blood alcohol levels, and taking steps for incremental change.

In moderation, motivation and confidence are important psychological variables in treatment for alcohol use disorder. Confidence appears to be especially key according to one study. "Individuals confident in their ability to reduce heavy drinking are most likely to respond well to a moderation-focused treatment," and, as the authors of the study point out, they may be more willing to try abstaining on certain days to reach their overall moderation goal.[36]

According to an online article from *Psychology Today,* fear of lack of ability to cope with stressors is a significant obstacle. "Professional guidance is an important part of learning moderation. It is best to find a psychologist who is informed about the best practices for learning moderation and who can support your progress." [37]

Moderate drinking could be more sustainable than abstinence. If someone is able to control how much they drink, they might find that they're better able to enjoy family gatherings, social events, and work events. Setting up personal guidelines and expectations—and tracking results—can make maintaining moderation easier, as can keeping track of what was accomplished and what still needs work.

Doing my best to set my long-time abstinence-approach bias aside is not easy here. Many people who wind up at the door of AA would probably not be good candidates for moderation. That is certainly true of me. As previously described, I made a concerted effort to manage, control, and otherwise normalize my drinking—massive failure. Based on years of experience and observation, I was not alone in my desire to turn the progression back to a point where moderation was possible. Somewhere in AA lore, it states that the dream of every *alcoholic* is to drink normally. For me, the simplicity of my abstinence-based recovery has become my way of life, and I expend literally no mental energy to maintain it. It's hard to fathom how someone in the moderation approach could settle into a similar groove, although it's possible.

A friend I've known for decades, someone I met in AA actually, has successfully returned to social drinking. She shared with me that she fixed things in her life, including toxic relationships and now drinks moderately after years of abstinence-based recovery. She reports that her family life is good, career is doing quite well, and relationships are fine. As is the case with almost seven out of eight people, alcohol is an enhancement, not a problem.

However, there is a clear distinction between what my friend did and the moderation pathway for someone initially coming to terms with problematic alcohol use. My friend stopped drinking completely, engaged in the recovery process for years, and did a lot of work on herself. Everyone's different, and technically anything is possible. It's a huge simplification, but it is a matter of degree. For someone attempting moderation, the challenges are following the guidelines, utilizing the tools, the need for guidance if not overt supervision... and constantly wondering if it's going okay. It's significantly more complicated than abstinence. Moderation requires a level of honesty and insight into one's own motivation that comes slowly to many in recovery, abstinence-based or otherwise.

In harm reduction, we think in terms of relationships with substances. My relationship with alcohol was destructive and harmful to me. However, harm reduction also holds that a bad relationship with one substance does not mean that relationships with other substances will necessarily also be harmful. This opens the door through which my office-based opioid treatment patients stepped with their use of cannabis while stable in opioid recovery. The same applies to those people who smoke weed and can't tell anybody. Or to me with my caffeine habit.

The harm reduction recovery pathway, an ongoing relationship with substances, lies at one end of the range of recovery pathways and overlaps the concept of many recovery options. While acceptance of many pathways to recovery is a newer concept, harm reduction is not. Moderation of alcohol use and recreational or medicinal cannabis use are just two examples of nonabstinence pathways. Promoting understanding of the broad range of recovery, and that each individual should have the best personalized approach, is equally as important as the elimination of stigma across the board. The public, treatment, and academic sectors are all in that process and in various stages of understanding the nature of addiction and recovery. The goal is an understanding and acceptance that recovery from addiction, the chronic medical condition, encompasses much more than the long-held ideal of abstinence.

Leonard is in his mid-40s and lives in a town near Manchester, England. He was one of the first members of my online support community back in 2018. He is a brilliant photographer, and he also writes fiction. Long ago, he was introduced to Xanax, taken for anxiety and what he describes as "mind pain," like depression that has a physical element. He tried opioids for the pain and soon became dependent. He detoxed from the opioids with buprenorphine, but the Xanax, a benzodiazepine, has been a long and difficult road. He continues to take the lowest dose he can tolerate under medical supervision, and abstinence is not a goal for him.

While trying to taper himself down, he experienced a type of post-acute withdrawal syndrome. We talked about his recovery. "I tried to detox on my own first, almost killed me. Then I found a free organization in town. It's been great."

Leonard describes himself as an introvert, and his family is back in Denmark. He describes his supports as "not much. Tried a few group meetings in the organization. But I don't have anybody locally

I can lean on."

Regarding AA meetings, he shared, "I don't feel at home in them. Too many people, not very personal." For this reason, Leonard has sought recovery connections online through Facebook and other social media. He said he found my group through another group he belongs to. He posts about his experiences, puts up inspiring photographs, and connects with other group members. He keeps me updated on his progress through personal messaging, and I first explained post-acute withdrawal syndrome to him. "I am very glad to learn of PAWS; it makes me more optimistic about the future."

In terms of outcome, successful recoveries don't automatically equate with the approaches and pathways used by the majority. Popularity of an approach does not equate, inevitably at least, with quality of results. Pathways to recovery are as numerous as people seeking recovery. However, for the majority, finding their way on a well-worn path can be safer. The whole experience is easier when someone else has blazed the trail—ask anyone who has snowshoed. Individualism and good decision-making are the themes of any alternative recovery pathway. Forging your own way forward is the most challenging. That's why they call them rugged individuals.

The paradox is that you can be recovering before you realize you are, but you need to consciously and deliberately try to succeed—it works if you work it. Like me when I was attending alumni meetings and questioning my choices, literally in the contemplation stage of change, the initiation of recovery might not be clearly defined. This is because recovery overarches, or brackets if you will, treatment episodes that can fall within the recovery process. Part of treatment's mandate is preparation for recovery to follow, whether orienting, directly training, or spoon-feeding the concepts. An individual needs to make the leap from substance use to recovery. Beyond the treatment process, this must be self-directed.

The recovery framework is distinctive from treatment. Both have infrastructures and organizations. There is some overlap, as treatment should facilitate recovery, but in the end, it's a "treatment industry" and a "recovery… ?" There's no corresponding word, but you don't need your insurance card anymore. Treatment is an intersection of the medical industrial complex and the healthcare business. Recovery is a different entity, looser, more informal, but vast. Recovery is its own world.

However, recovery requires a different kind of initiative. Engaging recovery is a pursuit that requires energy on my part. I can receive treatment in a passive way, but the quality of my recovery is proportionate to the energy I put into it.

Yeah, but do I have to go to a meeting every day for the rest of my life?

Sometimes I'm in the position of introducing and explaining recovery to someone who has no prior experience. We're starting at square one. When someone is first confronting their substance use disorder, it's like they're being assaulted in every conceivable way. Things in their life probably became... unmanageable, so that's stressful. They went through the detox process, an unknown that likely involved some anxiety and possibly physical discomfort. They are in some stage of that bad breakup with the friend (the substance) that betrayed them. And now, I have to explain to them that all of that was the easy part. Now comes recovery.

I approach this task with a strong sense of responsibility. My two objectives are to share information, objectively, about recovery options, as well as supporting someone's decision process. Every recovery professional has their own cherished approach that works for them—and emphasizing that over other alternatives is unethical.

Early in the treatment process, I like to initiate a discussion about a client's goals, particularly regarding abstinence in the longer range. This gives me an idea about what options to present. After getting to know someone through a few days of detox and learning about their personality and history, I start to get a sense of what they're open to and what might be a good fit.

Bearing in mind that the orientation to recovery that I provide comes toward the end of a detox treatment, the best option is aftercare, i.e., more treatment. This is the gray area where treatment segues into recovery. We know that longer structured treatment yields better outcomes. The best option is the highest level of care that is acceptable to an individual, and I run down the list from residential treatment through the various outpatient options. Then comes the discussion of the existing recovery infrastructure. If someone is open to exploring one of the existing recovery fellowships, either 12 Step or other, providing a direct orientation to this is desirable. Let's hit a meeting!

Exploring 12-Step options is often an exercise in overcoming bad public relations. For decades, the mainstream perception has been that recovery means a lifetime of daily meetings, the supervision of a sponsor, and living in apprehension of resuming the old behaviors.

Alcoholics Anonymous, the most successful and widely accessible recovery fellowship, is 90 years old. During the first decades, as a measure of self-preservation, it was engineered to be tamperproof. It doesn't change—deliberately. Its principal text, the eponymous book *Alcoholics Anonymous,* is stylistically closer to the Civil War era than contemporary times. People struggle with the vocabulary.

The traditional model, AA and NA, has a couple of significant elements presenting obstacles. Spirituality is hardwired into the 12 Steps. A power greater than ourselves—God, with and without the qualification, "as we understand him,"—is referenced numerous times.

The spiritual component of the Alcoholics Anonymous recovery approach is simultaneously a significant strength of the program while being a significant obstacle for many. It's both the secret sauce and the Achilles' heel of 12-Step recovery. Briefly, and from my personal experience, I've seen both sides of that double-edged sword. When I arrived at Alcoholics Anonymous, my stance on spirituality landed me in a murky no man's land somewhere between agnosticism and atheism. In other words, as far as religion was concerned, I didn't know enough to even believe there was no God. To succeed in the traditional model, it became increasingly more obvious that I would need to come to terms with spirituality.

AA originated in the Christian Midwest. According to *"Pass It On": The Story of Bill Wilson and How the A.A. Message Reached the World,* Bill W. sought guidance in the community for the treatment of spirituality in the book, *Alcoholics Anonymous.* A prominent Protestant minister approved an advanced copy. After the Catholic Committee on Publications of the New York Archdiocese previewed the book, Wilson acted on the minor changes they recommended. The result is that the program of Alcoholics Anonymous was impacted by the committee's cultural and spiritual influence, in essence, Christianity.

I was able to get around that. I needed to. My lack of religious upbringing and belief was offset by my open-mindedness and motivation to change. This is not true for some, unfortunately, who are averse to the religious context of AA's perspective on spirituality. Spirituality is enmeshed in AA culture as well as the 12 Steps, the program's model for recovery. For the many who find the spiritual elements of 12-Step recovery impracticable, this renders the approach useless.

In essence, I've been going along with it. To me, any mention of God merely references my conception of a creative intelligence of the universe. I am a scientific materialist. I guess I'm like the physicist who does his science job all week, then goes to church on Sunday; it's a little disconnected.

Yet, I am hardly an outlier in accepting the conditions of the traditional model. I made peace with spirituality in the genuine way I described in my story. Many are able to make this leap of faith. Abstinence was the right path for me, and my success in recovery is based on answering the God question with conviction. That millions have succeeded in the traditional model attests that others have resolved those issues as well.

## How *Does* It Work?

The other principal downside of the traditional model is that it's mysterious. There are no directions, and there is no way of being certain that you're doing it correctly. Other than remaining sober, that is.

After a point early on in recovery, we all think we know what we're doing. I listen to the people I work with and the people I encounter in my travels. From coast to coast, the common theme I hear people express is that they have confidence and a level of assurance that theirs is a good recovery.

Everyone believes that they are the expert on not only their own recovery but also recovery at large. This is, of course, bias.

Bias is a lack of objectivity where judgment or perception is influenced by preconceived notions or personal opinions. There are many types of bias. Confirmation bias happens when I accept information that reinforces my existing ideas, while denying the validity of things that contradict my beliefs. Asymmetric bias happens when I believe I know better than other people, or that I am less biased than others. Asymmetric bias leads me to believe I have insight into the thought process of others while believing that my thought process is too complex for others to understand.

I'm going to pick on AA a little bit here. Whereas my recovery journey started there and I have engaged in Alcoholics Anonymous for thousands of hours over decades, I think I'm qualified to make the following observations. Many in the traditional model are merely skimming the surface. They do not change to any substantial degree or depth. They have merely stopped drinking and substituted a set of conventions—meetings and social rituals and interactions. It's not that transformation is elusive; it doesn't seem to be the actual goal. Most people are tethered to meetings. It's not unusual to hear people say things like, "I haven't been to a meeting for five days and I'm losing my mind." Really?

Wouldn't freedom from that be the demonstration of actual recovery?

It seems that the point would be to become a version of myself who is okay, at least for five days, without the meetings. The point would be to become a version of myself who could be happy and contented without any constant need for external things like social rituals and interactions. The goal would be to become the generator of my own recovery.

The traditional model's approach to recovery is not wrong so much as incomplete. Recovery as holistic, as outlined in the SAMSHA definition. It's just not being practiced that way. It doesn't happen in a vacuum populated by a set of expected behaviors or attitudes. A version of or approach to recovery that omits understanding of addiction and principles underlying the brain changes during the healing process—based in science—leaves the outcome wildly to chance.

Recovery is not something I do. It's something I become, a state and way of being. It's okay to not drink or use one day at a time. That's how the traditional model does it, and it's perfect when you're new. Beyond that, I think it's reasonable to become a version of myself who would never drink or use again. Why would I? I'm transformed. I'm completely different than the old version of me who couldn't go a day without a drink.

My confirmation and asymmetric bias notwithstanding, multitudes of people do struggle to give up substance use and often lose that struggle. And for just as many, the tenuous grasp of recovery is lost, and they return to substance use. The power of addiction is on the scale of a force of nature.

Recovery comes without a manual, discounting the 90-year-old book. There are no standard instructions. For the person seeking recovery from substance use disorder, addiction, there is no actual set of directions. Whether in the traditional model, alternative peer-support recovery organization, or fellowship, or some unique variation or self-directed approach, it's up to the individual to find their way. But it is confusing, often verging on overwhelming.

Recovery, in summary, is fragmented in a contradictory manner. The trend toward silo effects for abstinence versus nonabstinence recovery only serves to raise the already considerable difficulty factor for people who just want to get better. Where treatment suffers from the underlying aspect of business motivation, recovery's inherent flaw is its nebulous nature in which the only crystal-clear thing is that each approach purports to be the best. Why can't we all just get along?

The best thing someone seeking support in recovery can do is to explore and investigate. Whether finding the right preexisting recovery style or creating a customized version, everyone needs their own personalized approach to recovery that meets their individual needs.

We need to do better in supporting that.

# Chapter 10
# Better Recovery

"There are no traffic jams along the extra mile."
~ Roger Staubach

The short answer to the question, "Do I need to go to those meetings every day for the rest of my life?" is no. NO!

However, there are better questions. What do people get from going to those meetings every day? What's the purpose? What are the foundational concepts behind it and how does that support people? If AA is a brand name product, what would the generic version be? Think of Alcoholics Anonymous as being like a trademarked over-the-counter cold remedy.

You've seen these products with catchy names advertised on TV, usually with *before* imagery of someone suffering with flu symptoms and an *after* shot of them sleeping peacefully. Nursing wisdom I like to share with people is that they should read the label of the cold/flu preparation they are purchasing. They will see that the ingredients of the product are commonly available generic medications. Typically, these cold remedy products combine a pain reliever, a cough suppressant, and one or more antihistamines as a decongestant and/or sleep aid. While people are free to shell out $15 or $20 for a three- or so-day supply, I like to point out the prudence of cutting out the middleman and just utilizing the basic medications to manage the symptoms directly.

AA, which is actually trademarked, is like a premade remedy with generic components.

Recovery in the traditional model has underlying fundamental—

generic—elements that confer the real benefits. Community is the most universal. That daily meeting that many choose to attend is a ready-made serving of community. It's not so much that I need the daily meeting, but I benefit from engaging in a community of like-minded people with the same goals and objectives. Furthermore, if that serves as a vehicle for healthy relationships, possibly even unconditional support, that's tremendously beneficial. Community is the rationale for the daily meetings.

The community then facilitates other fundamental elements of recovery. I engage in the community and I learn. Gaining knowledge about my addiction, what it is, and why it happened, helps me. Gaining knowledge about recovery and related skills helps me. Knowledge about addiction and recovery is another essential element.

Mentoring is the next element. I need someone to show me the ropes. The traditional model's set of directions is a 90-year-old book; to help people interpret that, they endorse mentoring in the form of a sponsor. The sponsor is like a preceptor, a walking, talking version of the orientation manual they don't have. While a sponsor is specific to AA, the concept of mentoring is universal to a wide range of pursuits. Business, education, athletics, and basic growth and development all utilize mentors as integral components. Here is another misconception where AA's public relations hasn't helped the cause. Do I need micromanagement and the supervision of a step-nazi taskmaster? Not really (in most cases). Would I benefit from a stable relationship with a role model who is invested in my success and shares their personal experience greater than my own? And do I benefit from making myself accountable to this person? Absolutely.

Service, in the form of helping others or serving a greater cause, strengthens the individual's recovery. Service is formalized in the traditional model. In general terms this takes a wide range of forms. Helping others isn't just good for other people—it produces physiological changes and emotional benefits for the helper. Helping behavior is known to cause the release of neurochemicals linked to decreasing inflammation, lowering pain threshold, and supporting immunity as well as emotional well-being.[38]

Whether one is religious, atheist, or agnostic, the experience of confronting an addiction or substance use disorder can be measured on some scale of existential consequence. It's a significant life event. Whether I regard this as merely circumstantial or something more, I'm probably going to be different after the event than I was before. To varying degrees, it's life-changing. Whether I call it my way of being, worldview, or belief system, etc., the way I view my life is likely to be modified. Questioning and defining one's belief system is something many people experience at some point. This might be merely a backdrop, or it might be redefined by the experience of addiction and recovery. If it's the latter, examining and defining one's belief system is a potential source of strength in the recovery process.

So that meeting that people might choose to attend every day is like a one-stop shopping version for checking all these boxes.

These are the generic elements of the traditional model, the reasons it works for so many. Community comes in unlimited forms and types. A church is community. A group of high school or college friends is a community. The alumni group of the treatment organization is a type of community. Books, YouTube videos, TED Talks, and websites are ready sources of knowledge. If you have a phone, you potentially have access to anything you might need for your recovery. Mentoring is available in a multitude of forms, easily sought out, as are opportunities to help others. Defining one's belief system is one of those inside jobs. We need only devote ourselves to thinking about it. These fundamental elements of recovery do not require membership in an organization or fellowship.

Better recovery starts in the process. The power of that process comes from intentionally and mindfully incorporating the fundamental elements of community, knowledge, mentoring, service, and some type of belief system. In the presence of these elements, and combined with certain skills, a stable, healthy recovery can thrive... without a requirement of daily meeting attendance.

## Deficit Modes

When people first detox, it is common for them to believe that they will be able to manage their sobriety and recovery by themselves. It's also common for them to resume substance use in a matter of days or weeks without some type of aftercare, support, or recovery plan. This is not about someone's level of resolve or good intentions; this is about behavior and how the brain functions.

The expression used in the recovery mainstream is that people

"Don't know what they don't know." In nursing, this is called knowledge deficit.

There are a couple of things going on when someone stops using the substance they were dependent on. The first one has to do with learned behavior. The skill of driving serves to illustrate.

The first time I got in the car for the purpose of driving was overwhelming. I sat in the driver's seat, confronted with the steering wheel, the controls, the transmission stick, and the pedals. In those days, we learned on standard transmissions, so there were a clutch and gears to contend with. Then, there were all the rules of the road, recently learned in a driver's education classroom. After the requisite clumsy practice with the clutch in first and second gear in an empty parking lot, I went out on a quiet back road near our house. I needed every ounce of my full attention to think about all the elements and details of driving. I was anxiously aware that I did not know how to drive. You could say that I was consciously unskilled.

Fast-forward to the present day. I get in the car and head to a routine destination. I think about what I'm going to be doing later when I arrive... or just about anything else. Last weekend, next weekend, a grocery list... I'm thinking about anything and everything except driving. That's because I'm driving automatically. I have practiced and rehearsed driving so much that I can do it without consciously thinking about it. I'm still obeying the rules of the road, signaling, stopping, merging; I'm just doing it automatically. Now you could say that I am unconsciously skilled.

As with the skill of driving, where I practiced until I did it automatically, substance use becomes an unconscious skill.

I practiced going to the liquor store, drinking on the way home, secreting the open bottle under the seat, and the other various skills of chaotic substance use—all unconsciously. I mastered them and did them automatically. Then, there were other associated skills that reflected my mental process and behavior. Maintaining adequate supply was always an important consideration. However, the most compelling behavior was the amount and level of deception practiced toward everyone in my life. I was completely dishonest about the quantity and type of drinking I was doing regardless of the situation. Most heavy drinkers are. This was completely automatic, as though it was firewalled from any critical analysis on my part.

Most people who have used substances to the point of physical dependency have learned all the unconsciously skilled behaviors related to that.

The same principles also apply to recovery from substance use, where we find ourselves consciously unskilled. The problem is we don't realize it; we don't know what we don't know.

After I've completed a detox and I am free of the symptoms of withdrawal, it feels reasonable to assume, "I got this." Many people think this way. In fact, in most cases they would pass a lie detector test—no, they don't intend to drink or use.

Carl, a businessman whose detox I managed a couple of years ago, is a good example. Over the prior year, as he took his private company public, his drinking and stimulant use escalated, prompting him to seek help. "I understand what happened and where I went overboard. I had no idea this would happen," referring to his daily alcohol consumption and frequent cocaine use.

He was open-minded and receptive to education and explanations of his various options for aftercare, i.e., continued support as he established recovery. "AA is definitely not for me." Neither were any of the other secular or scientific, peer-support approaches, and he was not interested in residential treatment or an outpatient program, a sober companion, therapy, or a recovery coach.

He said he would avoid alcohol. "I'm going to start working out again and stop going to the restaurant (that he was part owner of) every Friday afternoon after work."

Catching up on email the same day his treatment ended, he received bad news about his business venture and he drank. Over an email! Without ongoing support, this is not uncommon. Carl acknowledged our expertise but chose not to accept recommendations because… the answer is somewhere on a continuum between he thought he could manage and the right option doesn't exist.

So, what happens? Basically, it comes down to unconsciously skilled against consciously unskilled—automatic behavior versus having to consciously think through every step. A series of small, seemingly harmless choices and decisions take someone into a position where drinking or using seems like one more small choice or decision. The following example is almost verbatim what someone once shared with me. You need gas. You decide to stop at the combination gas station/convenience mart. This happens to be where you often bought beer or cigarettes or kratom, or you bought a little packet of powder from a guy you know who works there. You're just planning on getting gas. However, you make the small decision to go inside. Once inside to pay for the gas you could have paid for at the pump, you see that the guy you know is working. You don't want to be rude, so, of course, you say hello. Or you pass the beer refrigerators or the energy drink section. The cigarette display is in your face. Small decisions have put you in the position of going against your automatic behavior, which was to buy beer, cigarettes, kratom, or whatever the guy you know is holding. You now have to consciously decide to not do what you would normally do unconsciously.

Even if you make it out of the gas station/convenience mart with your recovery intact, you probably considered one more decision to resume using your substance of choice. You thought about it. More likely than not, this risky situation will leave persistent thoughts in your mind. You will now have to contend with a little devil on one shoulder and a little angel on the other, both trying to tell you what to do. By putting yourself in this situation to begin with, you put that devil on your shoulder and it's not going to shut up for a while.

But wait, there's more.

As if the conscious and unconscious behaviors and automatic thoughts weren't enough, there's an issue with your brain when you first stop using substances. The neurotransmitter, or brain chemical, that governs your motivation and sense of pleasure and reward is temporarily out of order.

Dopamine is the brain chemical that not only registers how much we like using substances but also lights a fire under our asses to chase those substances. Dopamine serves an important purpose, and it helped us to survive as a species and evolve. We maintain a baseline level. When we do something pleasurable, we get a boost, which in turn makes us want to repeat the process. We need to eat to survive; we get a dopamine boost from a nice meal. Most people associate greater pleasure with sweet-tasting food. In primitive hunter/gatherer times before supermarkets, if we found some sweet berries or fruit, we would chow down on them. We might store the extra calories as a little body fat and survive another day during lean times. That's dopamine at work.

On a quiet Friday night at home, dopamine is what makes me pause the DVR, find my shoes, wallet, and car keys, and drive to the store. I peruse the ice cream section, make a selection, pay and return home. Back in front of the TV with a bowl of chocolate-chip cookie-dough ice cream, I have fulfilled the biological imperative of dopamine, which motivated me to get up and go for the sake of pleasure and reward.

Substance use boosts dopamine. The first drink provides a noticeable bump; we feel like a million bucks. Unfortunately, the second drink falls short of making us feel like two million bucks, so the tendency is to keep trying. This is why some people just keep drinking once they start. Other substances raise the dopamine level by as much as 500 percent, 800 percent, even 1000 percent. This is not sustainable, and the pleasure reward system adapts. The body and central nervous system always want to stay level, so the dopamine response dials back. The result, when substance use ceases, is a dopamine deficit. The baseline level of dopamine goes down.

The dopamine deficit is temporary and lasts about 30 days in most cases. The possible results are mood disruption in the forms of depression and irritability, as well as lack of motivation and dysregulation of sleep and appetite. There is decreased sense of pleasure and decreased tolerance to discomfort.[39] The irritability might present as low tolerance for people and life's routine annoyances. This puts the individual experiencing dopamine deficit at high risk for resuming substance use.[40]

These two distinct conditions of early recovery, the knowledge deficit and the dopamine deficit, conspire to make the first weeks and months of recovery precarious. The stakes are high and the circumstances are adverse. It's like wandering through a minefield without even knowing exactly what your destination is. The desired outcome is that you know what to do, how to do it, and you do it automatically; you get exactly the opposite in the first days of recovery. These behavioral and physiological conditions are rudiments of neuroscience, and I teach them to every patient, client, or interested individual I encounter.

These notes are from my standard discharge instructions.

> "Remember the critical time frames.
> • Your brain will take 30 days to recalibrate your motivation/pleasure/reward center and dopamine levels. This is a high-risk time, so remember—if things feel strange or wrong, there's nothing the matter with you. That's just

how brains heal.

• The same applies to a lesser degree to the first six to nine months. Be kind, patient, and gentle with yourself while you learn the skills of recovery and unlearn the skills of addiction."

So, how do you navigate from knowledge deficit past dopamine deficit? How does someone transition from being consciously unskilled to unconsciously skilled? How do people learn and practice the skills of recovery automatically?

The first step is awareness and understanding. Numerous people have come back to share with me, "I'm so glad you told me about that." The tendency to feel isolated, that there is something wrong with you, is common to many in early recovery. Knowing what to expect changes the game. Incorporating a relatable example like learning to drive helps people to make the leap from learning new information to practical understanding. Later, when they catch themselves feeling moody or short-tempered, it clicks.

Sometimes this happens in a forensic context, when we are looking back at what went wrong. A young patient had started his recovery with our office-based treatment from day one. About a month later, he came in testing positive for cocaine in his urine drug screen. He was open and forthright about this.

"It was just like you said. It was like I was fed up with everything, but it was really nothing. I knew getting high would make me feel better. Temporarily, I mean." In these situations, it's not about someone's willpower, resolve, or intention. This is just how brains heal.

Information sticks better when people understand the why part. Better recovery starts with better information and understanding of leading-edge concepts. Many therapists and clinicians know and share this, but it's not in the mainstream yet. The future of recovery is a shift toward people understanding these basic principles of neuroscience and the empowerment of that understanding.

### Recovery Is a Skill

The skills of recovery are learned through practice. When we first learn information, it is stored as a distinct episodic memory. Each experience observing and being exposed to information is consciously associated with the occasion when it happened. It can be consciously retrieved. For example, when you are brand-new in recovery and faced with choices, such as getting gas where you bought beer, you might remember the time you heard someone say that has risks. This takes deliberate effort in the early going, however.

With repeated practice, episodic memory becomes procedural memory. The memory gradually becomes more automatic, requiring less conscious control to recall the learning experience. The associated brain activity shifts from areas of conscious control to regions handling automatic programs. This happens through an effect called neuroplasticity, the ability of the brain to change and adapt its networking pathways. In a literal sense, the brain rewires itself. This occurs best with consistent practice—many, many repetitions. As the memory of the specific learning occasion fades, the procedural knowledge remains. I don't remember learning to write my name, but I know how to write my name.

People in successful long-term recovery have often developed a modified version of the basic human skill of pattern recognition. Pattern recognition is the ability to identify relationships in information, in the present or from past experiences. Inherent in that is identifying that certain actions lead to certain outcomes (or consequences), or that events tend to occur in particular sequences. As a recovery skill, this can come in handy when deciding where to purchase gasoline, as an example. The ability to associate certain situations with their potential for undesirable outcomes is a considerable asset.

Mindfulness is widely thought to be a trainable skill. Paying full attention to one's thoughts, feelings, and bodily sensations in a non-judgmental manner promotes the self-awareness of better recovery. Introspection figures prominently in the process of changing one's relationship with a substance. Self-examination is significant in the stages of change and motivation previously referenced. People think about their feelings and well-being. People think about their lives. The capacity to engage in this process and corresponding self-awareness is directly proportionate to the ability to change and recover. The level of investment in the process is based in self-awareness. How intense is someone's conviction? Is the desire to move forward absolute? Is someone all in, mentally, physically and emotionally?

Better recovery is based in higher levels of motivation. On the first day of my recovery, while I couldn't lay claim to being in a state remotely as graceful as mindfulness, I was intensely self-aware. My decision to recover carried a level of conviction and intensity that was greater than the power my addiction held over me. I knew that recovery was the right thing for me to do. This form of motivation, sometimes referred to as ethical motivation—it's the right thing to do—is a higher form than my previous level of motivation, avoiding consequences. I had been like an amoeba, moving instinctively to avoid a threat in the environment. Experience shows that the lower forms of motivation like avoiding consequences and reward motivation do not translate to strong and sustainable recoveries. The only data I have to support that is 35 years of observation, but I will stand by that.

My early recovery, based in absolute conviction that it was the right thing for me to do, was the launching point. Soon, my recovery moved further up the motivational scale. Beyond ethical motivation, there is purpose motivation. I'm on a mission. I wake up every day with a burning desire to grow and improve, and even more important, to help people who live as I once did. Better recovery is a self-aware, self-actualized way of being that is based in a sense of purpose.

## Best Recovery

The skills of recovery are part of a continuum, a "recoverysphere" that includes numerous other elements. Realizing the full potential, the unlimited possibilities of recovery, requires integrating the new relationship with substances into the fabric of one's life. Skills alone have wonderful value, but I am not suggesting recovery be reduced to skills and behaviors. Recovery is holistic. As with the SAMSHA definition previously stated, recovery accounts for the wholeness we all deserve.

We must emphasize that recovery is an opportunity. Regardless of the damage addiction does or how much baggage might be accumulated, recovery is an opportunity to realize your full potential. You can be whomever and whatever you were meant to be. You need only be willing to roll up your sleeves and do whatever is necessary to achieve that. The stipulation is that you need to be willing to leave the old version of yourself behind. You can't bring your old life into your new life. You can step into your true greatness, provided you are willing to shed your old, addicted self and release anything and everything that was not based in love and your highest interest. You will be the person you were always meant to be.

The step-by-step directions for that transformation are more than this chapter can hold. I wrote *The Infinite Recovery Handbook* for that purpose (yes, that's a shameless plug). When I occasionally revisit that book, the third edition completed in 2023, I'm reminded of what is possible. I transformed in the truest sense of the word. I don't think about it in the course of my daily routine, but I am an ordinary man who has done something extraordinary. At age 30, I couldn't go a day without getting drunk or high; the sun rose and set on my open bottle of vodka, even though it was under the seat of the car. I was a slave; my addiction was the master. At age 30, I could not have conceived of the life I live today. I couldn't have scripted it any better than it's turned out.

As I return to referencing my personal experience, I understand that, in many ways, I'm like everyone else. I just happen to have dedicated myself to the pursuit of my personal recovery and the support of everyone else. I've done my best to realize my potential, studying Western medicine as a registered nurse, the practice of alternative and energy healing, and the principles of neuroscience pertaining to addiction and recovery. Most of all, I've manifested the experiences necessary to inform my perspective on addiction, treatment, and recovery.

Thinking, feeling, and behaving differently in a new relationship with substances is the basis for better recovery. The best recovery is a transformation. However, this is not likely to happen randomly. That's the rub.

I experienced numerous elements of transformation in my first year, and this was further solidified by the time I was five years recovered. I can attribute this to showing up every day. I did a ton of work. However, that was still largely random. That's why I went back in later years to study what had occurred. Why doesn't everyone do the same thing?

The answer is knowledge and understanding. Knowing what addiction did to my brain, body, and personality, as well as what it did to my life, is essential. Knowing what to expect in recovery and why it happens is also essential. That means rudimentary neuroscience. Unfortunately, the mere mention of that word can cause anxiety.

The other piece is motivation. We can help people to understand the importance of focus and getting crystal-clear on their desired outcome.

We also acknowledge that recovery happens in a recoverysphere, and the backdrop of culture is a significant part of that. On every level, we need to make society safer and more accepting of addiction and recovery. Let's talk about that next.

# Chapter 11
# Harm Reduction

"A new scientific truth does not triumph by convincing its opponents and making them see the light, but rather because its opponents eventually die and a new generation grows up that is familiar with it."

~ Max Planck

## The Struggle Is Real

In the fall of 2021, although the mandated wearing of masks had officially ended earlier that year, the practice of COVID safeguards continued in medical offices. The entryway to the primary care practice where I ran the outpatient substance treatment program had a little station where clients took their temperature, sanitized their hands, and put on a mask. People with cold or flu symptoms were supposed to be seen remotely, jargon for telehealth appointments. Anna had a temperature the morning she came for her check-in to get her Suboxone prescription.

Anna was a young woman in her mid-20s, the mother of an adorable four-year-old son, and separated from Jason, the boy's father. Jason was also in our program and had primary custody of their son. We were quite concerned about Anna after learning from Jason that he had revived her from an overdose with a NARCAN treatment that I had given him months earlier to have on hand for emergencies.

"She was over visiting and went into the bathroom. She must've shot up; she came out and passed out." Jason described the situation at his next visit, and he was obviously shaken up about it.

Anna had missed some appointments after her overdose, and we wanted to reconnect with her. She called into the office from the parking lot saying she had a fever. I asked her to meet me at a picnic table next to a corner of the building. We would do her appointment outside, the best we could.

A typical appointment would start in my office with a vital sign check, urine drug screen collection, and catching up on any concerns followed by a little recovery coaching. The prescriber would pop in at some point, and I would set up a Suboxone prescription for signature and transmission. This was not a typical appointment by any stretch. Anna said that she had used, then started back on her Suboxone.

When I saw the condition of her left arm, all the other concerns became secondary. Her arm had redness, swelling, and felt warm to the touch. These were the basic signs of infection and indicated the possibility of serious problems. Further discussion revealed that she had injected herself using water from a puddle. I texted inside to the doctor who was her prescriber, and she came out minutes later and diagnosed Anna with phlebitis, an infection of the veins of her arm. We appealed to her to go to an emergency room for evaluation.

This is an example of meeting people where they are. We made exceptions and bent and broke "rules" in the interest of supporting someone and reducing their risk of harm. We waived the urine drug screen; the presence of opioids or fentanyl was a given. Based on our established relationship, we prescribed one week's supply of Suboxone in the interest of supporting Anna to not use street drugs. In the best compassionate way we were able, we tried to impress upon Anna the potential seriousness of her symptoms, and that there could be dire consequences. There was no scolding, schooling, or talking down to her. We did the best we could to leverage the positive rapport and relationship we had established in previous months for her benefit. That was the last time I saw her.

I reached out to her later that day, but we didn't connect. She was off the grid until Jason updated us on the occasion of his next visit. Anna eventually went to the emergency room and was admitted to the hospital with a diagnosis of endocarditis, an infection of the lining of the heart. She was in the hospital for weeks and eventually had one of her heart valves replaced. She never returned to the program, at least not while I was there.

## The New Standard

The MAT program I worked in was termed office-based addiction treatment. This was an opportunity for me to work in a clinically structured setting with people who were beyond the inpatient phase of addiction treatment. The methodology of this program was based in harm reduction, as well a holistic, best-practice medical approach and the underlying philosophy of motivational interviewing.

This program, started a couple of years before I signed on in 2020, represents the new standard. Substance use disorder is a chronic medical condition and should therefore be part of basic healthcare. The office was one of three locations of a Federally Qualified Health Center organization and had to meet requirements for that. This actually made it somewhat leading edge. The region's larger, Boston-based organizations eventually caught up in the early 2020s, establishing their own office-based programs. The program where I worked was located in a region of southern New Hampshire that was hard-hit by the opioid crisis.

We understood that our patient population defied structure. When people were late or missed appointments, we adapted. Medical and prescribing decisions were based on individual needs and circumstances as opposed to hard and fast rules. We did more than one visit at that picnic table. Rather than project some ideal of recovery onto people (like an abstinence approach), we supported all minor positive achievements and helped people to recognize and work toward their personal recovery goals. The recognition part was based in allowing people to process by evoking aha moments leading to questions they might otherwise not ask themselves.

On a daily basis, we saw and handled numerous situations requiring harm reduction. This program, my colleagues, and I continually operated in gray areas just outside the rigid rules and old established practices.

Routine urine drug screens are part of best practice in MAT. Urine testing is invasive and even controversial in the framework of harm reduction. Collection in our program was unsupervised and therefore more respectful of people's dignity. The primary purpose of testing is to verify the presence of prescribed buprenorphine; secondarily, any present nonprescribed substances are detected. About three-quarters of our patients were typically positive for THC, the psychoactive component in cannabis.

The presence of THC and its indication of cannabis use was not considered problematic. The presence of opioids, cocaine, or methamphetamine was a concern, however, but always in the context of the question, "How can we support you?" It was about risk management (another way of saying harm reduction), not remotely punitive. The advantages of this form of collaborative relationship, built on genuine rapport and honest communication, were evidenced by the mere fact that we could have these ongoing conversations. When they came back the next week, I knew it was working.

I led this section with anecdotes about treatment and enhanced engagement with people because these examples are not the typical kind of association most people make with harm reduction. Yes, it's been around long enough to form stereotypes. To many, harm reduction conjures images of resuscitation from opioid overdose with NARCAN, needle and syringe programs, NSPs (formerly called needle exchanges), or even mythical overdose prevention centers, OPCs (formerly known as safe injection sites). And to many, these things are scary. They are scary because they are so counterintuitive to the longtime status quo that DRUGS ARE BAD. These things send a radically different message that seems to be accepting of substance use, even support it. I said mythical because as of this writing there are only three OPCs operating in the US.

The reality is that drugs are here, and they are not going away. What experts know, and I slowly found out, is that it's a much more efficient expenditure of energy and resources to work with people in a respectful, cooperative manner. A little dignity goes a long way. The alternative, limited or zero tolerance, has been proven to fail over and over.

Harm reduction has evolved since its original emergence in the 1980s. The HIV/AIDS epidemic reached public health crisis proportions, and injection drug use was recognized as a significant risk factor. Social activism was initially the driving force behind the movement to raise awareness of and reduce the harm associated with drug use. Social marginalization and the risk of infectious diseases have remained a constant for decades now, but with the precipitous rise in overdose deaths starting in the 2010s, harm reduction has stepped prominently into the light. The concept now has numerous meanings and applications.

You practiced harm reduction today if you buckled your seat belt in the car. If you were ever vaccinated for anything, you have practiced harm reduction. Brushing your teeth is harm reduction. Any action or strategy with the intention of preventing or reducing consequences or bad outcomes meets the definition of harm reduction.

In the substance use treatment arena, harm reduction is an approach that seeks to not only minimize the dangers presented by substance use but also to engage with people on different terms. The expression "meeting people where they are" has become widely used to summarize the strategy of validation and acceptance in the interest of supporting people who are somewhere on a continuum of substance use/recovery. We could think of this continuum as the entire range between active, chaotic substance use at one end, with stable recovery (possibly abstinence-based, possibly not) at the other end. Between the two ways of being, which might be thought of as polar opposites, is a limitless range of gray situations and conditions. In that gray area lies self-determination of complex, real-life relationships with substances. Harm reduction has supported many pathways to recovery, the multitude of nonabstinence approaches. While abstinence-based recovery does not support harm reduction, harm reduction supports abstinence as one of many pathways.

## Public Health

As harm reduction protects and improves the health and safety of individuals, this is reflected in their communities. Measures like needle and syringe programs, where an individual can safely dispose of a used syringe while obtaining a clean, sterile syringe, prevent that dirty syringe from being improperly disposed of in the community. The individual is not using a shared or dirty syringe, which in turn protects that person from a couple of potential health problems.

Using an unclean syringe can introduce bacteria into the body. This can cause an infection locally, i.e., at the injection site, or systemically. Local infections can cause abscesses (pockets of pus) or cellulitis, which is bacterial infection of areas of skin. Vein damage or collapse can also result. A systemic effect is called sepsis and can cause death from complications, including organ shutdown. Endocarditis, as previously mentioned, is when the infection affects the inside surfaces and valves of the heart and is also life-threatening.

Human immunodeficiency virus, HIV, and hepatitis are blood-borne diseases transmitted by unclean syringes. HIV, the pathogen that causes acquired immunodeficiency syndrome, AIDS, can be transferred from one individual to another by sharing syringes. Both hepatitis B and C viruses can be transmitted through shared needles, potentially causing severe liver damage, cirrhosis, and liver cancer. Those viruses can then in turn be passed to other people by sexual contact. Studies indicate that as many as 26 percent of injection drug users are infected with hepatitis C after one year.[41] This is a public health issue on a massive scale that could be prevented with sterile syringes and a little education on safe injection practices.

However, all of the above complications could also befall an innocent victim of a needlestick with a discarded syringe. An improperly disposed syringe becomes dangerous hazardous waste. Sadly, and this is a different discussion, the mindset and thought process of someone in the throes of chaotic substance use might not be capable of considering the possible consequences, for themselves as well as the potential domino effects of polluting the community with discarded paraphernalia.

Another significant public health initiative is the distribution of naloxone, trade name NARCAN. Naloxone is a medication that rapidly reverses opioid overdose. It's classified as an opioid antagonist and works by dislodging and replacing opioids in the central nervous system's receptor sites. This action is rapid and quickly restores consciousness and breathing to a person experiencing an overdose.

NARCAN is available without a prescription in most areas, and it is not considered a controlled substance. If the medication is administered to someone who is not actually having an opioid overdose, it is harmless and will have no effect.

NARCAN is distributed in communities and is available over the counter at pharmacies. Healthcare, civic, and nonprofit organizations often give NARCAN to anyone at risk or even the general public in the interest of overdose prevention. Programs are often administered by state-run or affiliated agencies. They provide NARCAN, requesting only some information such as ZIP Codes or demographics about where it goes to help them keep statistics.

Equally as important as having NARCAN is education on using it properly. Recognizing a suspected overdose is the first step. If you see someone who appears to be unconscious, verify by shaking them and asking them loudly if they are okay. Indications of overdose might include slow or no breathing, gurgling, blue lips, or gray color. If unresponsiveness is verified, immediately call 911 or have someone else do it while you prepare to administer NARCAN. Remove the NARCAN from the packaging. Gently insert the tip of the nozzle into one nostril, until your fingers on either side of the nozzle are against the bottom of the person's nose. Press the plunger firmly to give the dose of NARCAN Nasal Spray. Remove the spray dispenser and observe the person. If they do not regain consciousness in two minutes, give the other NARCAN. Place the person on their side and observe them. If they do not regain consciousness, assess, and initiate rescue breathing and CPR, if trained.

When they regain consciousness, explain what happened to the person. They may be confused and in withdrawal (and possibly agitated). However, they might have more opioids in their system than the NARCAN can handle; it's possible that the NARCAN will wear off and they will be unconscious again in as little as 30 minutes. This is why they should go to the hospital, or, at a minimum, be observed for several hours with more NARCAN available.

## Substance Use and the Public at Large

One element of the harm reduction philosophy is that we have relationships with substances. In the substance use disorder field, we've moved on from referring to drinking habits or drug addictions. Obviously, not everyone who drinks alcoholic beverages has problems. By the same token, not everyone who uses nonprescribed, mind-altering substances has a dependency. Some people just enjoy doing that. I know I did.

Altering our states of consciousness is basic and age-old. Think of children spinning themselves around until they get so dizzy they can't stand up or intentionally hyperventilating. They are literally experimenting with altering their consciousness, though there is no 12-Step support group called Hyperventilation Anonymous (the first breath gets you dizzy). Yet. The Greeks had a God of fermentation. There are references to Dionysus going back to the 14th century BCE. As well as being the god of winemaking, he was also responsible for festivity, insanity, ritual madness, religious ecstasy, and theatre. An Israeli scholar makes a case for Moses being on psychedelics while on Mount Sinai in the Bible,[42] and some of the oldest known cave paintings depict imagery associated with distinct stages of psychedelic experience. In colonial times, an employer's failure to provide sufficient quantities of ale was grounds for quitting. It is safe to say that modern people did not invent getting messed up.

Recreational use of substances is ingrained in our culture. It has progressed from the underground to the mainstream. The issue of what is legal or illegal is complicated. Also complicated is the issue of medications that must be prescribed by a doctor while other medications are available over the counter. People's choices and self-determination in substance use has overflowed the container of regulation in a tidal wave of illicit drug use.

It's not as simple as substances being restricted if they are harmful. Almost any substance can be harmful if used to excess or incorrectly. According to the CDC, there are approximately 2200 deaths each year in the United States due to alcohol poisoning.[43] This translates to about six deaths every day. The National Institute on Alcohol Abuse and Alcoholism, NIAAA, reports that there are tens of thousands of emergency department visits annually due to alcohol poisoning.

Going back to the 18th century, medicines were part of the free market, and there arose what came to be known as patent medicine. This was characterized by secret formulas and aggressive marketing, often with dubious health claims. The Pure Food and Drug Act of 1906 was the beginning of federal regulation. It mandated labeling of ingredients and prohibited adulterated or misbranded drugs. The Federal Food, Drug, and Cosmetic Act of 1938 created the US Food and Drug Administration, which oversees the approval, manufacture, and labeling of prescription drugs.

The Controlled Substances Act, CSA, of 1970 further defined drug prescribing, manufacture, importation, possession, use, and distribution of certain substances. It classifies drugs into five schedules based on their potential for abuse, medical use, and safety. Under the CSA, drugs listed in Schedules II–V can only be prescribed by licensed practitioners. Drugs listed in Schedule I were considered to have no medical value and high risk of abuse. The US Drug Enforcement Administration was created in 1973 and is tasked with enforcement and ensuring compliance with prescribing and distribution guidelines.

So then, does tobacco have medical value? High risk of abuse? And yet, it's legal and widely available with a minimum of regulation. Only since 2019 has it been illegal for people under the age of 21 to purchase tobacco products. I was a smoker of cigarettes by age 14, and this was not uncommon. I never had to lurk outside a convenience store and approach someone of legal smoking age surreptitiously and say, "Hey, can you by me a pack of Old Gold?" The history of tobacco production is enmeshed in the history of the country and culture, and today tobacco represents a big industry with a formidable legislative lobby. It's complicated.

Cannabis was demonized in the early 20th century for political and racial reasons. In the 1960s, psychedelics became synonymous with counterculture and radicalism. It's not a coincidence that the CSA came along quickly thereafter, and cannabis and LSD, the potently hallucinogenic lysergic acid diethylamide, headed the list of Schedule I substances. Others of the so-called recreational drugs were considered to have medical or therapeutic application and are classified as Schedule II or III. As examples, cocaine is a local anesthetic, while amphetamines are used in the treatment of attention deficit hyperactivity disorder, ADHD, and narcolepsy, a sleeping disorder.

The law of the free market dictates that if someone wants to buy something, someone will be willing to sell it to them. The demand for nonprescribed substances for recreational or even medicinal use is astronomical. The RAND Corporation reported that Americans spend approximately $150 billion annually on illicit drugs,[44] including cannabis, cocaine, heroin (fentanyl), and methamphetamine.

Who are the purveyors of drugs? International drug trafficking is controlled by sophisticated organized crime groups, including cartels, gangs, and old-fashioned regional crime families. On the drug side, key elements of global illicit trade are cultivation/production, manufacturing/processing, and trafficking/distribution. Heroin and cocaine are produced from plants, the opium poppy and the coca bush, respectively; they are cultivated and then processed. Fentanyl and methamphetamine are synthetic, made in labs.

On the socioeconomic side, the costs of the illicit drug trade are substantial, including law enforcement, healthcare, lost productivity, addiction, overdose deaths, the spread of infectious disease, and need for social services. Countries must also address the corruption and instability fueled by drug trafficking. The drug trade is associated with high levels of violence, particularly where rival gangs or cartels compete for control of territories. Countries like Mexico and Colombia have experienced significant drug-related violence. Drug-related crime includes not only trafficking but also crimes committed by users to support their addiction, such as theft and burglary. In the US, research shows that an estimated 65 percent of the US prison population has an active SUD.[45]

What are they selling to people? Whether obtained from a sketchy stranger on the street or from someone a user knows and believes to be reliable, what would that little plastic bag of white or brown powder say if it could talk? Would it tell us that impoverished people were involved in its production as their only viable option for economic survival? That it was smuggled in shipping containers or car trunks? That it changed hands literally a dozen times before reaching the end user? And regardless of how it started out or where it came from, how many times would that little bag say its contents were modified?

Whatever that little bag is advertised to be, chances are that it's not. A sample of off-white powder received by Drugsdata.org on April 29, 2024, called "Oreo" and sold as fentanyl, was analyzed as just over 50 percent dimethyl phthalate, which is used in solid rocket propellants, plastics, and insect repellants. Exposure via inhalation in humans and animals results in irritation of the eyes, nose, and throat, as well as headache, dizziness, and nausea.[46] The next most prominent component was acetyl fentanyl, a fentanyl analog 15 times stronger than morphine. The next ingredient by volume was xylazine, an animal sedative, comprising 15 percent of the specimen. There were nine substances in total, including trace amounts of fentanyl (1/70) and heroin (1/350). These trace amounts could actually be accounted for by their presence remaining in processing equipment from other drug batches. In other words, they weren't even intended to be there.

This was exactly the type of Wild West marketplace that led to the regulation of patent medicine by the Pure Food and Drug Act. The government stepped in to reduce harm. However, a couple of things are different now. People are addicted; they need substances or they will get sick with withdrawal, something that eliminates the element of choice. And suppliers of drugs, operating as criminals outside the law, do not care about consequences or harm that comes to drug users. This makes the case for a couple of controversial harm reduction concepts.

We have access to limited drug testing. The availability of testing strips specifically for fentanyl, and, more recently, xylazine, make it possible to know if substances have been adulterated with these specific additives. Because of its harmful side effects, xylazine should be avoided at all costs; it causes skin infections and does not respond to NARCAN in the case of possible overdose. The presence of fentanyl in substances like cannabis, cocaine, or others can also be detected. Multidrug testing cups can confirm the presence or absence of numerous substances. People could be checking their drug supply… if it was legal.

Drug-testing equipment in the form of fentanyl test strips and reagent test kits is considered drug paraphernalia in 34 states as of this writing. Possession and use range from misdemeanor to felony. Possible penalties range from fines to prison sentences. Sale or intent to distribute generally carries even harsher penalties. In North Dakota, for example, both possession and sale are Class C felonies. A person convicted of a Class C felony faces 1 to 10 years in prison and a $10,000 fine. Second-degree rape, robbery, and larceny are also Class C felonies. Numerous states have moved to take these laws off the books, and obviously someone using an illegal substance won't be concerned with the legality of testing strips. The problem is obtaining them. In states where they are permitted, harm reduction agencies, clinics, and civic health organizations distribute these. Even as a registered nurse working in the field providing direct care, I'm not allowed to have them, let alone give them to clients or patients in the restricting states.

People use drugs. That's the reality. It's true now, just as it was a century ago and a century before that. Looking at the timeline, we've taken a step backward. Regulations protecting the public at large are falling behind the prevalence of substances. The combined annual death toll of alcohol[47] and tobacco,[48] the legal substances, is about 640,000 people. Without regulation of the contents, quality, sale, and distribution of tobacco and alcohol, that would be higher. Essentially, the government is dodging the issue of all the other mind-altering substances by simply making and keeping them illegal. This is what opens the door for fentanyl, xylazine, and solid rocket propellant to find their way into the unregulated drug supply.

The fact that equipment for testing of drugs is against the law in two-thirds of the United States could not say any more clearly that the lives and welfare of the marginalized SUD and substance using population are not valued. This fact makes other harm reduction measures less likely here; in countries where drugs are not criminalized, they just don't have these problems. Portugal, Switzerland, the Netherlands, Spain, Mexico, the Czech Republic, and Uruguay are a partial list of countries that have decriminalized possession of small amounts of drugs for personal use.

To be clear, decriminalization does not mean legalization. Enforcement on the supply side continues with vigorous pursuit and prosecution of illicit trafficking. A United Kingdom report said that, "Since decriminalization, Portuguese law-enforcement statistics have also revealed an increase in operational capacity, resulting in more domestic drug trafficking seizures and an increase in international anti-trafficking collaborations." [49] However, no cup or test strip is going to detect the presence of solid rocket propellant or the like in a drug sample. This requires sophisticated laboratory testing, which, unfortunately, happens mostly in a forensic context—postmortem. The solution for that is on the other side of the line that was drawn in the late 1960s and early 1970s, when the official declaration of war on drugs began. "Countries have failed to recognize and correct the health and human rights harms that pursuit of prohibition and drug suppression have caused and in so doing neglect their legal responsibilities. They readily incarcerate people for minor offenses but then neglect their duty to provide health services in custodial settings. They recognize uncontrolled illegal markets as the consequence of their policies, but they do little to protect people from toxic, adulterated drugs that are inevitable in illegal markets or the violence of organized criminals, often made worse by policing." [50]

We need regulation of the drug supply. There, I said it.

Pushing beyond the simple ability of people to check and test substances before using them, the other much needed harm reduction concept is decriminalization and supply regulation. Understandably, it's an elephant in the room for states that won't even let people have fentanyl test strips. We need regulation of mind-altering, recreational substances for the general public in similar fashion to alcohol and tobacco. I suppose it sounded a little radical in the early 1900s when they started talking about the Pure Food and Drug Act too. No, it's not precisely the same circumstances. Yes, it is a public health crisis that we could be doing something about.

### Harm Reduction in the Treatment Field and Recovery

Amy Nichols (actual full name used at her request) is a woman in long-term recovery. She is like dynamite in a small bottle with big energy along with a keen fashion sense thrown in for good measure. She has worked as a peer specialist and recovery coach for a variety of organizations ranging from hospitals, nonprofits, and human services agencies.

"I take my abstinence hat off and open myself up to harm reduction," she said. For any accomplishment in recovery, "I would give positive feedback. How has it improved your life? I would encourage someone to weigh the pros and cons of their substance use."

Just like the early days of the Minnesota Model, with *alcoholism* counselors, today's treatment model utilizes people with lived experience of addiction and recovery. There is a range of titles and job descriptions that are variations on two basic disciplines—peer specialists and recovery coaches. "Participation of peers in recovery support interventions appears to have a salutary effect on participants and makes a positive contribution to substance use outcomes." [51]

Peer specialists and recovery coaches are utilized in numerous settings, including acute intervention, office-based treatment, recovery housing, recovery community organizations, and other outpatient formats. How does their personal recovery affect their disposition toward different recovery approaches and clients with different approaches? How do people who recovered in an abstinence culture work with and serve people who are not ready for abstinence or even reject abstinence entirely?

An initial hurdle might be that organizations or facilities support an abstinence approach. A principal tenet of the Minnesota Model is that it is abstinence-based. From the detox process on through clinical stabilization and residential treatment, it's absolute, zero substances except tobacco (and that devilish caffeine). In many situations, a peer specialist or recovery coach could find themselves working in a program where any harm reduction approach is like the proverbial turd in the punch bowl. More than just not fitting in, it's going to cause a little uproar. And in the zero-tolerance world of many programs, there is no actual option to meet people where they are. Support staff can just stay in their lane, and if the issue does arise, it's handled at a higher level. As an example, that might come in the form of a sober housing program that doesn't allow medications for addiction treatment. If a candidate who utilizes MAT applies to their residence, there's a policy in place and the matter is closed. A similar situation might occur with medical cannabis.

However, in the case of a residential program that embraces the harm reduction best practice of MAT, or has residents with medical cannabis cards, staff people in recovery might find their personal beliefs challenged. In office-based treatment, stable OUD clients who choose to use cannabis present a stark contrast to the experience and personal beliefs of a recovery coach whose own recovery is based in abstinence. Tasked with running therapeutic groups, the challenge for this recovery professional is to acknowledge their own bias and be neutral in support of the clients' highest interest. And beyond simply being neutral, a group facilitator should be well-informed.

Studies demonstrated that intervention stigma among healthcare providers was influenced by lack of training and abstinent treatment preferences. Providers equated medications for opioid use disorder, MOUD, with illicit substance use and at times refused to care for MOUD patients.[52]

Recovery professionals, whether in recovery themselves or not, are subject to the long tradition of abstinence programming and conditioning. While quantifying this has proven difficult, it's a safe statement that people decline treatment and avoid therapy for this reason. According to Patt Denning and Jeannie Little in their book, *Over the Influence*, the unrealistic goal of abstinence is "why the completion rate of programs is 30–50%, and why fewer than 50% of people achieve the stated goals of the programs when they do finish." [53] Isn't some recovery better than zero recovery? If the strategy of detoxes, rehabs and outpatient programs, and individual therapists is to compel people to go to AA, that strategy is clearly saying that complete abstinence is the shoe that fits everyone.

Everyone has a unique relationship with substances. Everyone is also in their own state of openness, or readiness if you will, to treatment and the concept of recovery. The transtheoretical stage of contemplation, where an individual is considering their own mental list of pros and cons, precedes the stage of action. Making the leap to initiate the treatment or recovery process can often be contingent on having the right options, and, for many, that needs to include some type of nonabstinence approach.

Treatment approaches are beginning to recognize the value of decreased number of drinking days, decreased overall alcohol consumption, not using alone, having NARCAN available, and testing substances prior to use. These things themselves are improved outcomes, whereas quitting completely has historically been the standard measurement.

As the fog over the recovery landscape slowly lifts, it's evident that the bias toward abstinence in substance use disorder treatment is just as much a form of stigma as are prejudicial attitudes and overt discrimination toward people living with SUD. It's just been more insidious.

In the recovery community, this translates to marginalizing a large segment of people who could otherwise benefit tremendously from widely accessible programs like AA and NA. Lack of complete abstinence is equated with failure.

In the previously mentioned Alcoholics Anonymous ritual, presentation of chips for lengths of sobriety, people are asked to identify themselves if they are returning to meetings after a drinking bout. This is commonly referred to as "coming back." While the ceremony is supposed to be well-meaning, it consists of a literal walk of shame as people leave their seats, walk to the front of the room, and receive a white poker chip signifying that they have 24 hours to 29 days of sobriety. As if to double down on this ordeal, someone among the onlookers invariably calls out, "no shame." Again, this is well-meaning, but the majority of people present probably were not thinking about shame... until the idea was introduced to the collective thought process. If I said to you, don't think about elephants, what are you thinking about?

Unfortunately, both the underlying and overt messages are that they are not working the program. Emphasis on perfect adherence to the AA program with its emphasis on powerlessness and requirement of surrender to a higher power simply doesn't work for everyone. The associated feelings of guilt, shame, or inadequacy associated with anything less than absolute sobriety are a setup for compounding someone's misery. Furthermore, AA says if you can't do it, it's your fault, not theirs. In a chapter titled "How It Works," AA's textbook,

*Alcoholics Anonymous*, says this.

> "Those who do not recover are people who cannot or will not completely give themselves to this simple program, usually men and women who are constitutionally incapable of being honest with themselves. There are such unfortunates. They are not at fault; they seem to have been born that way." [54]

It's not even something you did; they are saying it's something you are, the precise definition of shame.

The all-or-nothing mindset has spread to the collective consciousness as well. Family, social networks, work colleagues, and the community at large view any drinker who addresses their alcohol use as *not with the program* for any deviation from abstinence. The perception is that if they are not teetotaling, they're doing it wrong.

Speaking now from years of personal experience and to wrap up this section, I'll share a couple of personal observations and a cautionary tale. In three-plus decades of continuous, abstinence-based recovery while engaging with AA, my observation is that it's not a fit for everyone. There are a variety of reasons for this, and they do range to include lack of honesty, but not as a catch-all excuse when people don't succeed. AA fails more people than people fail at AA. It fails to engage and offer deep connection to people until they are ready to meet the real requirement for AA membership—a commitment to abstinence-based recovery. If they could make those church basements more welcoming, more accepting of people where they are at a given moment, they could probably accomplish their mission much better. On paper, that is AA tradition 5, "to carry the message to the alcoholic who still suffers." In reality, the unspoken message is that recovery should be pure.

Over the years, I've observed many people who did not maintain sobriety, but who benefited tremendously from the community, uplifting experiences, engagement, and the relationships they found in peer-support recovery fellowships. They came and took it in, participated and received value in return; unfortunately, they drank again after varying lengths of time. Some went on to stay sober permanently or at least for extended periods. In many instances, they eventually fell by the wayside due to the constant undercurrent and programming that they were failures. That chip walk of "no shame" probably gets old after a while.

AA is not going to change. The founders literally set it up to be tamperproof, though it's doubtful that they anticipated the explosion of substance use disorder that we are currently experiencing. The culture shift required to make it accepting of nonabstinence is just unlikely to occur given the history and structure of Alcoholics Anonymous. Mainstream peer-support recovery is certainly not a failure, but it could be so much more... and what's the price of that limitation?

## Use with Caution

Elements and forms of harm reduction have been listed and discussed. Harm reduction is NARCAN, NSPs, OPCs, and other direct measures that improve and save lives of people who use substances. Harm reduction is also stigma-free approaches to working with people who are in some phase of engaging with the healthcare system or treatment infrastructure.

Harm reduction is not saying it's okay to use substances. Or, at least not in ways that are potentially dangerous or harmful to people. Harm reduction is not intended to enable substance use in any instance or situation where substances would be used regardless. Harm reduction only enables increased safety in those situations.

Lastly, harm reduction is a recovery pathway. If recovery means a return to a normal state of health, the harm reduction approach to this means continued use of substances in some controlled or alternative capacity. Bearing in mind that there are many people who drink alcohol without any significant problems, and people who use mind-altering substances recreationally, any relationship with substances is an individual matter. Advocates for people who use drugs (PWUD—their term, not mine) would not include harm reduction as a pathway to recovery because the goal is not returning to a normal state of health. Substance use is the normal state.

The basis of the harm reduction recovery pathway is continuing the relationship with either the primary substance or alternative substances. Alcohol moderation is an example of continuing the primary substance use. Someone in remission from opioid use disorder who chooses to use alcohol is an example of using alternative substances.

A destructive relationship with one substance does not necessarily mean all substances have the same harmful effects. This is not simple. By comparison, abstinence is easier.

In the harm reduction approach, an individual must have a fairly high level of objectivity. They need the capacity to be honest with themselves about their substance use. There is a growing faction in the harm reduction community advocating for responsible substance use. Just like alcohol in the so-called "normal" world, people have the right to use substances as they choose. Also, like alcohol, there is the understanding that this right may be forfeited when society is negatively impacted. The responsibility factor also entails clear understanding of the harm the individual does to themselves.

This kind of ability for objective self-assessment is absent in many who enter recovery. It's fair to say that they have failed the tasks that a responsible user of substances is able to accomplish. These include assessing physical and cognitive effects, the actual and potential ripple effects on others, and the short- and long-term psychological effects. This requires critical thinking; this is work. And this is not mundane, like weighing the pros and cons or fine points of something like a purchase or a career decision. Mistakes are actually at the level of life, limb, and possible catastrophic consequences.

A man in my region's professional recovery community was a highly regarded harm reduction expert. His work on behalf of the recovery community was exemplary. He was instrumental in the formation of a regional recovery community organization, wrote and trained curriculum on harm reduction nationally, as well as various other noteworthy recovery initiatives. He was in a nonabstinence approach recovery.

We were personally acquainted through a small, tight network of recovery professionals; we spent time together at recovery events and socialized on a couple of occasions. When he resumed active use several times, we knew when it was happening. This brilliant young man, this expert in the field of addiction, recovery, and harm reduction, died of an accidental overdose.

He contributed so much and gave massive amounts of energy to a system that ultimately failed him. While he would have benefited tremendously from meetings, his expertise made him more keenly aware than most that he was a square peg in the round hole of an abstinence-based recovery community. Whether ostracism was reality-based or in his mind (more likely), he could not bring himself to seek support. Even among his close circle, he only confided in one person. I say that his feelings of isolation were more his subjective reality because he definitely kept me and others at arm's length.

A mutual friend observed that he "didn't die from an overdose. He died from shame." We would have done anything for him, but shame prevented him from reaching out. The untimely death of this man, a father of two, raises the question, how can the recovery community support individuals with alternative, harm reduction-based approaches to recovery?

Although cautionary, the real meaning of this anecdote is about the need for feelings and attitudes to shift in recovery culture. Must the best of us continue to be plucked out of the stream of life? A harm reduction intervention takes place in a moment that is like a snapshot in a longer story. It's not someone's best moment for sure, but if someone is saved from harm, better moments are almost assured. What would that man from my recovery community have accomplished? He had already done great things, and more of the same were a certainty... but we will never know.

Harm reduction is where we need to come together in the realization that there is more uniting us than dividing us. In recovery, in treatment, and in society, we need to look at the big picture, what's really important. Kindness matters. Compassion matters. Life matters.

# Chapter 12
# Tobacco, Smoking, and Vaping

"Quitting smoking is easy. I've done it lots of times."
~ Just about everyone who has
tried to stop smoking

## Where There's Smoke

"Hey, can I bum a butt?"

The first time I uttered those words in the early 1970s, a pack of cigarettes was $.50, perhaps $.55. I was asking someone for a nominal 2.5-cent outlay. Nowadays, a cigarette is a considerably larger investment, but still one that millions of people make many times daily.

This chapter covers another topic where I have personal experience, although not recently. The last time I purchased cigarettes for myself, over 30 years ago, I was buying by the carton (10 packs of 20 cigs) for about $15 at the wholesale club. I picked up a single pack for a friend just a few years ago, and there was scant change from a $10 bill. Despite a general uptick in inflation over the past few years, the price of cigarettes has outpaced the shift in overall buying power. This varies by state and is due to both taxation and pricing strategies of the tobacco companies. Smoking is down overall, but profits are not.

Smoking is the apple pie of substance use, as American as it gets. While it's hard to see the Marlboro Man as tobacco dependent, vaping, chewing, cheeking, and any other means of nicotine delivery is substance use that is so common we don't even see it.

Smoking has been around longer than just about every other substance except for alcohol. Millions of people use tobacco in some form. Along with the more recent development of vaping, smoking is, for many, habitual and difficult to stop. It could be described in a number of ways, but I'm going to just come out and say that it is an addiction that is legal and (marginally) socially acceptable.

According to 2021 National Institutes of Health statistics released in 2023, 46 million US adults reported using tobacco products, including cigarettes, e-cigarettes, cigars, smokeless tobacco, and pipes (including hookahs).[55] The World Health Organization estimated 1.3 billion people worldwide use tobacco products.[56]

Smoking and related behaviors are higher among the substance use disorder population,[57] as well as people living with mental illness. In general, there is a higher correlation with people who are socially and economically disadvantaged.[58]

One of the biases I have held on to until recently was that smoking and tobacco addiction are a lower priority. When treating people for alcohol, opioid, or cocaine use, their smoking habits seemed almost inconsequential in comparison. This was wrong. Smoking, vaping, and tobacco/nicotine use disorder are harmful substance use, accounting for more deaths than alcohol and opioids combined.

## Education Provided

I worked as a nurse in both inpatient and outpatient SUD treatment. Part of routine nursing duties is admitting new patients to facilities or programs, a process that can be complex. It entails a sometimes-lengthy interview in which detailed medical, social, and substance use histories are taken. While this is routine for the nurse, the process can be emotional, exhausting, or otherwise difficult for the patient. The patient might also be uncomfortable from withdrawal symptoms; the completion of the admission process stands between them and treatment.

So, after asking about allergies, surgeries, illnesses, family history, medications... have they ever experienced abuse or trauma in any form... and the standard 11 questions on substance use and detailed history of that... then the typical questionnaire arrives at the subject of smoking and vaping.

As with substances, the patient is asked when they started, how much they smoke daily, and if they have ever tried to stop. Whenever a patient acknowledges that they smoke, vape, or use other tobacco products, the nurse (me) is supposed to check a box that says, "Education Provided" and provide said education.

Bearing in mind that I might be having this conversation with someone who has been using large quantities of opioids, alcohol, or other significant substances daily, there was a certain trite quality about initiating a conversation about the 10 to 20 cigarettes they smoke most days. The very idea of telling someone who uses intravenous drugs, or is living with the physical effects of chronic alcohol use, that there might be consequences to cigarette use seemed stupid and pointless. Yet, there was that little box I was supposed to check.

People in early recovery would sometimes ask about quitting smoking. Sometimes they would ask right there in the admission interview. My response, which was based on personal experience and years of observing how this works for people in the real world, had always been something along the lines of *focus on your primary addiction first*. Get stable. Then you can work on the cigarettes. That's how it worked for me, and it just seemed intuitive. Quitting opioids or drinking is hard enough without taking away someone's legal and less harmful (we thought, though not really) secondary habit. It seemed like common sense that encouraging people to quit smoking at the same time might even jeopardize their recovery from drugs or alcohol. There was consensus supporting this; my colleagues agreed.

Back to the little box that required my nurse's attention. We don't check boxes that say we did something unless we do the thing. So, how to do the thing, but in such a way that it did not impose some varying degree of hardship on the patient? Then it came to me.

"We are almost at the end, thank you for pushing through, but we need to talk about your smoking for a moment." (Usually met with a "Are you f-ing serious?" look.) "We can probably agree that no one ever quit anything because anyone educated them, right? But I'm sure it's also come to your attention at some point that there are serious health risks associated with smoking and vaping." (Agreement is usually then verbalized.) "So, if you understand that we will provide information, support, and even nicotine replacement therapy, NRT, if you should decide you want to stop smoking, we can wrap this up." (Understanding was always verbalized.) ☑ Education Provided.

## But It's Legal

The question is why did I think that way, that nicotine addiction was less severe than opioid addiction? The answer is that I was like everyone else—concerned about the significant increase in catastrophic results of opioid overdose. Opioids were killing people immediately while smoking did not. Yet, smoking is the leading cause of death and disability in the US, killing 480,000 annually due to smoking-related causes.[59]

More than 1 percent of people using tobacco products die each year.

Cardiovascular diseases, including heart disease and aortic aneurysm, are major causes of death among smokers. Smoking is linked to lung cancer, chronic obstructive pulmonary disease, ischemic heart disease, stroke, and numerous other cancers (e.g., oral cavity, esophagus, stomach, pancreas, larynx, bladder, kidney, and leukemia).[60][61][62]

Whereas overdosing on opioids might be likened to Russian roulette, heavy, regular smoking of cigarettes is more like a death lottery with nasty consolation prizes, because the aforementioned illnesses are not universally fatal. And the payout comes over decades.

Nicotine is a chemical that occurs naturally in tobacco, and NIDA research in the 1970s identified nicotine as the primary component of tobacco responsible for sustained smoking behavior, i.e., addiction. Most smokers believe that cigarettes are addictive and generally acknowledge their dependence. Nicotine affects mood, and there is a withdrawal effect when someone discontinues using the substance.[63]

Aside from a physical need, addiction to cigarettes is thought to involve behavior and social factors. However, regular smokers differentiate tobacco use from other substance addictions, minimizing their own experience of addiction. According to one study, smokers are also focused on psychological aspects of their cigarette habit, responding to internal as well as external cues, with smoking being part of a routine. The smokers expressed, after being informed that cigarettes they had smoked had little or no nicotine, that the addictiveness was based in more than getting a fix of the chemical. They said that the behavioral elements, including oral fixation, were just as much a part of the habit as receiving doses of nicotine.[64]

Withdrawal symptoms such as irritability, difficulty concentrating, and cognitive impairments underscore the addictive nature of nicotine. Cigarette use becomes part of the fabric of the smoker's life. The difficulty of quitting is also indicative of nicotine's addictive properties. Anyone who has attempted to quit smoking will assert that it is no simple feat. Science supports that the addictive nature of nicotine is comparable to heroin, cocaine, or alcohol. Use can be compulsive, and withdrawal symptoms are only alleviated by nicotine replacement therapy.[65]

## Sacred Plant to Health Hazard

European explorers encountered Indigenous people using tobacco when they arrived in the New World in the 15th century. One of Christopher Columbus's Spanish crewmembers who sailed to the Americas on the *Santa María,* Rodrigo de Jerez, is credited with being the first European smoker. Jerez observed natives smoking and picked up the tobacco smoking habit. When he returned to Europe, the smoke surrounding him frightened his neighbors. He was imprisoned by the Spanish Inquisition, because "only the Devil could give a man the power to exhale smoke from his mouth." By the time he was released seven years later, smoking tobacco had caught on.

The tobacco plant has been cultivated in the New World for over 6000 years. Native American tribes, mainly in South America, smoked, chewed, and inhaled snuff made from tobacco and used it for religious and social rituals as well as medicinal purposes. Indigenous peoples believed that tobacco had spiritual significance; shamans and healers considered it a sacred plant.

By the mid-1500s, tobacco was gaining popularity in Europe. In the Americas, the settlers quickly took up the use of tobacco, as well as its cultivation. Tobacco soon became a mainstay of the colonial economy, particularly in Maryland and Virginia, where it became a cash crop for export to Europe. The resulting demand for labor contributed to the transatlantic slave trade. By the 17th century, tobacco smoking was widespread across Europe.

Up until the 1800s, most tobacco was smoked in pipes or as cigars. The cigarette was a more convenient form and means of consumption, and when rolling machines were invented later in the 19th century, manufacturing on a mass scale revolutionized the industry. Companies such as Philip Morris, American Tobacco Company, and R. J. Reynolds eventually emerged as global giants in a worldwide market. Big Tobacco had a great run through the middle of the 20th century.

Mounting and damning evidence began to emerge, or rather, not emerge, linking tobacco use to health problems, including cancer, respiratory illness, and heart disease. It was later found out that the tobacco companies themselves had been doing research and chose to suppress the fact that their products were harmful. In 1964, the US Surgeon General declared smoking a health hazard and mandated that a warning be placed on every package of cigarettes. That warning is still there to this day.

Smoking officially went from bad habit to addiction in 1988 with the publication of the Surgeon General's report, *The Health Consequences of Smoking: Nicotine Addiction*. Early research had been more engaged in determining a causal link between smoking and diseases like lung cancer.

In 1999, the US Department of Justice, DOJ, filed one of the largest litigations in US legal history against the tobacco industry. Initially, they sought to recoup billions of dollars spent by Medicare on care for tobacco-related illness. In the nearly five years between the filing of the suit and the start of the trial, spanning from the Clinton (pro-litigation) to Bush (anti-litigation) administrations, the case morphed into a Racketeer Influenced and Corrupt Organizations (RICO) Act proceeding.

The DOJ case against Big Tobacco is a remarkable story in that it survived intense political opposition. The tobacco industry has a small army of lobbyists in Washington, DC, and donates millions annually to political campaigns.

In 2006, the verdict found that the tobacco industry knowingly lied about the dangers of smoking, the addictiveness of nicotine, and the harmful effects of secondhand smoke. Furthermore, the tobacco companies manipulated nicotine levels to enhance addiction. However, under the RICO Act, instead of monetary damages, the court ordered remedies designed to prevent future misconduct. While this might have been the tipping point that has seen a gradual downturn in overall smoking, for Big Tobacco, this nominal price of doing business was well worth five decades of profits.

Another important point in the sordid history of smoking is menthol. Menthol is a chemical compound found in plants like peppermint but can also be produced in a lab. Going back to the 1920s, tobacco companies began adding menthol to cigarettes to make them seem less harsh.

Menthol cigarettes have been marketed to Black American people and new smokers. The tobacco industry sold menthol cigarettes through advertising media, culturally tailored images, and messages, leading to a disproportionate use among Black Americans; 85 percent of Black American smokers prefer menthol cigarettes.[66]

Menthol enhances nicotine absorption. According to the CDC, menthol cigarettes are harder to quit than regular cigarettes, and menthol smokers are less likely to quit successfully. Menthol smokers attempting to quit report more intense withdrawal symptoms. In 2022, the FDA proposed a ban on all menthol tobacco products, following trends set by Canada and the European Union, where they are no longer available.[67]

And finally, the tragic irony of the sacred tobacco plant is that it visits the worst problems on the Indigenous people. Native Americans have the highest smoking rates among all racial/ethnic groups in the US, as well as significantly higher rates of smoking-related diseases and mortality.[68] According to Lonnie Nelson, PhD, there is a prevailing belief that tobacco is a "powerful spirit." The powerful spirit carries powerful consequences; commercial smoking-related death accounts for half of all mortality for Native people, according to Dr. Nelson.

## Vaping

The idea for e-cigarettes goes all the way back to 1963. A smokeless, nontobacco cigarette was patented but never made it to the market. In 2003, the modern vaping movement began with a Chinese pharmacist who was himself a heavy smoker. His goal was an alternative means of inhaling nicotine without smoke, and his invention utilized a heating coil that vaporized a nicotine solution. E-cigarettes found their way to European and US markets by the mid-2000s, gaining popularity as a supposedly less harmful alternative to smoking traditional cigarettes.

The technology advanced, and vaping pens and mods showed up in the 2010s. Users could adjust power settings, customize airflow, and use a wide variety of products, both including and excluding nicotine-based solutions. Next came pod systems, appealing to younger users. JUUL, in particular, dominated the US market with a high-nicotine solution intended to mimic traditional cigarettes.

In 2016, the FDA began regulating vaping products, now referring to them as electronic nicotine delivery systems, ENDS. Sales to minors were banned and manufacturers were required to submit their products for approval. Vaping-associated lung injuries have become known as e-cigarette or vaping product use-associated lung injury, and hundreds of illnesses have been attributed in what the CDC considered an outbreak. It was later linked to the use of THC-containing products with vitamin E acetate, prompting calls for stricter regulations on vaping.[69]

Dave is a 78-year-old man in long-term recovery from alcohol use disorder. He was a lifelong smoker, starting at age 17 when he joined the Marines until three years ago, when he was diagnosed with an abdominal aneurysm and underwent surgery, which was complicated. On the other side of a long hospitalization, he traded cigs for vaping.

Dave explained that he went to a local vape emporium and received a tutorial. He purchased a device and an assortment of "juices" to try before he settled on Turkish tobacco. He said it's better for him than smoking but acknowledges that he understands it's merely a means of getting the nicotine into his system. He also acknowledges, as with cigarettes, there is a hand activity and oral-fixation element. He demonstrates how he likes to just hold his device in his hand even while not vaping. "It's a pacifier," he conceded. For Dave, vaping could be considered an exercise in harm reduction.

On the other side of the vaping coin, vaping by adolescents is rampant and escalating. Whereas vaping is a step back from the greater harm of cigarette smoking for Dave, it represents a dangerous health hazard for young people.

The attraction of vaping for young people, especially males, is compelling. Perusing the assortment of devices sort of made me want one.

It starts with the device itself, a gadget that is almost irresistible. These have evolved way beyond the cigarette look-alikes and "pens" of a decade ago. *Pods and mods and all-in-one systems, oh my!* One could spend as little as $15, or as much as $350 for a high-end, fully accessorized box mod with temperature variability, tactile carbon fiber, lithium-ion battery, and other bells and whistles. It's not just an addiction; it's a status symbol! And like Dave said, puffing aside, this habit gives you a little security blanket that you can hold in your hand or keep in your pocket. I would have been a sucker for this in my wild and misspent youth.

Then there's marketing—Dave didn't come home with a juice flavor called cotton candy or gummi bear (actual flavors). The sweet and fruity flavors mask the harshness of nicotine while names that evoke dessert-like associations are deliberately enticing to youth. Also appealing to youth is the colorful and eye-catching packaging, complete with cartoon characters and playful imagery. Social media imagery portrays young people modeling an attractive lifestyle prominently featuring vaping. Youth-oriented events such as music festivals are the platforms that vape manufacturers associate with, if not directly through sponsorship, often by virtue of access lounges and immersive experiences. They want the youth market and strive to zig when guidelines zag, often with one foot in the regulatory doghouse.

There is now a distinction between combustible and noncombustible smoking in the recovery field. Vaping/ENDS is, of course, noncombustible, as a heating coil vaporizes the vape juice on demand. With conventional combustible cigarettes, there is an ignition with a flame source, i.e., a lighter or match and attendant smoke and odor while the cigarettes burn. This gives vaping a more discreet element that people sometimes take advantage of. A crafty adolescent student can "hit" their vape while a teacher is facing the writing board at the front of a classroom. School restrooms are also tempting vape lounges. This is just another aspect of vaping that only conspires to endear it to young people. The appeal of outwitting stupid grown-ups is hard to resist.

## Recovery from Tobacco Addiction

You can officially add tobacco use disorder, TUD, to the growing list of disorders, along with SUD, AUD, and OUD.

I quit smoking at age 32; the year was 1992. Smoking was not only allowed but also commonplace in restaurants and most public places. It was still allowed on some domestic air travel. Smoking was allowed at many AA meetings. The corralling of smokers at workplaces to designated puffing areas was just starting. It seems almost bizarre to consider nowadays, because of social norms as well as my confirmed nonsmoker status, that cigarette smoking was so commonplace and such a part of the culture.

I was about 15 months into my alcohol recovery and stable in my abstinence from all other mind-altering substances. As I began to ponder the nature of addiction, both mine and the overarching concept, my smoking habit was becoming increasingly dissonant.

The swelling social friction was a backdrop. I worked with healthcare professionals and was part of a small proportion who smoked. In the preceding years, smoking had been more acceptable but was clearly transitioning. We used to light up in the doctors' and nurses' lounges. Smoking had shifted to a couple of designated areas. Eventually, it would be phased out and forbidden anywhere on hospital property.

I began to consider the possibilities of more physical activity. While I had never excelled at athletics enough to carry anything from childhood to adulthood, I thought about returning to cycling or taking up jogging... possibly even going to a gym! Fitness and healthy lifestyle were gaining popularity. Smoking was just not consistent with this. I began to see smoking as an obstacle to things I wanted to do.

Ignoring the health consequences was no longer possible. In a typical week in my role as a surgical technologist, I could literally see a dozen cancer procedures, including lung resections for tumor. Nor could I overlook the dark crap I was coughing up in the mornings.

Today, I know I was moving through the stages of change regarding my tobacco addiction. I was beyond the innocent ignorance of precontemplation and starting to think about what quitting would be like, referred to as contemplation. One day, I asked one of the surgeons I worked with regularly, "What do you know about transdermal nicotine patches?"

"Nothing, but I'll write you a script right now." His response was a strong indication that he supported my quitting. In those days, nicotine patches were available by prescription only, though not covered by insurance. I was not ready for that response; I was still in the contemplation phase, not yet ready to take action. I will say that the positive response helped my thought process. It's also one of my fondest memories of this man. A week later, I hit him up for the prescription.

A box of 21-mg transdermal nicotine patches, a 28-day supply, cost me $108 out of pocket. I can't recall exactly what I was earning back then, but I think that was more than a day's take-home pay at the time. This represented some commitment. I became ready, set a date, and stopped smoking. And I'm going to be honest—it was insanely difficult. For the first four weeks, even though I was getting nicotine, the habits and routines were the challenging part. Working on those while utilizing the nicotine patches was my strategy. Over the year and several months since I had stopped drinking, my 8 or 10 cigarette per day habit had escalated to a solid pack a day. My routine of having a smoke on the way to and from work, at coffee break, and after lunch, with maybe a late afternoon cig, and never smoking in the house, rose to 20 plus smokes daily with an ashtray on my coffee table. As mentioned previously, we smoked at AA meetings, so there was the ride to and from, with additional cigarettes before, during, and after.

By the time the 21-mg nicotine patches were gone, I had made inroads into modifying my habits. Rather than shell out another hundred bucks for the 14-mg patches, the usual tapering treatment, I thought I would be fine without them. However, and in hindsight, I significantly underestimated the effect that nicotine had on me. The withdrawal was real. Over the course of the first few days, I became irritable and moody; cravings were overshadowed by my general restlessness. Initially I had difficulty sleeping and lack of appetite, but that gave way to being tired and hungry to excess. While I don't minimize how miserable the experience was, I can't say enthusiastically enough that it was worth it. I'm so glad I gave up that addiction!

Within a few weeks, the smell of cigarette smoke was abhorrent. I still feel that way today, 34 years later.

Studies have determined that nicotine is a powerful drug of addiction, comparable to heroin, cocaine, and alcohol, with compulsive use and withdrawal symptoms alleviated by nicotine replacement,[70] but I could have told you that.

## Smoking Cessation

Although there has been a decline in the number of smokers in the US, there are still 28.8 million adults who smoke cigarettes according to the *Morbidity and Mortality Weekly Report* of July 25, 2024.[71] In 2022, 67.7 percent of the US citizens who smoked wanted to quit; 53.3 percent attempted to quit and 8.8 percent were successful. Among those who attempted, 38.3 percent used some form of treatment. That represents an improvement over 2020, when only 31 percent of smokers interested in quitting received counseling and/or medications.[72]

Smoking or vaping, essentially the act of absorbing nicotine through the lungs into the bloodstream, results in a nearly instantaneous spike in the neurotransmitter dopamine in the brain. Dopamine, as was previously mentioned, is the brain's currency for the sensation of pleasure. We maintain a baseline level of dopamine, which is bumped up with rewarding experiences, which in turn can start to wire in a response where we want to repeat these experiences.

So, smoking/nicotine use, like any of the addictive substances, is a trap in that we are motivated to continue the behavior, while at the same time the brain adapts. With repetition, the brain will produce less dopamine while the receptor sites, the areas that take up the dopamine, become less sensitive. This downward recalibration is the body's response to anything that changes its balance, referred to already as homeostasis. It's like the body wants to work smart instead of working hard. When we introduce something that increases dopamine, the response is an opposite action, again, aimed at restoring equilibrium. However, now the body needs that artificial dopamine spiking behavior, smoking, to stay in equilibrium.

Take away, or withdraw, the dopamine-raising action of smoking, and the body will work to restore equilibrium. But... not instantaneously. The resulting disequilibrium of quitting smoking causes the discomforts and real physical symptoms that we refer to as withdrawal.

The challenge of smoking cessation, quitting smoking and giving up nicotine, is managing those uncomfortable symptoms and simultaneously changing some significant behaviors. Recall earlier there was some discussion of the social and behavioral components of smoking—even the element of oral fixation. Smoking is something we do automatically in social situations; it's something we do habitually as part of certain routine activities; and, it's something we do with our mouth, kind of like a child with a pacifier. Deviating from these learned but often deep-rooted behaviors generates feelings of unease, even anxiety. Compounding that is the fact that we have, even if only temporarily, lowered our baseline dopamine level, which was maintained by the periodic influx of nicotine. Yeah, nothing is going to feel right.

So, how can we manage this? Fortunately, there are a variety of approaches and options.

There are numerous options for nicotine replacement therapy, NRT. That's precisely what I did with my 21-mg nicotine patches in a blunt and unsupervised manner. Transdermal nicotine, or nicotine replacement in general, is intended to be tapered. The dose of nicotine is gradually decreased. This provides an opportunity for people to begin addressing the behavioral component without nicotine withdrawal. You can literally try on life as a nonsmoker. As long as you're not lighting a cigarette, that's what you are. Not that it's easy. Every time you get in the car, go to coffee break, wait on hold on a phone call... every time and situation where you would routinely light a cigarette, or take a pull off your vape, and you do not—you are doing the work of quitting your nicotine addiction. And yes, it's work.

Nicotine replacement comes in other varieties. There are a couple of different dosages of gum, there are lozenges, and there is even a nasal spray. Most people find that a combination works well.

Nicotine gum comes in two strengths, 2 mg and 4 mg. For smokers of a pack or less per day, 2 mg is appropriate; 4 mg is appropriate for those who smoke more than a pack daily. The recommended way to utilize nicotine gum is to chew slowly until there is a tingling sensation, indicating nicotine is absorbing through the mucosa, or lining, of the mouth. Hold the piece of gum between your cheek and gums until the tingling subsides, then chew until it returns. Repeat the chewing/holding process for about 30 minutes.

Nicotine lozenges are another form of oral NRT, similar to nicotine gum. They also come in 2 mg and 4 mg dosages. They are intended to be placed in the mouth and moved from side to side without chewing or swallowing the lozenge. As the lozenges dissolve, nicotine is absorbed through the oral mucosa.

The above nicotine replacement therapies are available in most areas without prescription.

It is recommended to avoid eating or drinking for 15 minutes prior and avoid eating or drinking during the use of nicotine gum or lozenges.

The other variety of NRT is a rapid-acting nicotine nasal spray, indicated in cases of intense cravings where rapid onset is needed. The recommended use is one to two sprays per hour, not exceeding 5 doses in 1 hour or 40 doses in 24 hours. Nicotine nasal spray is by prescription only.

Nicotine replacement therapy is intended to help ease or manage cravings by maintaining a level of nicotine in the system. Transdermal nicotine patches are intended to be worn for 24 hours, then replaced, and there is a steady but slow release of nicotine. When a patch is first applied, the effect might not be felt or not be sufficient to ease cravings. Combining either gum or lozenges with patches as needed is an effective strategy for maintaining adequate nicotine levels and managing cravings. The long-term strategy is to gradually decrease the strength of the nicotine patches from 21 mg to 14 mg to 7 mg. The strategy with gum and lozenges is a similar tapering, except by spreading out the administration to longer periods of time between in a gradual fashion. Ideally, the nicotine replacement therapy is done over 8 to 12 weeks, giving the body plenty of time to adjust to increasingly lower levels of nicotine.

Two FDA-approved medications, available by prescription, are routinely utilized in smoking cessation. They are bupropion and varenicline, brand names Wellbutrin and Chantix, respectively. Bupropion is an FDA-approved antidepressant that has benefits for smoking cessation. It contains no nicotine but rather supports neurotransmitter levels in the brain, thereby easing cravings and supporting mood. Bupropion is typically initiated two or three weeks prior to smoking cessation. Possible side effects include dry mouth, insomnia, and headache but are not common. Bupropion is a great option for people who cannot tolerate the NRT options or simply prefer a non-nicotine method.

Varenicline works as a partial agonist for nicotine receptor sites. Where nicotine molecules would normally bind to structures in the central nervous system, the medication gets in their way while activating the receptor sites enough to suppress cravings. It's kind of like Suboxone for smoking. Patients start therapy a week before quitting smoking and gradually increase the dose. They might start with 0.5 mg for three days, then go to twice daily at the same dosage before upping the dose to 1 mg twice daily about the time they discontinue smoking. The possible side effects are nausea, vivid dreams, insomnia, and headaches. Patients utilizing this therapy should be monitored for mood changes, agitation, or even depression.

The effectiveness of NRT, bupropion, and varenicline are enhanced with behavioral support. Counseling or individual therapy, group therapy, and peer-support groups are some common examples. Behavioral support provides tools and resources to recognize and manage triggers, develop coping strategies, and build long-term habits for a smoke-free lifestyle. It's work, but it's worth it. Finally, there are also digital supports. Smartphone apps that provide reminders, track progress toward daily and long-term goals, and give coping strategies are becoming popular. Some people desire this type of assistance over the in-person approach and can customize these programs to meet their individual needs and preferences.

With the exception of the medications, which are one or the other but not both, all of these various therapies and approaches can be mixed and matched, customized to suit the individual. Wellbutrin, transdermal nicotine and lozenges for breakthrough cravings, along with a smartphone app and weekly check-ins with a therapist as an example. More is better.

As with quitting any substance use or addiction, preparation increases the chances of success. When I became completely ready to take action on my cigarette habit, I believe that made a difference. While support is a wonderful thing, pressure or influence from others is not a recipe for success. Doing it for myself works best. And remember, recovery from anything is nonlinear. There are going to be setbacks. If I light up a cigarette, or buy a whole pack, it's just one bad day. If I can remind myself why I'm doing it—for my health, for the activities I want to enjoy, or just to be free of a nasty substance—

I can always get back on track.

One of the most dreaded side effects of quitting smoking is weight gain. According to Luba Yammine, PhD, 80 to 90 percent of people who quit smoking gain weight: 5 to 15 pounds is the average at 12 months, while 13 to 14 percent of people gain over 20 pounds. The weight gain is because nicotine causes the release of epinephrine and norepinephrine; these neurotransmitters speed up metabolism and energy output. There is also a tendency for people to replace the reward of smoking with the reward of eating, a psychological effect enhanced by the increased reward value of food. So, it's a bit of a double whammy. Weight gain is likely to occur without eating one extra forkful, but the tendency is to use that fork. At the extreme end, there is increased risk for diabetes.[73]

The class of medications known as glucagon-like peptide-1 inhibitors, GLP-1, is the newest trend in front-line treatment for diabetes and, secondarily, medical weight loss. Almost ironically, this class of medications was found to inhibit the desire to smoke and is now under investigation as a smoking cessation medication.

A newer approach is transcranial magnetic stimulation, TMS. This uses magnetic fields directed to target the specific areas of the brain associated with addiction, impulse control, and reward. It is noninvasive and has been approved for smoking sensation by the FDA. TMS is new, and protocols are still being refined. It has promise and can be utilized in combination with other cessation approaches. Advantages to TMS are that there are no systemic reactions, and it does not interfere or react with medications or other smoking cessation supports. A possible disadvantage is that it is time intensive, requiring numerous treatments per week over several weeks.

### Providing Updated Education

According to the CDC, less than 12 percent of people in the US smoke.[74] According to one study, over 74 percent of people who use opioids smoke.[75] In fact, "97% of heroin users in one study of methadone or buprenorphine treatment used an average of 20 cigarettes or a pack per day. Co-occurring tobacco and opioid use creates an additive effect of increasing toxicity and related health consequences across all body systems, leading these users to face unnecessarily high mortality and morbidity." [76] These figures speak to a correlation between the use of opioids and tobacco that is statistically compelling. The science is now beginning to define elements of the connection between substance use and tobacco use.

"Using both opioids and tobacco may enhance subjective positive effects and satisfaction with drug use, reduce withdrawal symptoms for both substances, and act as a substitution when one drug is unavailable." [77] This is because both substances utilize the same neurological machinery. The two pathways, the opioid and the nicotinic-cholinergic neurotransmitter systems, "interact in important ways to modulate opioid and nicotine effects." In other words, "dopamine release induced by nicotine is dependent on facilitation by the opioid system." But here's the worst part: "Nicotine can serve as a prime for the use of other drugs, which in the case of the opioid system may be bidirectional." [78]

What that is clearly saying, albeit in a science-y way, is that using opioids triggers desire to smoke, and smoking triggers desire to use opioids.

The conclusion is that smoking among people in remission from SUDs is associated with a higher risk of resuming active SUD. Research indicates that both "continued smoking and smoking initiation are related to statistically significant increases in the odds of SUD relapse." [79] This emphasizes the importance of incorporating smoking cessation efforts into SUD treatment programs

Regarding alcohol use disorder, while outcomes are mixed on the longitudinal timeline, long-range data supports correlation between smoking and resuming active drinking. "Among adults with remitted AUDs, daily and non-daily use of cigarettes was associated with significantly decreased likelihood of alcohol use [short-term] and increased likelihood of alcohol abuse and alcohol dependence three years later. Concurrent treatment of cigarette smoking when treating AUDs may help improve long-term alcohol outcomes and reduce the negative consequences of both substances." [80]

When people detox and enter recovery from substance use disorder, quitting smoking and vaping improves their chances for success.

By today's standards and leading-edge knowledge, my beliefs, my practice, and the education I provided in the past were wrong. While everything I said previously hasn't changed—that initiation of treatment is a challenging time to broach the topic, that smoking is a coping skill for people who often don't have many others—this new understanding of the relationship of smoking and substance use can no longer be ignored. People entering recovery need to know this, and, just as important, people in the treatment sector need to know this.

Today, I share this information with clients and patients and recommend they examine their relationship with tobacco and nicotine products. The science says quitting smoking or vaping will enhance their outcome.

As daunting and difficult as this revelation sounds in terms of incorporating it into an upgraded standard of care, it's necessary. We need to change our minds about this. Every new bit of knowledge, every new understanding of how addiction and recovery work matter in the big picture. Even small, incremental upgrades in the way we treat people will eventually add up. It's time to recognize that smoking and vaping, tobacco use disorder, is every bit as threatening to someone's welfare as a drug of choice is.

# Chapter 13
# The Weed Chapter

"You can smoke marijuana, you can eat it,
you can wear it, it's a perfect plant!"
~ Tommy Chong

## The Cannabis Experience

Cannabis has a unique place in contemporary society and popular culture. First and foremost, it's a plant, and its cultivation goes back thousands of years. Principally known for its psychoactive properties, cannabis is the most used recreational substance and is central to drug culture. Smoking cannabis is the most common way to activate and administer the effects, which could be best described as euphoric, with varying degrees of intoxication.

Back in the day, we just called it getting high.

Mr. Chong is 100 percent correct regarding the versatility of the cannabis plant. In addition to being intoxicating, it is medicinal and even functional. Hemp, a non-psychoactive variety of the cannabis plant, can be used for textiles, paper, building materials, and even a form of plastic as an alternative to petroleum-based plastics.

*Cannabis sativa* is a flowering herbaceous plant native to Central Asia and the Indian subcontinent. It was introduced to the Western Hemisphere in colonial times. It belongs to the Cannabaceae family and includes three primary species or subspecies: *Cannabis sativa, Cannabis indica,* and *Cannabis ruderalis.* Each has unique characteristics. The plant has been around as long as history has been recorded.

As of 2026, cannabis is legal for recreational use in 24 states, as well as the District of Columbia, Guam, the US Virgin Islands, and the Northern Mariana Islands. Additionally, cannabis for medical use is legal in 40 states, the District of Columbia, Guam, Puerto Rico, and the US Virgin Islands, while 10 states permit limited forms of low-THC cannabis for medical purposes. The remaining states have either decriminalized or outlawed cannabis use entirely. Legal status is dynamic.

Federally, recreational cannabis remains a Schedule I substance under the Controlled Substances Act. The DEA has reclassified medical cannabis as a Schedule III substance (as this book was being prepared for final editing). An Executive Order expedited this. Currently, the federal government allows states to enforce their own cannabis laws, particularly regarding medical use, while recreational use remains federally prohibited. As previously mentioned, Schedule I substances are considered to have no medical value and high potential for abuse.

"Nearly six-in-ten Americans (57%) say that marijuana should be legal for medical *and* recreational purposes, while roughly a third (32%) say that marijuana should be legal for medical use only. Just 11% of Americans say that the drug should not be legal at all." [81]

Obviously, the regulations haven't kept pace with cultural trends, the marketplace, and popular demand. The US cannabis industry is expected to reach almost $40 billion in sales in 2024. Cannabis will add $115.2 billion to the economy in 2024.[82]

I entered a personal relationship with cannabis over 50 years ago. The weed of my wild and misspent youth was but a crude forerunner of today's sophisticated cannabis. The plant itself has literally been transformed; cultivation is more like an art form than mere gardening. Hybridization and refined growing techniques have elevated the cannabis experience.

## Got Pot?

When I was a kid, for a while anyway, we could actually get a "nickel bag." For five dollars, you received about a "finger" of weed in a standard sandwich-sized baggie, and from this, you could roll about five decent joints. The quality varied, but most of the weed in those days provided the desired "buzz." As the end product user, I had next to no knowledge of how the supply chain worked. I was strictly a consumer. I knew people who would sell it, and they always seemed to make it out like they were doing me a huge favor. In those days, an ounce was a standard retail quantity to purchase. The person who sold me that ounce had likely purchased (or been "fronted") a pound from someone who traded in larger quantities, etc. One can appreciate the challenges of this enterprise, as a dozen-and-a-half pounds of cannabis would probably fill an average suitcase.

In my 20s, I was renting a small house with a little space of land next to it, and I took up vegetable gardening. After the first year, with some tomatoes and zucchini to show for my efforts, I considered other possibilities. We were friends with a neighbor across the street, a woman who raised horses. With her kind permission, I lugged over numerous wheelbarrow loads of well-seasoned manure for deposit on the small plot, which happened to be discreetly positioned behind a wall of brush and shrubs. I prevailed on a friend to bring his rototiller by, and, with his help, I prepared a decent-sized plot with beautifully fertile soil. My plan was to grow some weed that summer.

Over the years, I've enjoyed gardening, but at that time, I was a complete novice. I don't recall how I started the cannabis plants, but I succeeded in establishing a dozen or so healthy plants. By today's standards of cultivation, my efforts were crude. The seeds were probably random, not from any special variety. Between full sunlight, daily watering, and the potently fertile soil, the plants thrived.

The one thing I did know to do was to observe the crop carefully for plants that were developing male characteristics. The formation and presence of little flowers with pollen sacks was the sign that I needed to remove those plants. Someone had explained to me the birds and bees of cannabis plants.

As the plants grew over the course of the summer, they would seek to fulfill their botanical biological imperative. Female plants grow flowers with little tendril or hair-like structures called pistils that act as pollen receptors; these are what formed the buds, the part of the cannabis plant with the highest concentration of psychoactive tetrahydrocannabinol, or THC. The act of denying the female plants pollination had two effects. The response of the pistils was to grow aggressively because they were becoming more desperate for pollination, and no seeds would form in the buds. To put it bluntly, the plants were horny. The result was more and larger seedless buds with higher THC concentration, i.e., higher-quality cannabis.

This weed-growing initiative could have had several possible outcomes. The stoner kid who lived a few houses down might have seen the plants and helped himself some late evening. That did not happen. The local constabulary could have somehow discovered them. That would have had legal consequences because cultivation was outlawed along with possession. People were being jailed for such things, something I failed to fully weigh due to my youthful exuberance. While neither of those negative outcomes occurred, I had not considered the full ramifications of the positive outcome I hoped for.

As the summer progressed, all was well in the garden. There were six or seven robust female cannabis plants, growing like weeds. They were taller than I was by late August. One evening there was a rainstorm with some moderate winds. The following day, the plants were fine, but several branches had actually collapsed and broken under their own weight. I collected them and hung them upside down in the little breezeway at the back of the house.

Several days later, Saturday morning, I was up early and remembered the branches on the breezeway. Somehow, in my mind, I was a little disconnected from the reality that these plant branches drying in the back of the house were a mind-altering substance, something I loved at that point in my life. I turned on the TV, spread some plastic on the floor, and began the laborious task of cleaning the cannabis buds off the branches. It was just mindless busy work, gently breaking the delicate buds from the branches and stalks, and TV was the perfect distraction.

About 20 minutes later, I suddenly realized that I was incredibly stoned. I mean, like almost tripping, it felt so intense. As we used to say—I was baked! But wait a minute, I hadn't taken a single hit... then I realized that my hands were sticky with the resin from the plants. The cannabis had entered my system through my skin. The full implication of this began to slowly dawn on me. The quality of this preliminary sample, the literal broken branches ahead of the actual harvest, was astounding. After the actual harvest, successfully accomplished without the previously mentioned mishaps, the full weight of the situation began to settle on me. This was beyond anything I'd hoped for. I had a huge supply of high-quality cannabis, as well as a secondary supply of lesser quality product, mostly leaves. This cannabis smelled heavenly, smoked smoothly, and was incredibly potent. This bumper crop of weed literally lasted me until I entered recovery years later, when I threw away the last of it.

## A Brief History of Weed

Cannabis has an old soul. There is much ado about weed these days. The last 120 years or so has seen big shifts in use, regulation, and attitudes toward cannabis. However, all the fuss is a contemporary development. It has been cultivated on every continent, even on Antarctica. Analysis of modern strains has traced domestication of cannabis to northwest China, corresponding with archaeological remains of hemp cord on 12,000-year-old pottery. Because it originated in Asia before spreading to Europe, cannabis did not make its way to the Americas until the Spanish colonization in 1545, when it was brought to Chile.

In the 17th and 18th century British colonies, low-THC hemp cultivation was high priority because it was used in rope, sails, and paper. In colonial times, the British Royal Navy was the world's foremost military force. Farmers in the colonies were mandated to grow hemp to meet the Navy's demand. The US founding fathers, including George Washington, Thomas Jefferson, Benjamin Franklin, and James Madison, all grew hemp. Whether or not they engaged in recreational use of cannabis remains the subject of conjecture.

Cannabis was utilized for medicinal value, or at least with that intention, in the 1800s. Tinctures for pain relief were commonly sold in pharmacies, and it was believed to be safe and effective, as we like to say today. THC is known to have analgesic, or pain-relieving, value. Cannabis products were aggressively marketed to women. Tinctures or salves were applied to the gums of infants for teething pain. Cannabis-based products and medications were a prominent part of the golden age of patent medicine.

A series of laws and new regulations began to rain on the cannabis parade in the early 20th century. The Pure Food and Drug Act of 1906 required honest labeling of tincture ingredients, as well as setting the tone for regulation to follow. Ironically, progressive thinking at the time was trending toward prohibition (I know, right?), and the writing was on the wall for cannabis-based remedies. Next came the Harrison

Narcotics Tax Act of 1914. It did not specifically name cannabis but rather regulated the production and taxation of opiates and coca products. It did pave the way for increased regulation in the Wild West world of patent medicines, setting the stage for the Marihuana Tax Act of 1937, codifying the spelling with an "h" as a legal precedent and to relate the word to Mexican culture. That law made the possession and transfer of cannabis illegal.

A 1917 Treasury Department report said that "Mexicans and sometimes Negroes and lower-class whites" were the only ones smoking cannabis. The same report warned that upper-class White women were in danger from these "drug-crazed" minorities. This kind of demonization planted seeds of stigma, but even worse—made the association of cannabis use with violence and insanity.[83]

A 1936 propaganda film, *Tell Your Children,* symbolized the moral panic that cannabis was causing in the early 20th century. The film portrays cannabis as a dangerous drug that leads to moral decay and aberrant behavior, including crime and promiscuity, followed by hallucinations and murder. The plot depicts young people who fall under the spell of the evil weed with tragic consequences. Originally intended as an educational film, it was eventually renamed *Reefer Madness* and became central in early antidrug campaigns. The film is seen as ludicrously comedic today.

Harry Anslinger was to cannabis what Joe McCarthy was to communism. He was on a mission, and it was personal. As notably chronicled in Johann Hari's *Chasing the Scream: The First and Last Days of the War on Drugs,* Anslinger is probably best known as an aggressive advocate for cannabis criminalization in the 1930s and beyond.

Anslinger began his buzzkill career working as an agent for the Prohibition Unit of the US Treasury Department. Realizing that position had an expiration date, he transitioned to the Federal Bureau of Narcotics, FBN, also part of the Treasury Department, as its first commissioner. This was likely facilitated by Treasury Secretary Andrew Mellon, a relation of Anslinger's wife. Anslinger felt the role of the FBN was too small; they needed a new threat, and cannabis was made to order.

Commissioner Anslinger began a campaign to convince his superiors as well as the public that weed was a threat to civilization as they knew it. He undertook an aggressive media campaign to spread his antidrug message, that cannabis caused insanity, violence, and immoral behavior. As his influence grew, he suppressed the scientific facts that cannabis caused none of the harms he asserted. He also leveraged racial biases, and his policies were harshly disproportionate to marginalized communities, and a principal driver of the trend toward incarcerating drug law violators. He had particular contempt for jazz musicians.

The Marihuana Tax Act of 1937 effectively outlawed cannabis by imposing heavy taxes on its sale. In the 1950s, the federal government also established mandatory minimum sentences for drug offenses, including cannabis. Cannabis went deep underground.

## It's Not Just for Hippies Anymore

In the 1960s, cannabis, "smoking grass," became synonymous with counterculture and the antiwar movement. Weed's underground status gave way to growing popularity. Hip suburban adults were lighting up after the children went to bed. It was a mainstay on college campuses. And, over in Southeast Asia, our boys in the armed forces were smoking powerful local cannabis.

The antiwar demonstrations, on and off college campuses, were becoming commonplace in the late 1960s, and smoking weed was a given. The drug itself became the source of protest in many instances, and a legalization movement was gaining momentum. Along with the war in Vietnam and segregation, the criminalization of cannabis was creating a significant fracture in the social backbone of the country. Top-down propaganda of the day asserted that the war was necessary, and cannabis use led directly to heroin use.

Dr. James L. Goddard, the FDA commissioner during the administration of President Lyndon Johnson, from 1966 to 1968, recommended vigorous and significant testing. He pointed out, "There is little scientific knowledge of its dangers or merits," and that the laws of the day were, "Unenforceable, excessively severe, scientifically incorrect and revealing of our ignorance of human behavior." [84] There seemed to be considerable momentum, not toward legalization but rather decriminalization.

Richard Nixon changed all that.

President Nixon considered cannabis an existential threat to the country and his presidency. He was on record, taped during a staff meeting, opining that, (insert Richard Nixon voice) "homosexuality, dope, [and] immorality in general" were undermining the nation. "That's why the Communists and the left-wingers are pushing the stuff, they're trying to destroy us." [85]

It gets worse. "Every one of the bastards that are out for legalizing marijuana is Jewish. What the Christ is the matter with [them]?... I suppose it's because so many of them are psychiatrists, you know... By God we are going to hit the marijuana thing, and I want to hit it right square in the puss." [86] It's easy for anyone old enough to remember Nixon to envision him saying this in his oft-imitated voice.

Nixon had Attorney General John Mitchell produce the Comprehensive Drug Abuse Prevention and Control Act of 1970, best known for its Title II, the Controlled Substances Act. This established the five-level scheduling system that rated drugs based on medical use and potential for abuse. The drugs synonymous with counterculture, such as LSD, heroin, and peyote were placed in Schedule I, considered to have no accepted medical value and high potential for abuse. This effectively made possession, use, and trafficking federal offenses, closing the loophole left open by the 1937 Marihuana Tax Act that left the penalties up to individual states.

Nixon also lobbied to have cannabis categorized as a Schedule I drug, and this was done temporarily, pending further congressional review. Part of Title II called for the establishment of a National Commission on Marijuana and Drug Abuse to undertake a two-year survey on cannabis. This working group was also known as the Shafer Commission, named for its chair, Raymond P. Shafer, former Republican governor of Pennsylvania and state senator.

Releasing its report in 1972, the Shafer Commission came out in support of decriminalization and stated that prevailing views on the harmfulness of cannabis were incorrect and invalid. The report basically concluded that people who use marijuana were in no way physically, biochemically, or mentally different from nonusers. Cannabis did not justify the manner in which the criminal justice system was intruding on private behavior, and that "the compulsive use" of alcohol was "the most destructive drug-use pattern in this nation." [87] (While there is no evidence that alcohol use regularly impaired Nixon's ability to carry out his presidential duties, biographers have described his drinking as problematic and becoming more intense in stressful times, such as the Watergate scandal).

Nixon was pissed. Prior to the commission's convening, Nixon had made his position clear to Senator Shafer. Shafer's commission had followed the science, not the political mandate. The report concluded that the country should abolish criminal penalties for possession of small amounts of cannabis—decriminalization. While Nixon could not ignore the report, he spun the conversation toward legalization, something the report did not advocate for. Nixon essentially dismissed the report and cannabis remained in Schedule I.

More and more people were arrested and jailed for possession of cannabis. Nixon's first term was a high point for the war on drugs. However, Nixon had other problems to contend with, and resigned in August 1974, just over a year-and-a-half into his second term. The realization that while cannabis seemed to symbolize the problem, the scope of the drug situation—trafficking, enforcement, use, and addiction—loomed larger than was previously understood. It was quickly realized that the war on drugs was not winnable. And yet, it waged on.

The Shafer Commission report sowed the seeds of serious doubt about draconian laws and penalties for simple possession, but arrests continued to escalate from several hundred thousand in the early 1970s to a peak of about 750,000 annually between 2000 and 2010.[88] However, from the 1970s on there has been a serious shift in perception of cannabis; people began to understand that weed was not heroin. At the state level, there were ongoing and more-or-less constant initiatives to decriminalize. In 1996, California became the first state to legalize cannabis for medical use. In 2012, Colorado and Washington became the first states to legalize recreational use.

## Weed Science and Medicine

When FDA Commissioner James Goddard advocated that research and better understanding of cannabis was needed in the mid-1960s, this was understatement. Tetrahydrocannabinol, THC, the primary psychoactive compound in cannabis, was only isolated in 1964, scant years prior to Goddard's FDA tenure. In contrast, the poppy plant yielded first opium, then morphine, a century-and-a-half prior in the early 1800s. Cocaine was first produced from coca leaves in the mid-19th century. Virtually nothing was known about how cannabis worked. An Israeli organic chemist, Raphael Mechoulam, is credited with the discovery of THC. Working at the Weizmann Institute of science outside Tel Aviv, he isolated numerous substances from 11 pounds of confiscated Lebanese hashish donated by the national Israeli Police. He injected these separately into rhesus monkeys, discovering that THC made the normally aggressive monkeys mellow.

Mechoulam dedicated his career to studying cannabis and is responsible for many discoveries, earning him the nickname the Godfather of Cannabis Research. In addition to THC, he studied numerous other cannabinoids including cannabidiol, CBD. Previously discovered CBD stands out because of its nonintoxicating properties; it does not produce the high associated with THC. Now widely known, CBD has gained attention for its potential therapeutic effects.

So, how does cannabis do what it does? It was Mechoulam who first sought to understand the mechanism of action, i.e., the interaction between a drug and its target as well as what that target is. Most drugs interact with specific biological targets, such as receptors or enzymes, and bind with them in a way that modifies or blocks the target's normal activity. Mechoulam's early work laid a foundation that he and others built on to gain understanding of how cannabis and cannabinoids interact with the human body.

The study of cannabinoid molecules in cannabis led to the identification of the endocannabinoid system, ECS, in the human body. Endo means inner or within; endocannabinoids are natural cannabinoids produced by the body. They bind to cannabinoid receptors to influence various bodily functions. The ECS is a complex signaling system of chemical messengers in the body that plays a crucial role in regulating a wide range of physiological and psychological processes. Some of its key roles include pain regulation, mood and stress responses, appetite and metabolism, memory and learning, inflammation and immune response, and sleep! The close chemical resemblance of cannabinoids to endocannabinoids is the reason cannabis can have effects on the human organism.

Tommy Chong didn't know how correct he was—cannabis mimics our central nervous system. The ECS is now a growing area of medical research. Potential treatments are being explored for numerous conditions, including chronic pain, epilepsy and seizure disorders, anxiety and depression, neurodegenerative diseases like Alzheimer's and Parkinson's, and autoimmune disorders like multiple sclerosis.

Considering the above information, it's a remarkable coincidence that the components of cannabis correspond so well to human biochemistry. Cannabis might hold a bounty of potential benefits, and continued research is the key to unlocking the medicinal mysteries of the cannabis plant.

The FDA has approved a short list of cannabis-based medications. Epidiolex is essentially CBD and is approved for treatment of a couple of specific diagnoses, Lennox-Gastaut and Dravet syndromes, rare forms of childhood-onset epilepsy characterized by frequent, treatment-resistant seizures. Syndros and Marinol (the generic name is dronabinol) contain synthetic THC and are approved for treatment of nausea, vomiting, and lack of appetite, side effects of chemotherapy. Cesamet (generic nabilone) is also used for treatment of nausea and vomiting. Again, these were Schedule I medications, and I have observed these kept in locked medication drawers alongside opiates and benzodiazepines with count verification required every time the next shift comes on duty.

Another important area of research is continued study of the effects of cannabis use, particularly prolonged cannabis use, and cannabis use by younger people, especially adolescents.

Marijuana Investigations for Neuroscientific Discovery, MIND, was started by Dr. Staci Gruber in 2014. She said MIND remains the only program in the United States dedicated to studying the long-term effects of medical cannabis use in patients who live with a wide range of conditions and symptoms.

Dr. Gruber has focused on examining the etiologic bases of neural models of dysfunction in patients with bipolar disorder as well as cannabis-using adolescents and adults. She has also been involved in applying behavioral science to help shape policies regarding juvenile advocacy and defense. "Everything we know about cannabis and its impact basically comes from studies of recreational consumers. I found little things here and there where cognitive performance was assessed, but not in a comprehensive way." [89]

MIND supports numerous projects designed to address the impact of medical cannabis on a number of important variables, including cognition, brain structure and function, clinical state, quality of life, pain, sleep, and other health-related measures. As director of MIND, Dr. Gruber has generated major contributions to the field as the first to assess medical cannabis patients longitudinally, first to acquire neuroimaging data in medical cannabis patients, and as principal investigator of the first clinical trial of a full-spectrum, high-cannabidiol product, which she specifically formulated to treat anxiety. Dr. Gruber is known as the "pot doc" to her many patients.

Dr. Yasmin Hurd is the director of the Addiction Institute of Mount Sinai in New York City. Dr. Hurd's multidisciplinary research investigates the neurobiology underlying addiction disorders and related psychiatric illnesses, focused on understanding the contribution and interplay of epigenetics to the development and treatment of addictive disorders.

She is a leader in the field of cannabis research, particularly involving children and adolescents. She sees "growing evidence in the field that cannabis use puts children and adolescents at risk for a variety of psychiatric problems, from dependence on that drug and others to schizophrenia. In utero exposure, she believes, can ignite mental health problems in childhood and beyond. In studies with rats, human fetal tissue, and children, her lab has begun to uncover changes in gene expression, as well as alterations in the brain's chemical communication systems and wiring, that may underlie some of these effects."

Dr. Hurd opposes the criminalization of cannabis use and possession, but believes legalization has downsides. "I am worried about how cavalier we're becoming and that there is a cannabis smoke shop now practically, in some places, on every other block," she said. "I feel frustrated that people are willing to sacrifice kids and young people for their quote-unquote right to get high." [90]

Like almost everything else in the continuing evolution of substance use, treatment, and recovery, the ongoing story of cannabis is complicated. It's not as simple as "drugs are bad," but it's also debatable that cannabis is the perfect plant.

I have mentioned working in office-based addiction treatment, where some patients in stable remission from chaotic opioid use continued to use cannabis. While the conversations with them were always about safety and support, I never failed to point out that, "If you were 16, this would be a much different conversation." With adolescents, the conversation needs to be different because the human brain doesn't fully mature until about age 25. On the way to growing up, young people experience psychological and social milestones that are crucial to healthy growth and development, as well as meeting the demands and responsibilities of adulthood.

Even moderate cannabis use can have negative impact on growth and development. Researchers David Ferguson, PhD, and Joseph Bowden, PhD, performed a study of a New Zealand birth cohort between the ages of 14 and 25. Measurements of cannabis use were correlated to level of education, income, welfare dependence, and unemployment. The study concluded that cannabis use in late adolescence and early adulthood is associated with a range of adverse outcomes. Of study subjects who never used cannabis between the ages of 14 and 21, 36 percent had attained a university degree by age 25; for subjects who used cannabis 400 times or more during the same age range, the statistic for university degrees was 2 percent. For subjects who never used cannabis, 21 percent were unemployed sometime between the ages of 21 and 25; 52 percent of subjects who used cannabis over 400 times were unemployed between the same ages. And 57 percent of study subjects who used cannabis 400 times or more were welfare dependent, as opposed to 25 percent who never used cannabis.[91]

There is no formal detox for cannabis use. However, cannabis withdrawal is real. Therapeutic elements utilized for treatment are containment or restriction from cannabis use or THC in any form. The symptoms of mood disruption with irritability, sleep disruption, appetite disruption, and generalized physical discomfort are addressed symptomatically. Benzodiazepines might be utilized, and another antianxiety medication, buspirone (brand name BuSpar), has been shown to be effective. The most intense physical symptoms, which can include tremors, headache, sweating, and nausea, can last up to a week. The effects can linger for a month, and the psychological adjustment period can take several months.

## The Cannabis Industry

The cannabis industry in the United States is still in an early, formative phase. Nevertheless, the fledgling industry has already evolved significantly in the scant decade that cannabis has been legal for recreational use. Medical marijuana required the building of a cultivation infrastructure from essentially nothing. Initially, growing was informal, often home-based and outdoors, and without quality control. Other states followed California's 1996 legalization, prompting more organized cultivation with grower licenses, plant count limits, and regulatory oversight.

Today, trained horticulturists grow a stable and consistent product in commercial settings consisting of industrial-scale, controlled indoor/greenhouse environments. Products are tested in compliance with guidelines and strict licensing.

This rapid evolution began as a dynamic between a purist approach and a business approach. Viewed as an art form, the cultivation of cannabis had been the underground, guerrilla pursuit of intrepid pioneers. As the game changed, the trend toward legalization offered open potential for legitimizing what had previously been an illicit, underground market commodity. The business perspective reduced cannabis to that commodity, a proposition in agricultural.

Not surprisingly, the business perspective has won out over the art form for the most part. The challenges of navigating this turbulent, constantly changing marketplace require technical prowess, business expertise, and entrepreneurial spirit. Even today this enterprise still operates in a gray area somewhere between the rock of state regulation and the hard place of federal law. Imagine being an innovative startup company, but banks and payroll companies won't work with you. If you want to go into the cannabis business, you better bring some deep pockets.

Cannabis is being rescheduled while this book is being written. The Controlled Substances Act states the US government's policy on cannabis as having no medical value and high potential for abuse, per Schedule I. Licensed medical cannabis is now Schedule III. Therefore, cannabis regulation is complicated. A color-coded map of the US with the breakdown of legal statuses looks like a patchwork quilt. The distribution, in 2026, is as follows: recreational use in 24 states and the District of Columbia; medicinal use in 40 states, DC, and three territories, low-THC/CBD use in 10 states, and two lonely states (Idaho and Kansas) with absolutely no legal use permitted. The individual states determine the legal disposition of the substance. Each state sets possession limits, home cultivation rules, and licensing requirements. As far as cannabis is concerned, we are "united" states in name only. The maze of individual regulations makes crossing state lines as complicated as foreign travel, perhaps more so.

Texas is a low-THC/CBD state. During a recent visit to El Paso, I crossed the state line into New Mexico, where both medicinal and recreational use are legal. Immediately upon crossing into the Sunland Park area, I saw numerous cannabis dispensaries and establishments, an obvious cannabis-friendly zone. My host explained this and also described the area as having a high crime rate, owing to the fact that cannabis is largely a cash business. Federally regulated banks want nothing to do with federally outlawed cannabis businesses, which have to find workarounds such as small, independent credit unions. Customers can't pay for their products with credit cards. The establishments' employees are often paid in cash, without tax withholding. It's a mess.

The cannabis industry has seen some significant developments from a cultivation perspective over the years. Today's sophisticated cannabis products are a far cry from the weed of my youth, even my windfall bumper crop. THC content is probably three times higher, between 15 and 25 percent. The consumer experience has been enhanced by cultivation techniques and hybridization, crossbreeding with the intention of bringing out certain characteristics. Growers usually produce three generations per year, so can intentionally manipulate the evolution of plants toward a desired outcome. The presence of organic hydrocarbons called terpenes influences how the product will affect the user. Different strains will have specific benefits, such as relaxation, focus, and enhancing creativity as examples. This is where the art form meets the business venture in the competitive marketplace.

Cannabis products have expanded to meet different markets and consumer preferences. In addition to "flower," the smokable dried buds, cannabis companies are producing pre-rolls, edibles, concentrates, self-enclosed vape pens, vape cartridges, topicals, tinctures, capsules, and... beverages. That's right! Nonalcoholic THC beverages are being produced from low-THC hemp. Products made from hemp are legal across the United States, thanks to the Farm Bill (officially the Agriculture Improvement Act of 2018), and these beverages now account for 2 percent of the cannabis market, according to Forbes magazine.[92]

The takeaway is that cannabis is here. While it always has been, the pendulum has swung in the direction of more liberal policy. There are still many details to work out and kinks to iron out. The confusing maze of regulations between federal and state oversight remains a barrier to the acceptance of cannabis on a scale like alcohol or cigarettes. Issues like zoning—where the public use of cannabis might negatively impact others—need to be addressed. No one ever got drunk from secondhand alcohol, but a cloud of cannabis smoke in a public place can impact bystanders.

While the gateway drug idea is a myth, we need to encourage responsible use among people in recovery who choose to use cannabis and recognize the potential negative consequences for young people.

We should continue to investigate cannabis in its many forms for beneficial and therapeutic applications. The fact that there is a human endocannabinoid system is significant and suggests there is much more to understand.

Weed has impact. The potential for harm is real, and awareness of risk versus reward is essential, but again, no more so than alcohol or cigarettes. It's apples and oranges, and it comes down to freedom of self-determination. This is where the responsibility lies with the individual user to understand and recognize the differences between substance use and substance use disorder.

# Chapter 14
# The Psychedelic Chapter

"No account of the universe in its totality can be final which leaves these other forms of consciousness quite disregarded."
~ William James

Lysergic acid diethylamide, LSD, was discovered by Albert Hofmann, a Swiss chemist and researcher for Sandoz Laboratories in Switzerland. He first synthesized the psychedelic drug in 1938 by isolating compounds found in ergot, a fungus affecting rye. Because he was actually looking for new medications to control uterine bleeding, and because LSD had no such benefits, it was set aside. Five years later, Hofmann was revisiting the compound and accidentally exposed himself to a small amount. He experienced some dreamlike hallucinations.

Hofmann was intrigued. He decided to use himself as a subject, a guinea pig, for an experiment. He deliberately ingested what he thought would be a small quantity, but the 250 micrograms he took was actually a whopping dose. The drug started to take effect, and he headed home… on his bicycle. He experienced the typical effects now commonly associated with the compound—visual and spatial hallucinations. He reported that he saw kaleidoscopic colors and the buildings appeared to ripple. He made it home and experienced intense anxiety, paranoia that his neighbor was a witch, and a fear that he had poisoned himself. A doctor was called, but, aside from his agitation, Hofmann's only physical symptom was dilated pupils.

Dr. Hofmann's wild bicycle ride home on April 19, 1943, henceforth referred to as Bicycle Day, initiated the modern era of psychedelic drug culture. Following his auspicious first (intentional) LSD experience, Dr. Hofmann continued his research. He believed that LSD, and eventually other psychedelic compounds, could have therapeutic benefit for various psychiatric conditions. He went on to author books and became an advocate for the legitimate study and application of psychedelics (not recreational use).

Psychedelics are a class of drugs that work at the neurotransmitter level to affect specific parts of the brain in ways that alter function, perception, and consciousness. There are a number of substances in the psychedelic classification, also called hallucinogens. The general effects are increased stimulation of the neocortex (executive function), enhanced sensory processing, altered neural network connectivity, and increased neuroplasticity, among others. A primary job of the brain is the interpretation of our internal and external reality; psychedelic substances alter that interpretation.

Psychedelic substances have been around since before recorded history. Dr. Hofmann's "problem child," as he termed LSD, served as a vehicle to bring psychedelics to modern culture. In terms of cultural significance, there are those who would rank the discovery of LSD as momentous as the first splitting of the atom.

Psychedelic substances, hallucinogens, also referred to as entheogens, are a fixture in the modern culture of substance use. Yet, these substances are not considered addictive. Psychedelics have been on a roller coaster in terms of popular perception and acceptance since arriving in the mainstream in the 1950s. Initially thought to be the promise of deliverance from a host of psychological conditions and mental illnesses, they wrongfully became the pariah of the drug culture before coming full circle. Today, hallucinogens are under robust investigation for their therapeutic value; these substances can rightfully be called medicine today.

As they set about conquest of the New World, the Spanish sought to suppress hallucinogenic practices of the Indigenous people that were tied to cultural and spiritual tradition. Viewing psychedelics as incompatible with Christianity, the Spanish aggressively prohibited substances and rituals as a measure of social control. The altered states induced by religious ceremonies were perceived as demonic possession. All indigenous hallucinogens, including the key substances psilocybin mushrooms, ayahuasca, and peyote, would have been effectively stamped out and forgotten had they not gone underground. The forbidden practices continued clandestinely, adapting as necessary to keep the traditions alive.

Following Hofmann's discovery of LSD, early research focused on hopes that it might offer therapeutic benefit for psychosis, because it was known to induce psychotic symptoms and is termed psychotomimetic. In the late 1940s and 1950s, researchers began looking at potential benefits for treating anxiety, alcohol and drug use, and enhancing creativity.

Meanwhile, an author and ethnomycologist named R. Gordon Wasson *rediscovered* psilocybin. His interests combined the study of mushrooms and human culture. In central Mexico, he participated in a sacred mushroom ceremony led by a local shaman. Not surprisingly, he found the experience transformative and became a believer. He published an article, "Seeking the Magic Mushroom" in the May 13, 1957, issue of *LIFE* magazine. He went on to collaborate with Albert Hofmann to isolate the psychoactive ingredient in psilocybin mushrooms, psilocyn. The stage was set for academic interest and mainstream acceptance. What could possibly go wrong?

In 1960, Dr. Timothy Leary began the Harvard Psilocybin Project. This initiative conducted experiments with graduate students and faculty with the goal of understanding the effects of the substance on the human mind. Of note were separate experiments with prison inmates and divinity students. The majority of results and outcomes were positive. However... concerns arose over experiment methodology, storage of substances, inclusion of undergraduates, coercion of graduate students to participate, and graduate students running experiments unsupervised, blurring the line between research and social events... and Dr. Leary's personal use of psilocybin. The project had gained significant notoriety, and Leary was attaining "guru" status in mainstream culture. At first other faculty questioned the scientific validity of the work, then complained openly to administration. Harvard pulled the plug and ended all psychedelic research in 1962. Accounts vary, but Dr. Leary was dismissed in 1963 for abandoning his teaching duties, using unorthodox scientific methodology, or his contract was not renewed, or a combination. He moved to New York and continued advocating publicly for psychedelics.

The legacy of the Harvard research was mixed. The legitimacy of psychedelic research was seriously damaged. While much useful and positive data emerged, the lack of disciplined protocols cast a shadow that is still debated today.

In a broader social context, Timothy Leary had become a prominent symbol of counterculture. As referenced in the previous chapter, grassroots disenchantment with segregation, the Vietnam War and drug laws was sowing the seeds of social upheaval or at least fear of that. There was top-down linking of drugs with the antiwar movement, perpetuated through conservative media in an effort to discredit counterculture. Psychedelic research found itself squarely in the crosshairs. While Leary pulled Harvard noisily into the public eye, good research was quietly still underway at other institutions, notably Spring Grove State Hospital in Maryland.[93] While other investigation of psychedelics wasn't abruptly stopped, regulation became more stringent, funding became more difficult. The ripple effect was undeniable, and the study of psychedelics eventually did grind to a halt.

History repeats itself, and the up-and-down saga of hallucinogens is a regrettable example. As Richard Nixon took office in 1968, the backlash was in full swing. It's urban legend, but Nixon is widely attributed as referring to Timothy Leary as "the most dangerous man in America."[††] The paranoia over counterculture that Leary symbolized was great.

Leary was arrested twice for cannabis possession. The first time was for less than half an ounce, which he claimed was planted. Under the 1937 Marihuana Tax Act, he was sentenced to 30 years with a $30,000 fine! He appealed this all the way to the US Supreme Court and won. He was busted a second time in 1968, this time for two roaches (vernacular for the remaining end pieces of mostly smoked cannabis cigarettes). Probable cause for the search was questionable. For this offense, he was sentenced to 10 years and imprisoned. The punishment meted out to Leary was draconian, even for the day, when typical sentences were months, not years or decades.

The message was clear. The conservative establishment considered psychedelics integral to counterculture, and drug laws were used to suppress dissent. This paved the way for the Controlled Substances Act and the inclusion of hallucinogens in Schedule I—no medical value with high potential for abuse.

[††] There is no evidence that Nixon ever said these words. This quote is more of a legendary pop culture response that shows the animosity that Nixon and his administration felt about the drug culture.

Timothy Leary was busted for weed, but it was really psychedelics that the system wanted to send away. The saga of Leary and the question of his credibility was never borne out. He escaped from prison after two years and became an international fugitive. Like Leary, and just as it did centuries ago during the Spanish persecution of Indigenous people in South America, psychedelic substances went underground again.

## The Power of the Experience

As with other substances discussed herein, I have lived experience with psychedelics. My abstinence-based recovery, of course, precludes current use, so it's been a while. Although... I have given thought to the use of psychedelics. Ceremonial ayahuasca has been credited with a host of benefits, especially spiritual development. Recovery authorities and experts from Bill Wilson to Gabor Maté have used psychedelics to open "the doors of perception," as Aldous Huxley wrote in an essay about his psychedelic experience. For me, future use of psychedelics is off the table, but it's another of the many things my mind is now completely open to. I personally know people who are benefiting.

In high school, I had a couple of experiences with a substance referred to as "purple microdot." While this was purported to be mescaline, that was clearly just marketing. Actual mescaline is the psychoactive compound in peyote and a couple of other cacti found in the Southwest, Mexico, and South America. In the day, we called taking the substance a "trip" or tripping.

I ingested psilocybin mushrooms several times when I was 18 and 19. During these experiences, I typically took what was considered a standard dose, about one gram. According to psychoactive plant authority Michael Pollan, a gram of psilocybin mushroom contains about 10 mg of psilocybin. I've since learned from research that 10 mg is a low dose. The requisite dosage for a more transformative experience, nicknamed the "heroic" dose, is about 50 mg.

During my last experience, in the fall of 1978, I ingested about two grams of mushrooms or about 20 mg of psilocybin. This was for the best, as I was alone, and got the bright idea that I should go to the nearby high school, specifically the ropes course out in back. The ropes course was a set of obstacle-type challenges intended as a component of physical education designed for teambuilding and instilling self-confidence. Strictly meant to be used with supervision, spotting, etc., it consisted of things like rope ladders and bridges, balance beams, four-inch-wide elevated pedestals, and the like. Many of the stations involved varying degrees of elevation—doing the structured training back in the day tended to eradicate and cure one of any fear of heights. I don't recall precisely what I was thinking, but I was likely entertaining some hope of defying gravity. I was certainly under the influence of the psychedelic substance but fortunately not enough to attempt flight.

So, what is all the fuss about? The experience might be described as an amplification and alteration of the senses. That which is usually in the background—visually and auditorily, along with smell, taste, and tactile sensation—can come to the forefront of attention. Along with that, cognitive association, both good and bad, can become powerfully prominent. There is a much greater level of intensity wherever the attention is directed or drawn. Perception of patterns can occur. Compelling thoughts and feelings about things both important and insignificant might occur. Sense of time becomes distorted. Memories can feel like they are occurring in the present.

Synesthesia is a neurological phenomenon where stimulation through one of the senses is perceived as stimulation from a different sense. Examples are "hearing colors" or "seeing sounds." This is more than just a perception. Hallucinogens are known to have psychoplastogenic effects; they stimulate neuroplasticity. They enhance connectivity between different individual brain cells and between areas of the brain, including different sensory areas.

Within the experience, thoughts can bypass normal cognitive process with the typical emotional components. Normally, acquiring conviction or wisdom requires experience and reinforcement over time. Ideas are compelling and burrow in deeper than simply altering mood or temperament. In this way, personalities may be significantly altered. According to LSD psychotherapy pioneer Stanislav Grof, psychedelics are nonspecific amplifiers of unconscious mental material that impacts conscious contents. Thoughts can become clearer, more meaningful, and more significant.[94]

In recovery and specifically the area of personal development, there are differences among simple awareness of information, comprehension, belief, and finally conviction; these are different levels of cognition. People with awareness and understanding of information can have an interesting dinner conversation. A person with conviction can start a religion.

## The Spirit Molecule

In the upper Amazon region of South America, Indigenous people consume a hallucinogenic drink as part of their religious practice. Ayahuasca is considered sacred and is prepared and administered by shamans according to centuries-old spiritual tradition in multiple South American countries. The beverage is prepared from plants and vines, and each shaman has his own unique recipe. The common element is the psychoactive molecule, dimethyltryptamine, DMT.

The term shaman refers to spiritual and ceremonial leaders among various Indigenous cultures worldwide. Anthropologists coined this term, which originates from the Tungus tribe in Siberia. Anthropological studies recognize shamanism as one of humanity's oldest spiritual practices, with archaeological evidence suggesting shamanic traditions dating back tens of thousands of years. The role of shamans in their communities is deeply respected. They serve not just as healers but also as spiritual guides, keepers of traditional knowledge, and bridges between the seen and unseen worlds.

Ayahuasca is the gateway to these unseen worlds.

The sacred brew is consumed in community ceremonies, often involving ritual. "Ayahuasca fulfills, to perfection, the purpose of incarnating an indigenous identity, but it does so by means of a much more flexible strategy than dances or traditional body painting, opening out to a broad pan-indigenous identity." [95] Each participant then has a personal spiritual experience induced by DMT, which is actually short-acting, less than an hour. Common themes in these experiences are visions of and interactions with spirits and entities from beyond our reality. This underpins the cultural identity of these tribal Amazonian people that the Spanish conquistadors sought to crush.

There is quite a bit to unpack regarding DMT. First, we produce our own endogenous DMT. That's right, we make our own powerful hallucinogen, and it's present in our brains, cerebrospinal fluid, and blood. Dr. Rick Strassman proposed that it is produced in the pineal gland in the middle of the brain, but this has yet to be proven. Also yet to be proven but theorized is the presence of a DMT neurotransmitter system similar to those of serotonin and dopamine. Where serotonin regulates mood and dopamine regulates motivation and reward, it's been proposed that DMT regulates reality. A common theme in subjective reports of subjects of DMT research was that it felt "more real than real." [96]

Before psychedelic research came to a halt in the early 1970s, DMT was investigated for a suspected relationship to psychosis. DMT concentrations in lab rats were observed to be elevated at the time of death, and a theory emerged on the phenomenon of near-death experiences that DMT acted as a mediator. Reality regulator indeed.

Early in the research process of identifying and isolating DMT, human testing determined that the substance was effective when administered intranasally (snuff) or smoked. DMT taken orally had no effect. It was eventually discovered that a common digestive enzyme, monoamine oxidase, MAO, breaks down DMT in the gut. This raised the question of how DMT in ayahuasca, consumed orally in liquid form, could be effective. The answer was in other ingredients in the brew. Shamans knew to include plants with compounds that acted as MAO inhibitors, thereby allowing the DMT to go through intact.

The obvious question was how did the shamans know to do this? When researchers asked, the response was, "The plant told us."

Unlike serotonin and dopamine, we don't know the purpose of DMT in the human body. As with the endocannabinoid system previously discussed, here occurs something in nature that duplicates something in our physiology that we don't understand fully. Or vice versa. Either way, this suggests some fundamental connection between human beings and the natural world. The role of shamans in their cultures is literally the responsibility to offer people guidance in their natural world, including divination, healing, and death.

Consider how the invention of the microscope opened up a new dimension of our reality. The upgrade in understanding that came with awareness of the cells (and smaller components) that we are made of is now part of our everyday reality. The same could be said of telescopes and the cosmos. Before we could visualize and assimilate these previously unknown dimensions into our paradigm, they were there, nonetheless. This suggests the possibility of other dimensions or aspects of reality that remain undiscovered. When people interact with entities or spirits during DMT experiences, is this another form of the microscope or telescope? Are these people accessing a wider aspect of reality?

Our reality is broadcasting a signal that is comprised of a wide range of vibrations. Depending on the frequency of these vibrations we can see them or hear them. Smell, touch, and taste are simply variations on that theme involving waves and particles. What we see with our eyes is the result of a complex decoding process. Looking at something in our environment involves numerous steps before it registers as an image in our thoughts. The brain functions as a receiver. As with all receivers, it's tuned to a frequency or range of frequencies. Like tuning in a station on an old-fashioned broadcast radio, all the other stations are still there even though we are not receiving them. What if DMT modifies the range and capabilities of our receivers/brains?

Schizophrenics hear and see things that others cannot; we call that hallucinating and say they are delusional. This is a horribly difficult way of life with strong medications and frequent hospitalizations. Researchers are looking at the role of DMT, specifically how it's regulated and metabolized in people living with psychosis. We produce minute amounts of DMT. If the brain produced too much DMT, it would interfere with normal function. Like the people in the Amazonian ceremonies who lie down while others monitor their safety, we would be incapacitated. Could schizophrenics be living with some degree of perception of a wider reality than most people?

Just as we occupy our tiny location in the vastness of our galaxy, and the microscopic world teems beneath our awareness, we might be living alongside a separate reality. The key to accessing this reality might be solving how DMT, or other psychedelics, could let us change our receiver's channel setting. And maybe it already has.

The Upper Paleolithic era is the last subdivision of the Paleolithic era, and spans from 50,000 years ago to 10,000 years ago. It is also referred to as the late Old Stone Age. This time frame saw the emergence of anatomically and behaviorally modern *Homo sapiens*. It was characterized by advancements in art, technology (tools), and social structure. Primitive humans began drawing and painting on rocks and the walls of caves during this time frame.

Expert theories of the symbolic, social, and spiritual significance of the cave paintings vary. The neuropsychological model, according to archaeologist David Lewis-Williams, is a leading explanation, which proposes that this ancient art originated from altered states of consciousness. Imagery that is common to shamanistic altered states termed entoptic phenomena—originating within the visual system—is depicted in cave and rock paintings dating back as much as 35,000 years. Entoptics, manifested as geometrical shapes and patterns, are the first stage of Lewis-Williams's model of trance. The therianthrope, a being that is half human and half animal is in the third stage. While people living in the Upper Paleolithic era might routinely see bison, a man-bison type of being was not part of everyday life. And yet, therianthropes are frequently depicted in cave paintings.

The presence in cave paintings of psychedelic imagery also suggests that hallucinogens played more of a role than mere muse for subject matter. Lewis-Williams posits that the motivation for the act of painting itself was stimulated by the psychedelic experience. For anyone who has experienced the effects of psychedelic substances, this is not only plausible but also intuitive. This would have powerful significance. Life was hard 30,000 years ago, and the concept of leisure time was nonexistent. Something needed to matter for people to take time out from hunting and gathering—i.e., surviving. These cave paintings are not only among the oldest known representation of art but also of spirituality. The effort involved in creating these paintings—making the materials and lighting the dark space, not to mention the painting itself—would endorse that this was important.

Do the *Mona Lisa, Morning on the Seine*, *Starry Night*, and *Dogs Playing Poker* trace their lineage to caves where primitive people attempted to reproduce their hallucinogenic visions? Do the world's religions somehow link back to shamanistic connection to a spirit world that was facilitated by psychedelic substances? There's a strong case that these substances are part of our heritage as human beings and possibly part of a genetic memory.

## The Stoned Ape

In his book, *Food of the Gods: The Search for the Original Tree of Knowledge*, ethnobotanist Terence McKenna explored the role of psychoactive plants in human evolution and consciousness. His central thesis became known as the "Stoned Ape Theory." He made the case that psychoactive plants, psilocybin mushrooms in particular, played a catalytic role in human evolution.

Dramatic changes in the human brain occurred between 500,000 and 250,000 years ago with the emergence of early *Homo sapiens*. In addition to increased size of the prefrontal cortex, neural reorganization provided capacity for more advanced symbolic and abstract thinking, language processing, memory, and complex social cognition. Neural connectivity became more complex, with enhanced communication between different brain regions. The development of more sophisticated neural networks enabled distinctive human capabilities and provided recognizably different survival advantages. The speed of these changes is among the most dramatic examples of rapid evolutionary change in the fossil record. There has been intense scientific interest and debate about how such accelerated development occurred.

McKenna's hypothesis proposes that early hominids who consumed psilocybin mushrooms experienced enhanced cognitive abilities, leading to rapid brain development. He suggested psilocybin mushrooms were an "evolutionary catalyst" that triggered language, imagination, the arts, religion, philosophy, science, and other components of human culture.[97]

Many of the psychedelic substances are psychoplastogens. The term refers to medicines that produce rapid changes in neuroplasticity following as little as a single therapeutic administration. Ketamine, DMT, LSD, methylenedioxymethamphetamine or MDMA, ibogaine, and psilocybin are all psychoplastogens. They stimulate the growth of new neurons, the production of new connections between neurons, replace lost myelin or insulation on neurons, and turn dormant synapses into active synapses. It sounds like Bradley Cooper in the 2011 movie *Limitless*. However, two different studies have demonstrated enhanced neuropsychological function in regular ayahuasca users compared to nonusers.[98]

Needless to say, the scientific establishment did not embrace this theory when McKenna published his book in the early 1990s. McKenna had attained status as a counterculture figure and spoke on college campuses, as opposed to scientific meetings and conferences. The scientific community dismissed his idea, coining the term "Stoned Ape Theory." McKenna leaned into it.

The critics, unable to dispute the plausibility of McKenna's theory, point out that the cultures that embrace the use of psychoactive substances like psilocybin and ayahuasca/DMT are not considered to be advanced. However, this is cultural prejudice and based on the assumption that technology equates to advancement. A deeper understanding of our connection with the natural world seems like a more enlightened perspective. Awareness of subtle energy, humility, and perspective of one's true place in this world and beyond are attributes that render our modern stress culture and techno-toys trite by comparison.

### Trip Therapy

Ketamine is classified as a dissociative anesthetic that possesses hallucinogenic properties. Technically not a classic psychedelic substance, it causes feelings of detachment from the environment and self (dissociation), along with visual and auditory hallucinations, especially at higher doses.

Michael is a 59-year-old who recently retired. We are acquainted through the local recovery community. Like me, he's been in long-term recovery for over 30 years. He's an interesting guy; he has a background in engineering and technology and was teaching at the college level when he decided to retire. We met to catch up over coffee (me) and Mountain Dew (him). "I like playing with stuff and solving problems," he said. He has run information technology for one of the major universities in Cambridge, Massachusetts, and taught robotics at various points in his career.

Michael has lived with depression since he was a teenager. "I connected pot and drinking with relief from the pain I was feeling. It was like a switch was flipped—I smoked and drank for a reason, self-medication. I was 18, I drank until I was 24 when I realized that pot and alcohol were causing more problems than they solved. So, I decided to stop. I lasted three days and then spent a weekend trying to kill myself. In the psych unit I was given antidepressants, but depression was not talked about that I remember."

He treats his substance use disorder in AA. His depression has been treated with conventional antidepressants, but, more recently, he has utilized ketamine therapy.

Michael's depression is characterized by seasonal affective disorder. February has historically been his critical month. "Every December 21, the shortest day of the year, I always knew it was going to get bad."

He's tried to take his own life four times. "I felt like a failure, they kept reviving me. I said all the things I needed to say [to be discharged from the psychiatric unit] but thought next time I'm driving off the Tobin Memorial Bridge."

He heard about ketamine therapy from his therapist. For his first experience three years ago, he opted for an intravenous treatment.

"It was the highest dose of ketamine, and, of course, being an alcoholic, I wanted the most I could get," he said jokingly while stating the truth. He described, "wild hallucinations" during his first treatment, which was just an infusion of ketamine, no talk therapy. He described meeting with his therapist weeks later. "I didn't think it did anything, and I told my therapist who pointed out that it was February and I wasn't suicidal."

He continued, "What I like about ketamine is that, at least to some extent, it's a cure." Michael has since transitioned to a different type of ketamine therapy, which he does periodically. He takes oral ketamine called troches, dissolvable lozenges, to a therapist and self-administers them under supervision. He is debriefed at the end and then has a session the following day to help integrate the experience. After living with depression for decades, ketamine has been a game changer for Michael. He describes his quality of life as "amazing" and has not been suicidal since he began ketamine therapy.

Ketamine poignantly illustrates how a substance can be both a "drug" and medicine, depending on the application and setting—set and setting in treatment parlance. Therapy, treatment, substance use, and substance use disorder are distinctly different concepts although the distinction can blur. Ketamine is a drug that has been widely used in a nonmedical manner. The frequency that this at least starts out with therapeutic intention is known only to the people using the substance.

Alcoholics Anonymous endorses the need for a psychic shift for recovery to take hold. The depth of the hallucinogenic experience seems to facilitate this in a chemically induced manner. Researchers are working to understand this. AA founder Bill Wilson, who lived with depression his whole life, utilized medically supervised LSD.

Dr. Stephen Ross is the associate director of the NYU Langone Center for Psychedelic Medicine and the director of the NYU Psychedelic Medicine Research Training Program. His research interests include the treatment of addiction, the interface between pain and addiction, and the development of novel interventions for treating personality disorders and psychological distress in patients with life-threatening illnesses.

Dr. Ross has been leading recent and ongoing trials of psychedelic-assisted therapy, including a groundbreaking trial of psilocybin-assisted therapy for anxiety and existential distress in patients with life-threatening cancer and psilocybin treatment for major depressive disorder. He was a principal investigator and study therapist on trials of psilocybin-assisted therapy for alcohol use disorder and MDMA-assisted therapy for posttraumatic stress disorder, PTSD. MDMA is commonly known as ecstasy, a popular substance taken at parties and rave events.

Dr. Ross has acknowledged, "My own mental sufferings helped me be a better psychiatrist." He became interested in the therapeutic potential for psychedelics despite the knowledge and research vacuum left in the wake of President Nixon's war on drugs. He has a healthy respect for the power of psychedelic medications to cause disturbing emotions and hallucinations, but he believes in their potential benefits and is determined to make psilocybin an approved medical treatment. "It's still illegal, and you cannot take it unless you are participating in a clinical trial," he said. "We have to take this to the next step." [99]

At the moment, the next step is facilitated psilocybin experiences.

There is a small, underground group of people who will privately facilitate your psilocybin treatment. I know this because I met one.

I have had two lengthy conversations with a trained psilocybin facilitator. She shared that she heard Dr. Ross at a conference and spoke with him afterward. She went on to pursue training in Canada and (I believe she said) Mexico. When I asked to speak with her on the record for this book chapter, she declined for several reasons. Primarily, she is passionate and dedicated to what she is doing as a larger cause. My interpretation is that this overflows the vessel of ethical consideration, bordering on something sacred and personal. She expressed that my limited and clinical rendering of this topic fails to do it justice. I have weighed this against my goal of informing people and raising awareness; I've elected to include this short description.

She also works as a registered nurse, although maintains highly independent status, usually working under temporary contract in a supervisory capacity or a highly technical specialty. Her skill set also includes end-of-life care, experience that overlaps with the essentials of the psilocybin experiences she facilitates. She said that she administers psychedelic treatments infrequently; she can't exactly market these services on a website. Psilocybin remains a Schedule I substance; however, two states have decriminalized it. In sporadic areas, there is an ambiguous status of "deprioritized" enforcement.

Psychedelic psychotherapy is legal in Canada and Mexico.

I perused the website of TheraPsil, a Canadian treatment organization. They offer therapy as well as professional training. "Psilocybin-assisted psychotherapy refers to the professionally guided use of psilocybin in combination with psychotherapy and differs greatly from the recreational use of psychedelics. Psilocybin-assisted psychotherapy involves a rigorous and clinically tested treatment protocol that encompasses careful medical oversight of the treatment session." [100]

Psychedelic psychotherapy has four elements—screening, preparation, the actual medicine session, and integration. Psilocybin-assisted psychotherapy is utilized for treatment-resistant depression, disordered eating, PTSD, and end-of-life distress.

For substance use disorder, ibogaine is the hallucinogen with direct benefits.

Ibogaine has been described as an "addiction interrupter" by patients who have taken the drug to treat opioid and other substance use disorders. Ibogaine is a dissociative psychedelic that has multiple anti-addictive mechanisms, which target the stages of the addiction cycle, including withdrawal/negative affect and preoccupation/anticipation of the rewarding effects of substances.

Ibogaine is made from the roots of the iboga plant, which is native to Central Africa. It has been used for millennia in shamanistic rituals. It is illegal in many countries.

Ibogaine works through multiple mechanisms simultaneously resetting neural pathways altered by addiction, reducing withdrawal symptoms, decreasing cravings, and affecting dopamine and serotonin systems. A study designed to examine treatment effects over a 12-month period found that "A single ibogaine treatment reduced opioid withdrawal symptoms and achieved opioid cessation or sustained reduced use in dependent individuals as measured over 12 months." [101]

Currently, ibogaine is not approved by the FDA for any medical purposes, including addiction treatment, but there are clinics in Canada and Mexico. Ibogaine can cause heart arrhythmias, so medical monitoring and access to qualified care and emergency intervention are essential. One patient enrolled in the 12-month study died during treatment. Ibogaine is a proposition in consideration of risks versus benefits.

Researchers are working hard to isolate the benefits of ibogaine and synthesize new ibogaine-like chemicals to help in the fight against addiction. A laboratory at UC Davis "set out to create a synthetic analog of ibogaine which retained therapeutic properties without the undesired effects of the psychedelic compound." [102]

The therapeutic promise of hallucinogens is finally starting to be realized after a 50-year hiatus. While the suffering of traumatized veterans, people in end-of-life existential crisis, the clinically depressed, and the addicted could have been alleviated, dedicated researchers are working to make up for lost time.

I can agree with my acquaintance that my limited and clinical rendering of this topic indeed fails to do it justice. I weigh this against the need to inform. The experience of hallucinogenic substances may be fundamental to the human experience in ways we are only just coming to understand. The same way a child might hyperventilate to experience the dizziness that follows, it seems basic, almost innate, that we seek to alter our consciousness. Dr. Hofmann's "problem child" may yet hold the solution to many of our real problems.

# Chapter 15
# Kratom

"The road to hell feels like heaven.
The road to heaven feels like hell."
~ Unknown

Robert is a Southern gentleman in his early 50s. He's a businessman, a family man, and uncannily intelligent. He has the ability to understand anything. Almost. Typically, he's large (tall) and in charge. Kratom, or specifically the synthesized concentrate of its active ingredient, 7-OH, has been a dominant force in this man's life for the better part of the last year. While there is no other area of his life where he is unable to problem-solve, he is unable to solve his kratom problem.

Robert had a successful alcohol detox in the prior year. He began working with a recovery coach and attended Alcoholics Anonymous meetings. At some point, he started purchasing these innocuous little energy drinks (7-OH) that were available seemingly everywhere he went. He obviously liked the effect, which he described as a "pick-me-up."

He's the type of person who doesn't really even like to take Tylenol. "Angry" best describes his feelings toward the little drink that's had a big effect on his life. "I want to be able to walk my daughter down the aisle. I had no idea this could happen."

Over the course of several months, he signed himself out of a rehab after three days and failed to complete two in-home detoxes. Kratom has its hooks in this man, and, so far, it's winning. His recovery is jeopardized, he's not present for his children, and his marriage is at the breaking point.

Kratom (*Mitragyna speciosa*) is a tropical evergreen tree in the coffee family native to Southeast Asia. Its leaves contain mitragynine and 7-hydroxymitragynine, 7-OH, which interact with opioid receptors in the brain producing psychoactive effects. It produces a stimulant effect at low doses (the pick-me-up) but is sedating at higher doses. Kratom is sold in the US in various retail forms—powders, capsules, extracts, and beverages—in smoke shops, specialty stores, and online. The vast majority of kratom sold in the US comes from Indonesia. There is some domestic cultivation in Florida and greenhouses, but because the plant prefers a tropical environment, it's cheaper to import.

The use of kratom has increased markedly in recent years in the US.

Kratom is legal at the federal level. While the DEA has listed it as a Drug and Chemical of Concern, kratom and its active compounds are not scheduled under the Controlled Substances Act. Therefore, individual states regulate it as they currently see fit. The legal status in states with outright bans, states with consumer protection restrictions, and states with local community bans could shift markedly before I finish writing this chapter. The FDA has not approved kratom for any medical use. Kratom falls into a gray area because it's also considered an herbal supplement, which is regulated much differently than pharmaceuticals.

## The End of the Trail

Marcus is a 34-year-old whose experience with kratom and substance use in general illustrates issues and problems that many are facing. Marcus said, "Things could be better, things could be worse." As of this writing, it's been "about six weeks" since he last used kratom. Based on the seven-year history of his relationship with the substance, he's not out of the woods yet.

Marcus began using cannabis and alcohol in high school, and said it started, "Because I just wanted to fit in." He describes how his use escalated, particularly alcohol, and that he would get "very drunk" three or four times a week. He was sent to a treatment facility that he described as high-end. "But I wasn't ready for that." During his 20s, he discovered pain pills, Perc 30s, and eventually heroin. He overdosed the second time he injected and reported that he was in a coma and, "I guess I actually died." He again described that he was "not ready" for recovery and settled into a pattern of "mostly functional" drinking.

He discovered kratom in 2019. He was interested in getting off alcohol and opioids, and it worked. While he did a little reading on it, he thought, *It's a leaf powder, for God's sake. This can help me.* It worked until he became addicted to it. "It gave me a sense of comfort, ease, and a warm sense of security. It quickly became a daily necessity."

He describes how it took more and more of the powder compound to get the effect he needed, increased tolerance. "I was having to use a ton of the powder, and it was nauseating. Then I discovered the 7-OH in late 2023," readily available in Texas where he was living. "I switched to capsules but started needing more and more pretty quickly. Soon I was taking it two or three times a day. It was a better buzz, but I realized what was happening."

When he tried to stop, "The withdrawal was horrible. I couldn't do it." He described the classic opioid withdrawal symptoms of sneezing, sweating, restless legs, and muscle aches. His habit became more expensive, a few hundred dollars a day, and he maxed out credit cards, got loans, and pawned belongings. During the last years of his run, he let go of a teaching job, and his marriage suffered significantly.

Marcus attempted to detox himself with Suboxone, unsuccessfully. He separated from his wife and went back to the Northeast where his parents helped him. He went into a facility for a medical detox. He stayed with his parents for some weeks before returning to Texas, where he lived in a sober house and attended AA. Eventually, he moved back home with his wife and young son. As mentioned, his recovery remains tenuous. He takes Suboxone daily, a moderate dose, but said, "I still have cravings."

Like others, he thought he had found the magic bullet, the end of the trail for substance use. Instead, he lived a new and equally nasty nightmare. Also, like others, he said, "I didn't have the slightest clue what I was getting into."

My personal connection to Marcus is a 20-year friendship with his mother, Linda, an occupational therapist. Periodically over the years, she would share her son's trials and tribulations but also his successes.

For a time, she believed he was doing well—married, teaching, and living in Illinois. When the train started to come off the tracks and she first heard about his kratom use, she reached out to me for information and support. Eventually, she connected Marcus and me directly. He was halfway across the country, and all I could do was answer questions and offer support and some guidance.

It's an understatement that Linda felt frustrated and powerless. She experienced every form of fear and heartbreak that loved ones go through except one. Living in fear of a late-night phone call with the worst possible news is the common dilemma for many parents and loved ones in this day and age of chaotic substance use. All the willingness in the world to do whatever is necessary to help a struggling child avails nothing to people in Linda's situation.

"His addiction is buried deep in me and affects every part of my life." She shared that she has been pulled into her son's financial issues and took out 401(k) retirement money for a rehab treatment. Now she struggles with boundaries.

There is something disorienting about kratom and the whole situation currently unfolding. Alcohol, cannabis, and certainly opioids came with some inherent warning. Society has always known about and emphasized a cautionary perspective on alcohol. Cannabis and opioids have carried the stigma of decades of illegal, illicit status. Everyone knows this (thank you, Nancy Reagan). Kratom comes to us as a wolf in sheep's clothing, legal with the almost irresistible promise of solving addictions. What could possibly go wrong? Well, plenty has and continues to.

What about the promised upside?

My online support community weighed in.

> "My late husband used kratom a handful of times to get through opioid withdrawal, as he was a chronic pain patient."

> "I've used it to very good effect. Powdered leaf has been a big part of me not using much more addictive opiates, and the times I haven't had kratom available to me hasn't produced any withdrawal symptoms that are all that severe (my eyes get a little more watery than normal). However, there is a huge difference between kratom leaf

> and 7-OH, which is a lab created approximation of kratom's active ingredient. Kratom in its natural form, from my experience of ingesting very moderate amounts, is a fairly benign substance. 7-OH is not."
>
> "A solution with side effects..."

There are those who report positive experience, but they are a minority.

In a recent article, David Kroll, PhD, professor and director of the master's degree and certificate programs at the University of Colorado Anschutz Skaggs School of Pharmacy and Pharmaceutical Sciences went on the record. "In an ideal world, kratom powder would be a well-regulated drug. But we have a very complicated healthcare system now, and people are hurting, and there are gaps in access to care. For good reason, the pendulum has swung on opioids the other way toward more of a controlled system. At the same time, we have so many people who became opioid dependent and are cycling off the drugs and can't access buprenorphine… are suffering from chronic pain and depression, or don't have health insurance. We should still have some compassion and empathy for our patients, friends and neighbors in these positions." [103]

Dr. Kroll, in summarizing his perspective on kratom, encapsulates much of today's dilemma of substance use and treatment. The trend in kratom use is simultaneously an outcome and a symptom.

I can see myself as having easily fallen under kratom's spell back in the day. As someone who had that compulsion to alter my consciousness, my reality, it would have had strong appeal. The gray area of it being both herbal and legal might have been something I could have rationalized in the early days of my abstinence-based recovery. Marcus's history suggests motivation similar to mine, the need for the warm hug and drive for the perfect buzz. Kratom use is a logical manifestation.

Jackson is another individual I know who shares that compulsion to alter his consciousness. He's in his late 20s and hails from Oregon. We met two years ago when he and his significant other, Maura, began attending a local hybrid support meeting. Maura had lost a close friend to overdose, and, in addition to seeking support for that, had drastically reconsidered her relationship with substances, specifically alcohol. Jackson had recently quit opioids. Their complex personal substance issues contributed to complications in their relationship. Maura was native to my region; Jackson came back east with her and desired making a fresh start, opioid-free. Later, it emerged that he was not kratom-free.

Jackson shared that taking prescribed Suboxone was successful as far as treating his opioid use was concerned, but it got messy. He described how he would hold off on his morning Suboxone and buy some kratom. He was direct about the reason for this—he missed feeling high. It's that altered consciousness thing again, the draw of the warm hug. What's interesting is that we know that Suboxone stays in the system a long time. It would partially block the effects of opioids or, presumably, kratom.

Jackson accepted a job managing a construction project that took him to New York City. His plan for maintaining abstinence was that he would be too busy, occupied with the demands of his work. What Jackson didn't count on was how things work in NYC. Permits and licenses for his company's project wound up being perpetually a week away. "Every week, they would tell us that the permits are coming, sit tight. That went on for months. I was in a strange city, no social circle, and the paychecks just kept coming in. We did the demolition, but that only took up so much time, so I had nothing to do."

In the meantime, Maura was back in New England working on her codependency. Although they kept in touch, she'd made the decision to step away. Their relationship had been based in substance use. They had met at a wedding and connected over going out for drinks. "I knew he used drugs, but I never thought we would become serious." I saw her one evening at the hybrid meeting, and she was clearly having a difficult time. She was worried about Jackson in New York, and knew he was using kratom there and becoming more dependent.

Jackson described his kratom use as unrestricted during his time in New York. He entered treatment in January 2026, 30 days of combined detox and residential. He experienced a brief resumption of kratom use in the subsequent months but was stable on Suboxone at the time we spoke. Maura and Jackson agreed that, substance-free, "things are really good" between them. They fight less and exercise more and have seemed to hit their stride in terms of a mutually supportive dynamic. Time will tell if Jackson can distance himself from kratom.

Kratom is sticky. Making a clean break seems universally difficult. "If I could go back and do it over, I would never touch that shit," said Marcus.

Savvy, well-informed individuals have utilized kratom to successfully discontinue opioid use, although this is not straightforward, and success doesn't seem commonplace. Self-determination in kratom use is a blank canvas—there's no guidance, no equivalent of a Surgeon General's warning. It's ironic that cigarettes come with a warning about possible consequences that are years away when tolerance for a 7-OH drink will double in a matter of days.

# Chapter 16
# I'm Not the Language Police

"Words are, of course, the most powerful drug used by mankind."
~ Rudyard Kipling

A long time ago, I worked as a technician in the local hospital's operating room. I vividly recall an occasion when, upon seeing that a patient had tattoos, a coworker remarked, "Oh, she's a patron of the arts." My colleague was making a sarcastic and demeaning observation regarding an anesthetized patient's body art. I heard this *patron* phrase often enough that it stuck with me. Body art was less common than it is today.

At the time, organizations and facilities like hospitals actually had rules that employees' tattoos could not be visible. This is much different today, of course, and suggests that over time the negative beliefs tend to shift in response to what people are used to seeing.

The Merriam-Webster online dictionary defines *stigma* as "a set of negative and unfair beliefs that a society or group of people have about something." The body art anecdote is one example. In the context of substance use disorder, stigma refers to negative attitudes, beliefs, and stereotypes, as well as the discriminatory behaviors directed toward people living with SUD. Stigma can be societal, institutional, and interpersonal.

Human beings are naturally wired to be social creatures. As we climbed the evolutionary ladder, being part of a tribe was necessary to survive. A significant vestige of this, a remaining sign, is an almost instinctive drive or desire for the approval of our group, or at least avoidance of disapproval. This is what psychologist Abraham Maslow referred to as "esteem" or "social needs" in his hierarchy of needs. Being ostracized, or cast out of the tribe, in primitive times was a threat to survival, so maintaining a good standing in one's group or tribe was an important matter. In light of this, the phenomenon of stigma has a significant undercurrent that taps right into something basic in us, something survival related.

Substance use, problematic substance use, that is, puts people in subtle and unsubtle opposition to their tribe. Addiction is socially unacceptable. Addiction is stigmatized.

We have all heard the words *junkie* and *drunk* used in reference to people with opioid or alcohol use disorders. Used in many contexts, those two terms are now considered prejudicial and marginalizing—stigmatizing. Some people even continue to identify themselves in that manner, possibly with the unintended consequences of perpetuating negative stereotypes while subconsciously reinforcing feelings of unworthiness and inferiority.

## Language

As described previously, my recovery began in the traditional model approach of 12-Step peer support, Alcoholics Anonymous, AA. The custom at meetings of the AA fellowship has always been identification as an *alcoholic*. When introductions are part of a meeting's format, it is customary to go around the room with each person in turn saying, "I'm _____, an *alcoholic*." On first entering recovery, uttering those words aloud can be tremendously difficult. Once in the routine, it becomes automatic. Typically, all present at the gathering then respond by saying, "Hi, _____."

Many choose their own little variation. "Hi, I'm a grateful recovering *alcoholic* named _____."

This ritual, while more or less a formality today, signifies that person is identifying as a member of AA, as an *alcoholic*, and has taken the first step, admission of powerlessness over alcohol. This type of identification is also customary at other peer-support fellowship meetings such as Narcotics Anonymous.

To an uninitiated observer, this ritual might seem a little strange but not overly significant. However, to some, this identification ritual might seem counterintuitive. "You are identifying as your problem," someone once said to me. My response was that, to me at least, the identification is synonymous with being in recovery.

A few years ago, I began working in a primary care-based addiction treatment program led by a forward-thinking behavioral health clinician. This program sought to follow and observe leading-edge approaches across the board. This included language that was person-centered and strengths-based, as well as best practice in terms of medical addiction treatment. It was made known to me, in a tactful manner, that some of my peer-support vernacular wasn't up to spec. In other words, my *alcoholic/addict* way of talking about people and addictions, the product of years of recovery in the traditional model and beyond, was no longer going to work in that behavioral health context of clinical treatment.

I didn't know how to feel about that. To be truthful, I was a little bent out of shape.

*So let me get this straight*, I thought. *People with no lived experience are not happy with the way someone with lived experience talks? The people who know about addiction from classrooms and books are upset with my language?*

*Just so I'm sure I understand, the people I've been seeing for years, who, when it comes to their turn to identify themselves at a meeting, say "I'm ______, and I'm a nursing/social work/fill-in-the-blank student here to observe," have now decided they don't like the way I've been speaking about my alcoholism for half my life?*

Yeah, that's pretty much it.

Well, okay then.

I had to sit with it for a little bit. Initially, it didn't seem like a big deal; they were just changing up a few words. We weren't supposed to say *alcoholic* and *addict* anymore. However, it was actually a lot more than that. It is a significant and sweeping change. It started to sink in.

I took baby steps. The first thing I could do was accept that there was a duality, two separate approaches to language. There is this new way that academics want to talk about addiction, and there's the way people with addiction talk about addiction. And, of course, I do appreciate that smart, qualified, highly trained people with no addiction issues of their own were devoting their expertise to helping people with addiction. Duh, I woke up to that pretty quickly. Sure, I can make a few word substitutions... *It'll probably change again in a couple of years anyway.*

But it was actually more significant, deeper, than just making a few substitutions. It taps directly into stigma. Societal, institutional, interpersonal. And self-stigma.

So, what are we talking about here? It's a lot more than avoiding saying *addict* or *alcoholic*. However, that's a good place to start. An *addict* has impaired control over substance use, and calling someone that, in a sense, reduces them to that. We're talking about a person who is living with an addiction, or more specifically, a substance use disorder or some other reward-seeking behavior. *Alcoholic* also carries stigma and reduces an individual to the problems they have with alcohol despite harmful consequences. You don't think it carries stigma? Given the choice, most people would rather have family, friends, and coworkers know that they had shingles, excessive sweating, or chronic flatulence before sharing that they have alcohol use disorder. That was certainly true of me.

It continued to sink in. I know firsthand that substance use disorder is horrible. And I also know that amazing recovery is possible and exactly what that means. And I certainly understand, have even been known to say, that the experience of addiction does not define me. It's something that happened to me, not who I am.

The recommended approach is to bear in mind that we are describing a person who is experiencing something. Who I am is primary; what I experience is secondary. "Hi, I'm Keith, and I'm a person in long-term recovery from alcohol use disorder." I know, it doesn't exactly roll off the tongue, and it's a little convoluted. That's why it's still considered acceptable to identify myself in the old, standard way if I am at a peer-support meeting.

Another element in that identification, after being a person first, is stating that I'm in recovery, a strength by any definition. By ordering my identification person first, followed by strength-based, and, lastly, including my chronic condition, I am basically flipping the script. I also chose to avoid the stigmatic terms *alcoholism* or *alcoholic*.

But wait, there's more!

Some of the commonly used language of people with substance use disorder and people who work in the field of substance use disorder treatment confers stigma. While there is no malicious intent, many routinely used expressions and jargon are now considered to be, by implication, socially discrediting.

Consider this statement, which might be how someone describes their own recovery: "I've been clean for six months." This is a perfect example of language that has been used for ages. The concern is this implies that someone is clean as opposed to *dirty*. The suggestion of something being dirty is stigmatic, if even subliminally. They have a chronic medical condition that is now in remission; they weren't dirty. The same clean/dirty description is often used in the clinical area to describe the results of a urine drug screen—a *clean* urine specimen or a *dirty* urine specimen. While I am not the language police and would respect someone's right to refer to people or themselves as they choose, I would refer to anyone as a *person in recovery* as opposed to a *clean addict.* A urine drug screen is negative or positive, not dirty or clean.

Harm reduction adds a further element to the clean/dirty descriptor. In the harm reduction framework, a urine drug screen that is positive for a nonprescribed medication (as opposed to the stigmatic *dirty with an illicit drug*), while a reason to initiate a supportive discussion, is not a problem or proverbial strike against someone, implicit in the word *dirty*.

This is how language influences the way society and culture view substance use disorder and indirectly and directly influences treatment and, ultimately, those receiving treatment.

## Words

Moving on, consider the word *drug*. This can mean a prescribed medication or a substance used for psychoactive effect in a nonmedical context. Given that there are numerous appropriate indications for the medical use of psychoactive substances, using the term medication can prevent confusion or ambiguity. *Illicit substances* conveys judgment. In documentation, I've used *nonprescribed substances.* Sometimes *street drugs* is a good descriptor, but it's in the gray area. Baby steps.

*Marijuana* has a past negative association and historical connections to discriminatory practices with Mexican migrants. Historically, the term marijuana was deliberately used to associate cannabis with Mexican culture, playing upon *Reefer Madness* (the 1938 antidrug movie) type fears. Perception varies, and people still say marijuana without intending stigma. Last I checked, there is still a Marijuana Anonymous, but I've been saying cannabis for a while now.

*Relapse* is another term that has been in common usage for a long time. The term was used to denote the recurrence of active substance use disorder symptoms, or, in vernacular, *returning to active drinking or using*. Implicit in the word, there has always been an undercurrent of moral failing or weakness. Substance use disorder recovery is now widely understood to be nonlinear, often with a series of smaller successes and failures early on. Susceptibility to resuming active use of a substance is high in the first 90 days of recovery, and especially so in the first 28 days according to Stanford professor of psychiatry and behavioral sciences Dr. Anna Lembke and National Institute on Alcohol Abuse and Alcoholism Director Dr. George Koob.[104] People are now encouraged to say *resumption of,* or *resuming active use,* or *reoccurrence of symptoms*.

MAT was called medication-assisted treatment until recently. While it is a treatment for substance use disorder, and it does include medications, the concern was that it somehow draws a distinction between SUD and other chronic medical conditions. As an example, diabetes is treated with medications, but it's not called assisted treatment. Hypertension, high blood pressure, is treated with medications, but it's simply termed treatment.

When I worked in office-based addiction treatment, I would reinforce to my patients that they had a chronic condition that required treatment. Even going a little further, I would encourage them that, as people in recovery, this was an important concept, and that they belonged in that office waiting room every bit as much as people living with diabetes and hypertension. Medications for addiction treatment work just as well, and organizations can still call their programs MAT.

*Substance misuse* refers to use for intended or unintended purposes, or in quantities or dosages differing from directions. The term is negative and implies blame or judgment. The terms nonprescribed use, nonmedical use, or substance use are suggested instead. Also, negative and implicit of judgment are the terms *substance abuse* and *substance abuser*. These words have been demonstrated to create negative attitudes, the literal definition of stigma. Again, the best approach is person first, followed by strength-based, and then the problem or diagnosis.

It bears mentioning at this point that all these terms are still more or less in common usage. Everything from book titles to organizational mission statements contain the words *substance abuse* and *substance abuser.*

## Stigma

I am not the language police, as I mentioned earlier. However, I frequently find myself in situations where highly qualified recovery professionals are communicating with phrases like "the dirty urine screen indicates relapse to substance abuse." Well, okay, that was dramatized for effect, but the point is that stigma is alive and well in the language of recovery professionals. The same people who are supposed to provide care and model attitudes and behaviors for the SUD population and general public alike haven't gotten the memo yet. I'm not the language police, but I feel like I'm deputized. We're all responsible.

The real purpose of redefining and reframing the way we communicate about substance use disorder is because there is a direct relationship with stigma. SUD "is the most stigmatized health condition in the world, with alcohol use disorder not far behind at fourth in the world," [105] according to the Recovery Research Institute.

Dr. John Kelly and his team undertook a study comparing subjects' responses to questions about two hypothetical people; one person was presented to the subjects as a "substance abuser," while the other was presented as "having a substance use disorder." The study discovered that participants felt the substance abuser was less likely to benefit from treatment, while more likely to benefit from punishment. The substance abuser was also more likely to be blamed for their substance-related difficulties and was more likely to be socially threatening. Interestingly, 69 percent of the study's subjects also answered that those having a substance use disorder would benefit from treatment, and 79 percent of subjects said the person with substance use disorder was not responsible for their condition.[106]

The real question Dr. Kelly was asking is whether the language of stigma causes bias that affects clinical treatment. His Recovery Research Institute study shows that it does. How we talk about people affects how we think about people, and that affects how we treat people.

So, back to my coworker from years ago, who made the remark about someone with body art being a "patron of the arts." There was nothing else memorable about that surgical case. I think the surgeon, the anesthetist, my body art maligning coworker who was the circulating nurse, and me passing the instruments all did our jobs. However, I also think my coworker's remark stigmatized that patient, negatively affected my perception, and possibly the perception of others. While the effects of that type of stigma are subtle, believing someone won't benefit from treatment is not.

What about self-stigma, when a person with a condition is exposed to stigma from society, an organization, or other people resulting in a negatively impacted self-image? One study found that individuals with alcohol disorders who perceived high stigma in the community were less likely to seek alcohol treatment services. Also, the likelihood of seeking treatment decreased as the perception of stigma increased.[107] Perceived stigma was assessed using the perceived devaluation-discrimination (PDD) scale. The PDD scale is a 12-item tool that measures how much someone believes that most people will devalue or discriminate against someone with a mental illness. When people's decision to get help is influenced by negative public opinion, this is a highly personal consequence of stigma.

Medicine has specialties that are considered high risk. The conditions, treatments and interventions, or populations might be complex; there is high potential for complications and poor outcomes, that is, serious harm. An example is treating gallbladder disease, which accounts for 1.8 million hospital visits annually.[108] Gallbladder removal surgery is one of the most common operations. However, during this routine surgery, the surgeon must identify and ligate (tie, clip, or otherwise close off) involved structures called the cystic artery and the cystic duct. Damage to or failure to control these delicate bits of anatomy can result in uncontrolled bleeding or spillage of corrosive bile into the abdominal cavity. Not good! This illustrates how incorrect mechanical treatment can result in serious harm. It's a clear-cut cause and effect.

In substance use disorder, language causes the unintended harm. Unfortunately, there is no definitive mechanical correction for substance use disorder. It can't be removed surgically. While people with SUD do suffer physical effects, behavior is the focus of treatment. Just as the most skilled surgeon can inadvertently damage delicate structures causing harm to a patient, negative or inappropriate language is the equivalent for the person in treatment and recovery. Self-image and self-esteem are the delicate structures that can be damaged by stigmatizing language, even when it is accidental or well intentioned. The real harm of stigma is insidious, subtle, and cumulative but no less cause and effect. And no less high risk.

## Common Usage

The shift in commonly used recovery and mental health language is a top-down phenomenon. Part of the trend is a byproduct of research at high levels like the National Institute on Drug Abuse (NIDA) and the Substance Abuse and Mental Health Services Administration (SAMHSA). To be fair, it also reflects the trend toward political correctness, but there is science supporting it. The rationale is sound.

So, it's complicated. While it's definitely seeping into the clinical and academic sectors, the new jargon is only halfway here. SOS Recovery, a New Hampshire recovery community organization (RCO) issues language guidance for its conference speakers that is spot-on and right up to the moment, requesting that *addict, alcoholic, clean, substance abuse,* etc., be avoided, and offering suggestions for the acceptable substitutes.

However, while facilitating a remote counseling appointment for a residential client, I heard a graduate-level clinician from Boston Children's Hospital use the term "clean time." She was referencing AA meetings, saying there were people, "with a lot of clean time there." As opposed to dirty time, I guess. The irony is that the RCO is a grant-funded, folksy place run by people with lived experience. Boston Children's Hospital is recognized internationally as a clinical and academic hub.

At the extreme end, it's getting a little disproportionate, and it is just hard to communicate information at times. I've seen guidance that suggests that instead of manipulative, I say *resourceful*. Instead of resistant, I should say *chooses not to*, *isn't ready for*, or *is not open to*. Hostile or aggressive should be expressed as *protective*. Sometimes, we just need to say the word.

What I can totally get on board with is that *suffers with* really means *working to recover from,* or *living with,* and that an *addict* is a *person living with substance use disorder.* Victimization is turned into empowerment. I never heard anyone with a high body mass index called a food abuser; there is no place for expressions like substance abuse and substance abuser. We can be encouraged that something like body art, once heavily stigmatized, has become commonplace and accepted in our culture. It gives me hope that substance use disorder can make a similar progression in terms of understanding and social acceptance. It's a process.

Finally, I had been wondering about the terminology in the names of the top federal agencies. The National Institute on Alcohol Abuse and Alcoholism (NIAAA) and the National Institute on Drug Abuse (NIDA) were formed in 1970 and 1974, respectively. The Substance Abuse and Mental Health Services Administration (SAMHSA) is a newbie, formed in 1992. They are doing some wonderful work, but their burnt orange shag carpet names need to go.

It's not a matter of having stationery they want to use up. It literally takes an act of Congress to change the names of these agencies. According to an email response from the NIDA Public Inquiries Team, "A proposal to rename NIDA the 'National Institute on Drugs and Addiction' was included in the President's Fiscal Year 2024 Budget. Congress, which established NIDA's current name in 1974, will need to pass legislation in order to implement a name change."

Fewer than six years ago, I was taken aback that people working in the recovery field, having no lived experience themselves, seemed offended by the way people in recovery commonly spoke. Today, I have to stop and think about context when I see or hear the word *alcoholic.* I cringe at the term *substance abuse.* As evidenced by my 2018 *Infinite Recovery Handbook*, now in its third edition, with hundreds of language changes to the original manuscript that was started the year prior, my thoughts and beliefs have changed. I'm not the recovery language police, but I respect the power of words. Just as my approach to recovery language has shifted, so must the language of culture in general and recovery culture specifically. Stigma is the barrier to breaking old habits as well as the price we pay for not seeing people and their strengths ahead of their illnesses and problems.

# Chapter 17
# The Cold Hard Truth Chapter

"We lead the world in only three categories:
number of incarcerated citizens per capita,
number of adults who believe angels are real,
and defense spending."
~ Will McAvoy [109]

"Courtney wanted to be Hawaiian when she grew up," said Doug Griffin, Courtney's father, who I've known for about 10 years. Doug described how Courtney had experienced bullying, found drugs as a way of fitting in, and how they could talk about her situation openly while playing pinball together.

Doug said, "She loved everything about Hawaii. She wanted to study there and live there someday." Instead, she descended into chaotic opioid use, enmeshed in her relationship with boyfriend Chris, also an opioid user.

Courtney fought addiction. She made a decision to join the Marines. This was a clear choice to change her life for the better. Discipline, service, and freedom from substance use were the motivators. Doug said Courtney knew the Marines would take her in the positive direction she wished for. Courtney prepared for her induction by hitting the gym for months under the guidance of her recruiter. After she was at boot camp for a month, Doug received word that she was being discharged for an induction urine screen that was positive for THC. He said she was crushed. She picked up with Chris and resumed substance use.

At that point in our conversation, Doug became visibly emotional, his eyes welling up. He does this for the greater good, not because it's easy.

A couple of months later, she entered treatment. However, she was quickly discharged when insurance refused to cover her hospitalization. They said, "It's not a matter of life and death," according to Doug. They were wrong. She overdosed and died weeks later. She was 20.

Doug mourned, then got to work. First, he educated himself, attending local support and prevention groups. He soon joined the policy board of the Addiction Policy Forum. He began traveling several times a year to Washington, DC, to talk with congressmen and senators about substance use and the opioid problem. He's been to the White House five times and met with the drug czars of every administration. He also currently serves on the advisory board of the New England node of the clinical trial network of the NIDA, as well as the New Hampshire Opioid Abatement Advisory Commission, the organization overseeing distribution of opioid settlement funds.

"I'm a firm believer in letter writing. And connecting with lawmakers' staff is key."

He wrote a letter to President Joe Biden, and First Lady Jill Biden invited Doug and his wife Pam to the 2023 State of the Union address in Washington. I happened to be watching live on TV and experienced a surreal moment. The president of the United States was on live television introducing someone I knew personally and relating a story I was sadly familiar with. Biden introduced the Griffins as he solemnly related how their daughter had died of a fentanyl overdose. The moment was intended to be one of reverence. Then, the surreal abruptly became outlandish.

"Murderer!" Georgia Congressperson Marjorie Taylor Greene screamed at Biden from the gallery. This was a showstopping stunt.

She was standing in front of her seat in the House of Representatives chamber. She was impossible to miss, wearing an eye-catching white jacket with a fur collar. Like a boisterous schoolgirl whose boyfriend happened to be the quarterback for the opposing team, she'd come prepared to disrupt the Democrat's pep rally. She wanted attention, and she wanted to rain on the parade.

Ultimately, however, the people who lost their moment were Doug and Pam Griffin.

Courtney's story symbolized the thousands of young souls lost in what is often referred to as the opioid epidemic; Doug and Pam symbolized even more thousands of loved ones who were collateral damage from the brutal rash of overdoses.

Greene's insensitivity shattered what should have been a moment of solemn tribute. The look on Doug's face, a mixture of bewilderment and abject sadness, spoke volumes.

Regarding the Greene incident, "She totally ruined the moment. The place was silent when Biden was telling Courtney's story." Doug is visibly frustrated. "Biden never recovered from the interruption, moving on in the speech." The impact of this poignant human story of a major problem facing all of us was squandered in puerile partisan attention seeking. The moment, and the opportunity, was lost.

Courtney's story, along with Doug's subsequent activism and on through the tawdry Greene political theater escapade encapsulates much of what's wrong with our system and our culture today. The stigma, the broken system, and the lack of understanding at the leadership level are just as much obstacles to progress now as they were a decade ago. Doug, and the many like him who have mobilized in response to the addiction problem, is the bright spot.

What have we learned in a decade? According to Doug Griffin, "We need to channel loss into boots on the ground." He believes we can make a difference, but we need to work smart. "It's best if people can support an existing organization or nonprofit instead of starting their own. It's better use of energy and resources."

My takeaway is that we don't know when it's life and death or someone's last chance.

## Tourists in Addictionland

In April 2019, the Merrimack Valley Prevention and Substance Abuse Project, MVPASAP, held its quarterly in-person gathering. MVPASAP is a nonprofit organization with over 4000 followers. A hundred-plus people assembled in the auditorium of a trade school in Andover, Massachusetts.

The organization formed in 2013 in response to the opioid crisis, bringing affected people together to raise awareness. I began attending meetings and following on social media in 2016. I spoke at a couple of events, networked, learned, and, most important, met people like

Doug Griffin.

Meeting attendance had outgrown the folksy senior center where it started, and this first meeting at the new auditorium would be a town hall, featuring the newly sworn in US representative from the district. After the requisite picture-taking, she addressed the audience of parents of the overdosed, treatment professionals, and first responders. She introduced herself briefly, took questions, and listened to heart-wrenching experiences of people from the audience. She said she would fight for us, and, among other rhetorical statements, said, "I will be the voice for those who have no voice."

A year or so later, I watched a streamed panel discussion featuring this US rep. The panel featured another congressperson, along with a treatment specialist and someone from law enforcement. My district's representative spoke about a bill she was working on, which sounded promising. Then, she said something quite puzzling when she referred to "*sud*," as in the singular of suds, like bubbles from detergent. She said it again a minute later, and I realized she was referring to the acronym for substance use disorder, SUD. Anyone in the addiction field or knowledgeable on the topic would state the letters, S-U-D, when invoking the initialism. The congressperson's usage indicated that she was referencing something written, and when she saw the acronym SUD, pronounced it phonetically like the soap bubble. She was unfamiliar with the term. I know she was trying, but this did not bode well for the voice of the voiceless as having any credibility or working knowledge of the issue. It was actually embarrassing.

The promised bill, the MATE Act, passed three years later, with fanfare and a staged press event. The US rep from my district was a cosponsor and wanted to make sure we all knew it. This is from the website of the American Medical Association: "The Medication Access and Training Expansion (MATE) Act requires physicians, including residents and fellows, and other health care professionals who prescribe controlled substances, to complete a one-time-only eight hours of training on the treatment and management of patients with opioid or other substance use disorders." [110]

While substance use disorder is considered a chronic medical condition, and therefore the medical establishment is responsible for treating it, medical providers are a small proportion of addiction, treatment, and recovery. The MATE Act addresses such a tiny fraction of the issue that it is inconsequential. Three years! Eight hours!

We're not going to prescribe our way out of this.

The MATE Act is not directly helping people living with substance use disorder. It is not providing more treatment options or improving existing treatment. It is not easing the reentry process for criminal justice-involved people with substance issues. It's not expanding the narrow range of recovery options. It is not educating the public at large in the interest of combating stigma.

It amounts to legislators telling doctors what to do, and that seems to be a standard go-to when elected officials want to appear involved. It gives the appearance of doing something about the problem but does little for the substance of the issue.

Perhaps the theory is that they are somehow leading horses to water with the expectation that they will drink. Other recent legislation has made it so any prescriber can write for medications for addiction treatment, where a DEA waiver was previously necessary.

In 2000, the Drug Addiction Treatment Act (DATA) was enacted, allowing physicians who obtained an "X-waiver" from the DEA to prescribe buprenorphine in office settings. They were required to complete specific training on the treatment of opioid addiction. Later legislation, the Comprehensive Addiction and Recovery Act of 2016, expanded prescribing authority to nurse practitioners and physician assistants.

The 2023 Consolidated Appropriations Act amended the Controlled Substances Act to eliminate the requirement for qualified practitioners to first obtain a special X-waiver to prescribe medications for opioid use disorder such as buprenorphine. This means that any prescriber can prescribe medications for addiction treatment.

That means your primary care doctor could prescribe Suboxone. Or your dentist, technically.

Unfortunately, eight hours of mandated education does not mean that doctors will use that prescriptive authority. I don't think you'll leave with a prescription if you ask for one at your next teeth cleaning.

According to Dr. Arun Gupta, a practicing addiction medicine specialist and best-selling author of *The Preventable Epidemic: A Frontline Doctor's Experience and Recommendations to Resolve America's Opioid Crisis*: "An eight-hour course is not sufficient to teach addiction to providers. The AMA had opposed mandated education on addiction about a decade ago. Eight hours is certainly not enough education to make doctors comfortable to practice addiction medicine or provide effective care to save lives... There are no incentives for doctors to learn and practice addiction medicine. But there are too many disincentives that doctors will not jump in large numbers." [111]

In fact, the training might have the opposite of the intended effect.

A few years back, I decided to replace the original linoleum flooring in my bathroom with tile. After a friend said, "You could do that yourself," I signed up and took a tiling class at The Home Depot. My takeaway from paying close attention in the class was that installing tiles had lots of fine points and was potentially complicated. There was a lot that could go wrong. I hired a professional to install my bathroom tiles.

Boston Medical Center's Grayken Center for Addiction Training and Technical Assistance offers courses such as Screening, Assessment, and Treatment of Substance Use Disorders, Buprenorphine 101, Alcohol Use Disorders 101. These offerings meet the requirements set forth by MATE. I audited a couple of the actual courses required of prescribers.

When a primary care doctor or internist sees the short list of commonly co-occurring psychiatric disorders that include anxiety and mood disorders, schizophrenia, bipolar disorder, major depressive disorder, PTSD, and ADHD, they're going to think the same thing I thought about tiling my own bathroom. These are complicated people with complicated problems and complicated lives. There is a lot that can go wrong.

The eight hours of training will convince general practitioners to refer people who screen positively for SUD to an addiction medicine specialist. Better understanding is good, but the desired outcome of expanded care from more providers is not happening. Prescribing medication is no definitive answer to substance use anyway.

The lawmakers mean well, but they're the ones who need eight hours of training. They're having no success telling the doctors what to do. We're not going to legislate our way out of this either, at least not without thinking outside of the box we're stuck in.

## Why Don't We Lead the World in Addiction Treatment?

Anyone who wants addiction treatment should be able to receive it. We should change the way this works in the US. We need to make this a priority.

Why should we restructure and reprioritize addiction care? Since the year 2000, there have been over one million reasons, because that's the death toll.[112] Courtney Griffin and the scores of others should be all the reason we need. Once people decide they want help, they can't find treatment, can't afford it, and it doesn't work.

In bottom-line terms, there is the cost, which is estimated at $2.7 trillion for opioids alone. The figure is less staggering when you deduct the subjective costs of deaths and lost quality of life, but it still leaves $277 billion.[113] Annually. Again, for opioids alone.

The death toll and cost aside, we're really talking about human suffering. This ruins lives on a scale without precedent. Addiction comes in under the radar and changes people in ways that set them on a different trajectory. Then comes the ripple effect. Partners, family, friends—communities all feel the effects, both recognized and unrecognized. This country is collcctively living in an alternate reality from what it could be experiencing without the scourge of addiction. The negative impact is incalculable. Try to imagine a reality without substance use disorder and addiction; it's almost impossible.

In that hard-to-envision reality, quality addiction treatment is a basic right, something that one in seven people would benefit from or will need at some point in their life. This is something we must figure out.

In the hospice field where I worked directly, the basic values and mission were that everyone should die with dignity, free from pain, and in the setting of their choice. The concept occupies a unique place that is not quite a right, not quite an entitlement, but still a universally held value. The Centers for Medicare and Medicaid Services, CMS, sets the standard for this, and it is accessible to anyone who meets the requirement of terminal illness. Whether through Medicare, Medicaid, or private insurance, people are eligible to receive end-of-life care.

Another similar concept is that everyone should receive urgent medical care in an emergency. The Emergency Medical Treatment and Labor Act is a federal law enacted in 1986 to ensure public access to emergency services regardless of a patient's ability to pay. Hospitals with a dedicated emergency department that accept Medicare funds are required to perform a medical screening examination, stabilizing treatment and appropriate transfer. This is just basic humanity.

We need a universal addiction treatment initiative.

Whether we call that a right, entitlement, or simply an expanded human service, we need to make it so anyone who wants it can receive quality substance use disorder treatment.

Quality SUD treatment means individualized, evidence-based treatment by trained, qualified, competent professionals who recognize the correlation between length of treatment, level of support, and successful outcomes.

This treatment needs to be rendered by accountable organizations and facilities that are incentivized by positive outcomes rather than potential for repeat business.

In fashion similar to the restructuring of hospice in 2008, where CMS introduced new conditions of participation, we need restructuring and redefining of substance use disorder treatment. And we need to do this in such a way that the objective is true motivation to support the substance use disorder population while discouraging the opportunistic business element that hamstrings addiction treatment today.

The CMS took a hard look at what was going on in the hospice industry. One of the principal problems was organizations carrying people on their rosters who just weren't dying. Ideally, a patient's decline is identified, and they are enrolled in hospice for about six months. We heard about people who were on hospice for two years while the organization just bills Medicare every quarter.

That's not much different than treating the same patient 12 times for substance use disorder. Although that bill went to private insurance in that situation, it's reasonable to question who is being served. It's not the patient in this instance. We know that recovery from substance use disorder is bumpy and nonlinear. Yes, people resume substance use after treatment. The question is, was it the person or the treatment that failed? I personally admitted a man for his 12th treatment episode at the same facility. He wanted recovery. I believe that had he received competent, evidence-based treatment along with individualized support and follow-up, he would not have needed 12 treatments (plus however many more that I didn't hear about). Making that facility accountable for his treatment, or at least somehow incentivizing his success, would have improved the facility's treatment as well as his outcome.

Much of what's wrong with treatment could be fixed with accountability. Holding treatment organizations responsible for effective, evidence-based treatment starts with making them responsible to tell us what they're doing. My suggestion? Most organizations and facilities have alumni coordinators. Modify their job descriptions. Instead of following graduates' progress in the interest of readmitting them when they fail, this role should document assessment, individualized evidence-based care, discharge planning, and the warm handoff to the next appropriate level of care. Make it about quality control, not business development.

One out of seven people, 48.7 million US citizens over the age of 12, meet the criteria for substance use disorder. But then—those one out of seven impacts the other six. This equals EVERYONE being affected directly or indirectly. When we consider every aspect of what addiction is doing to us, it literally makes no sense that we fail to take drastic action.

While bold action is indicated, this would need to be done in carefully measured increments. As with hospice, we would anticipate that entities whose presence in the treatment field is driven by profit motive would rapidly lose interest and depart. A proportion of the 43 percent of for-profit organizations that treat 56 percent of patients are likely to react by selling or just closing their doors. Simultaneously, we will need more treatment. This needs to be measured and thoughtful. We need to figure out how to make this a win-win.

During times of national emergency, such as war, the federal government has compelled the private sector to prioritize the needs of the greater good. This has happened in times of war in an organized fashion. The federal government historically has formed organizations like the National Defense Advisory Board, the Office of War Mobilization, the Supply Priorities and Allocations Board, and a War Production Board. The Defense Production Act, DPA, of 1950 gives the US president broad powers to ensure the industrial base meets defense needs. The most common way the government commandeers the private sector is through the Mandatory Contract Prioritization, Title I of the DPA. While the intention of this was to compel automobile plants to make tanks instead of cars, it was utilized during COVID to boost production of ventilators and personal protective equipment.

During the Second World War, representatives of industry and labor were recruited to collaborate on national emergency situations. This would be optimal in the case of addressing our broken treatment system. Enlisting both the finest scientific minds and the top business minds to lead us in innovative fashion is obviously the best way forward. Again, we would have to recognize the level of urgency for what it really is, but the mobilization part has precedent.

Paul Revere's midnight ride to warn that the British army was coming started a revolution. Ronald Reagan famously stated, "Mr. Gorbachev, tear down this wall!" The wall came down. John F. Kennedy famously declared, "We choose to go to the Moon in this decade and do the other things, not because they are easy, but because they are hard." We went to the Moon. This is no less of a call to action. Addiction treatment should be made a basic right in this country. That shouldn't be as hard as going to the Moon.

We need to recognize that addiction is a major barrier to our greatness as a nation. We could lead the world in this area. We just need to understand how important this is.

### Recovery Friendly Culture

The following is from the West Hartford, Connecticut, website.

> "We are proud to announce that the Town of West Harford was recently designated as a Recovery Friendly Community. We support those who are in recovery from substance misuse and/or mental health disorders by 1) raising awareness of the nature of such conditions, 2) promoting health and recovery by reducing stigma and discrimination and 3) building or improving the environmental factors necessary for recoveries to flourish. Expected benefits of a Recovery Friendly Community may be reduced substance use, reduced overdoses, reduced crime, an improved sense of compassion, humanity and citizenship and positive statewide visibility." [114]

This is exactly what it sounds like—recognition that substance use exists and, more important, that recovery exists. Recovery friendly communities make it easier for people to stay sober. The needs of the recovery community, when appropriate, are considered when creating new policies, licensing, and town-sponsored events are planned. Public health language is inclusive of recovery. Civic goals, policies, and recommendations reflect this.

Do zoning regulations allow for recovery housing? Does the town prohibit alcohol and smoking in public spaces and town-owned properties? What about zoning for retail cannabis? Consideration focused on age-restricted products, including drug and tobacco paraphernalia for places like schools, childhood centers, libraries, playgrounds, sport fields, and even recovery locations, is a reasonable accommodation.

What does a town or city do to support its recovery community? Are public spaces made available for peer-support meetings and activities? AA groups want to pay their way but are seldom flush with funds. By nature, a recovery community is a silent but not insignificant proportion of the general population; civic leaders would probably be surprised at how much constituency is discreetly connected to and supports people in recovery.

How does a community approach prevention? Police forces now frequently employ social workers or clinicians to follow up after overdose incidents. However, uniformed law enforcement going into schools to warn about drug use has never worked.[115] Young people want to see a sermon not hear one. When a community has the best interest of youth at heart, it's obvious in the nature of an open, supportive, and accepting culture.

Recovery friendly workplaces are a logical extension of recovery friendly communities. Steady jobs, stable income, and supportive work environments are among the most valuable forms of recovery capital people can have.

Encouraging local employers to support individuals can lead to fundamental changes in the way they hire, engage with, and support employees living in recovery from substance use disorder. Training on SUD and ongoing support benefit everyone involved. Substance use disorders cost the US economy an estimated $93 billion in lost productivity in 2023—approximately $3703 per adult with a SUD. According to the *American Journal of Preventive Medicine,* that was the price tag for loss of productivity due to substance use disorder.[116]

It seems logical, intuitive, even natural, that in a society where people living with a disability are not only protected from discrimination in the hiring process but employers must also provide accommodations... that employment would be inclusive of recovering people. Restructuring of jobs, modifying of equipment, interpreters, and allowing leave are all considered reasonable accommodations under the

Americans with Disabilities Act. In the community, state and local services, programs, and activities must be accessible to people with disabilities, including physical access and communication aids if needed. Private businesses also must ensure accessibility.

And yet somehow, both historically and contemporarily, the substance use disorder population is still treated like lepers who wandered out of the colony. Recovery friendly communities and workplaces are rare. The sober truth is that we are still mired in stigma.

After six years of living with addiction, 34-year-old Alicia transitioned from a 30-day program into a sober residence in Plymouth, Massachusetts. When she had earned time away, she left on a weekend pass. The following Monday morning, her parents received the call that no parent wants to get.

The owner of the sober residence called to inform Alicia's parents, "She wasn't back at midnight. Is she with you?"

The residence owner then went to the police and was told, "She's an addict. She's partying somewhere. She'll turn up in a day or two." Alicia's parents called the police as well and were told the same thing. They called the state police and received the same response. They spent the next four days calling several times daily and received no assistance. "Finally, our police department talked to Plymouth and asked them to be on the lookout for her car. Within an hour, they were able to tell us our daughter had overdosed in a rest stop and had been in the ICU for the last four days," said Alicia's mother.

"SHE'S AN ADDICT. SHE'S PARTYING SOMEWHERE." No, she was in a coma while her parents went through four days of needless hell. This is the reality we still live in. Recovery friendly anything is a long way off.

Yes, the line between substance use and recovery blurs. The truth is that recovery is nonlinear (at the risk of being a broken record and repeating that yet again). In the first weeks and months of recovery, as Alicia was, guardrails and supports are vital, as is understanding when someone has a chronic health condition. We have a long way to go to overcome the sort of judgment inherent in a police department's refusal to assist in locating a missing person. Recovery friendly culture is only an ideal at this point.

## What Is Addiction?

I worked for two years running an office-based addiction treatment program, cited throughout this book. I was the SUD RN at one of three southern New Hampshire locations of a federally qualified health center, responsible for leading and coordinating the program at my office. In hindsight, this was a remarkable and forward-thinking program staffed with talented and dedicated people. The best parts of my day were always meeting with patients as part of their scheduled appointments. This involved holistic nursing and recovery coaching.

The office program was nestled in a primary care setting, where the general public came for routine annual physicals, follow-up appointments, and urgent visits for the typical issues ranging from sore throats to foot fungus. In a federally qualified center in southern New Hampshire, substance use disorder treatment met a significant need of the community. Our particular location had the distinction of the highest response, as tracked via quality assurance, when patients scored positive on the short SUD screening tool given to every patient at every appointment, organization-wide. This was directly attributable to my availability to respond when a provider came knocking at my door, essentially saying, "Do you have a minute to see someone in my exam room? They have questions about alcohol use." This type of collaboration and my role in this type of primary care setting tends to validate the notion that substance use disorder is a medical condition.

Somewhere toward the end of every nursing intake, I would emphasize that substance use disorder, the patient's reason for being there, was a chronic medical condition. This had the dual purpose of checking the box regarding expected conduct, but, more important, I wanted to provide something motivational. These people of different ages, different life experiences, and different paths to treatment all had stigma in common. They'd all encountered it in various forms, and they'd all paid some price in terms of their sense of self-worth and emotional comfort level. My message was that they belonged in that waiting room every bit as much as the person there for a diabetic checkup, the parent with a couple of coughing, sniffling kiddos, or anyone else with any medical condition needing treatment. They were entitled (a word I do not often invoke) to dignity and the best possible treatment we could provide.

The chronic medical condition conversation became something I would routinely revisit with patients to further reinforce the motivational piece. Placing emphasis on the treatment element while deemphasizing disease or illness, I would reference medical condition. I would further attempt to instill a sense of responsibility, because these patients were becoming the models of behavior for people in treatment. Their families, their employers, their other medical providers, in essence anyone who knew why they came for treatment, would see them as a stark contrast to all the stigmatizing stereotypes.

The disease model of addiction has been the medical/scientific paradigm for over 60 years. *The Disease Concept of Alcoholism* by E. M. Jellinek (1960) is a foundational text that established the modern understanding of *alcoholism*, and SUD by proxy, as a disease rather than a moral failing or character flaw. This was subsequently influential in the American Medical Association's designation of *alcoholism* as a medical diagnosis and ultimately the coverage of addiction treatment by insurers.

I see the disease model as reductionist. Substance use disorder is a condition that simultaneously affects the body, the brain, the emotions, socialization, and has ramifications for one's relationship with the authority structure. Do diabetes, cancer, or heart disease do all that? Disease doesn't do justice to the scope and complexity of SUD, but it's the best descriptor we have.

I had the opportunity to speak with John Kelly, PhD. Dr. Kelly is the Elizabeth R. Spallin Professor of Psychiatry in Addiction Medicine at Harvard Medical School and has published over 200 peer-reviewed articles, reviews, chapters, and books in the field of addiction medicine. He was an author on the *Facing Addiction in America: The Surgeon General's Report on Alcohol, Drugs, and Health*—and I'm omitting half his credentials. He had some light to shed on the disease model.

"Is it a disease? By the dictionary definition, yes, it is."

He continued, "Jellinek actually advocates against using the word disease in favor of something like illness, because he felt, and it's a point with which I agree, that when people hear the word disease, the schema that's activated cognitively is more around the idea of infectious disease, which is a biomedical phenomenon. Whereas we think about addiction as having more behavioral components and effects, of course. So, I think that's a good point he made. Perhaps we should be referring to it more as an illness or disorder as opposed to a disease. Now, the intention, as you know, with the focus on disease, is to place it in the biomedical realm and move it out of the criminal justice realm. What we have shown in studies is that when you emphasize the biomedical aspects of the disease, or disorder, or illness, or whatever you want to call it... you emphasize the biomedical nature, the genetic components, which affect cause, and the neurobiological components, which affect controllability. When you emphasize those, stigma goes down. You can study stigma, and you can show that the self-stigma goes down, the public stigma goes down."

So far, so good, but then the caveat, and I did see this coming.

Dr. Kelly went on, "But here's the kicker, the interesting thing on the other side. When people are getting into stable remission and recovery, if you keep referring to them as having a brain disease, then people re-stigmatize them as not being able to integrate properly into society. They view them as being less likely to stay in remission if they have a brain disease. And they're more afraid of them. They view them as more dangerous and to be more likely to be socially excluded."

He concluded, "So, NIDA and others who have emphasized the disease aspect of it through the brain wanted to destigmatize it. They wanted to get more people into treatment; they wanted to reduce that shame and blame and all the rest of it. And so, there was good intention of that emphasis. But it's a double-edged sword. You know, it is good for reducing shame, stigma, we can show that, but on the flip side, it can actually be a barrier for people for reintegration and assimilation back into society."

I was simultaneously blown away by his response and validated in my perspective. Something crystallized as he described the downside of the disease model, rooted in the complexity of substance use disorder.

People do not understand addiction and people tend to fear what they do not understand. It's been said that fear is the basis of intolerance. Stigma is the public relations campaign of intolerance.

We're not solving the addiction problem, and perhaps fear is one of the reasons. The mayor of my community does not attend the monthly meeting of her civic task force on the issue. I point out that it's one hour per month for something affecting one out of seven of her constituents. She insists she's too busy, but her unease is evident. It's like a catch-22; to overcome fear, one must face fear. If she acknowledges the problem, she's obligated to at least work on solving it. The same is true of the US representative. No one on her staff can seem to tell me what else she's done about SUD (not suds) in six years besides the little eight-hour training bill. Compartmentalizing seems to be the theme. A little bill, a one-hour meeting...

I think about the waiting room of the southern New Hampshire primary care, and how I got my patients thinking about their roles in the solution. We in recovery are responsible for modeling the behaviors and providing cues about how people should think, feel, and behave toward the substance use disorder population.

Apparently, we are the people we've been waiting for.

# Afterword

"The task of breaking a bad habit is like
uprooting a powerful oak within us.
And the task of building a good habit is like
cultivating a delicate flower one day at a time."
~ James Clear

## We Have a Choice

Why is it stupidly hard to change my mind?

In 1991, I did something that is considered extraordinary by anyone who understands it. I quit drinking, as well as the use of any other mind-altering substances. I quit smoking cigarettes the following year.

The hold that alcohol has on someone who is dependent is like a jackboot on the throat. For anyone who understands the physical, psychological, social/cultural, and personal ramifications of a toxic relationship with substances, a complete and permanent breakup is a remarkable and courageous human accomplishment. There are no medals or parades for those who do this, but it is a remarkable human accomplishment, nonetheless.

Recovery from any substance use disorder is unique to each individual accomplishing it. The experience of addiction is equally unique. The subjective nature of addiction and recovery adds another layer to the difficulty factor. I got drunk and high in my own special way; the same is true of my recovery.

How someone thinks and feels about their substance use, the subjective element, is another way that addiction is different from other chronic medical conditions. Substance use versus substance use disorder is ultimately deeply personal.

In recovery, for every individual I encounter who is just trying to get started and find their way, there are a dozen who believe they've got it nailed. The confidence and clarity are evident as they relate their perspective. There are many who believe themselves to be the experts of their own recovery and everyone else's. If you bought this book (thank you!) online, it was probably one of many on a crowded page. This is a popular subject.

Part of the reason we have so many confident authorities at all levels is because of the bias we all have. Bias is that lack of objectivity where judgment or perception is influenced by preconceived notions or personal opinions. As mentioned previously, confirmation bias and asymmetric bias affect all of us and lead us to believe we are experts. This can be to our detriment. It's almost miraculous that anyone actually changes their mind!

I was able to recover in the face of my bias. Later in recovery, I was able to first open my mind and eventually change my mind about a few things. My ideas about treatment have undergone significant revision. I now support harm reduction and many pathways to recovery, including nonabstinence approaches. My beliefs about smoking cessation during treatment, cannabis, hallucinogens and other things discussed here are just about completely opposite what they were a decade ago. I physically cringe when I hear certain stigmatizing language; maybe that's a form of bias, but I'm keeping it for the moment.

Many still cling to the notion that addiction is chosen. Psychology says it's not, and neuroscience has proven it's not a choice. We are making gains here, but slowly. Stigma shifts slowly.

We need to choose progress. We need to embrace change.

In recovery, the idea of remaining teachable is considered a virtue. We all have that choice. This is something we could all benefit from. Stigma will not change until we start to recognize our bias and recognize ideas and beliefs that no longer serve us. Dr. Adam Grant said, "The moment you believe you're not biased, you are incapable of seeing any of your biases." [117]

My goal is to remain teachable. The day they give me my medal and parade I could stop trying to learn, but I won't. For every individual who is just getting started and finding their way in recovery, somewhere, someone is experiencing the sensation of the warm hug and beginning their personal pursuit of the perfect buzz. It's like a horrible circle of life. Addiction is an endless, constant problem. Recovery must be an endless, renewable resource.

Thank you for reading.

# Notes

[1] Grant, BF, Dawson, DA. "Age at onset of alcohol use and its association with DSM-IV alcohol abuse and dependence: results from the National Longitudinal Alcohol Epidemiologic Survey." *Journal of Substance Abuse,* 1997, 9, 103–110.

[2] https://www.samhsa.gov/data/sites/default/files/reports/rpt42731/2022-nsduh-main-highlights.pdf

[3] https://www.samhsa.gov/data/sites/default/files/reports/slides-2020-nsduh/2020NSDUHNationalSlides072522.pdf.54

[4] https://nida.nih.gov/research-topics/trends-statistics/overdose-death-rates

[5] https://www.niaaa.nih.gov/alcohols-effects-health/alcohol-topics/alcohol-facts-and-statistics/alcohol-related-emergencies-and-deaths-united-states#:~:text=The%20Alcohol%2DRelated%20Disease%20Impact,behind%20tobacco%2C%20poor%20diet%20and

[6] https://benwesthoff.substack.com/p/fentanyl-crisis-is-the-border-the?nthPub=11

[7] https://www.ncadd.org/about-addiction/alcohol-drugs-and-crime

[8] https://news.gallup.com/poll/1675/Most-Important-Problem.aspx

[9] Cold Spring Harbor Laboratory Archives. (n.d.). Eugenics Record Office records. https://archivesspace.cshl.edu/repositories/2/resources/67

[10] White, WL. *Slaying the dragon: The History of Addiction Treatment and Recovery in America,* second edition. (Bloomington, Illinois: Chestnut Health Systems, 2014). 261–278.

[11] https://www.samhsa.gov/data/sites/default/files/reports/rpt35313/2020_NSSATS_FINAL.pdf

[12] https://www.samhsa.gov/data/sites/default/files/reports/rpt35313/2020_NSSATS_FINAL.pdf

[13] https://www.drugabuse.gov/publications/principles-drug-addiction-treatment-research-based-guide-third-edition/frequently-asked-questions/how-long-does-drug-addiction-treatment

[14] McLellan, AT, Skipper, GS, Campbell, M, DuPont, RL. (2008). "Five year outcomes in a cohort study of physicians treated for substance use disorders in the United States." *BMJ.* 337:a2038. doi: 10.1136/bmj.a2038. PMID: 18984632; PMCID: PMC2590904.

[15] National Academies of Sciences, Engineering, and Medicine. (2024). "FAA medical certification standards for pilots and air traffic controllers: Assessing the

efficacy of substance misuse monitoring programs." *The National Academies Press.* https://www.ncbi.nlm.nih.gov/books/NBK598904/

[16] https://www.samhsa.gov/data/sites/default/files/reports/rpt35313/2020_NSSATS_FINAL.pdf

[17] Socias, ME, Volkow, N, Wood, E. (2016). "Improved health outcomes among individuals with opioid use disorder in a community-based program that combines methadone maintenance treatment and peer support." *Journal of Substance Abuse Treatment*, 63, 74–79.

[18] Kranzler, HR, Van Kirk, J. (2001). *Alcoholism: Clinical and Experimental Research,* 25, 9, 1335–1341.

[19] National Institute on Drug Abuse. (2018). Drugs, brains, and behavior: The science of addiction (NIH Publication No. 18-DA-5605). US Department of Health and Human Services, National Institutes of Health. https://nida.nih.gov/publications/drugs-brains-behavior-science-addiction

[20] Substance Abuse and Mental Health Services Administration. (2023). Key substance use and mental health indicators in the United States: Results from the 2022 National Survey on Drug Use and Health. US Department of Health and Human Services. https://www.samhsa.gov/data/report/2022-nsduh-annual-national-report

[21] National Institute on Drug Abuse. (2018). Drugs, brains, and behavior: The science of addiction (NIH Publication No. 18-DA-5605). US Department of Health and Human Services, National Institutes of Health. https://nida.nih.gov/publications/drugs-brains-behavior-science-addiction

[22] Interview with John Kelly, PhD, March 12, 2026, via Zoom.

[23] https://www.samhsa.gov/data/sites/default/files/reports/rpt35313/2020_NSSATS_FINAL.pdf., 105.

[24] Substance Abuse and Mental Health Services Administration. (2021). National Survey of Substance Abuse Treatment Services (N-SSATS): 2020. Data on Substance Abuse Treatment Facilities. Rockville, MD: Substance Abuse and Mental Health Services Administration. Table 4.10, 74.

[25] Moyers, TB, Miller, WR (2013). "Is low therapist empathy toxic?" *Psychology of Addictive Behaviors,* 27, 3, 878–884. https://doi.org/10.1037/a0030274

[26] Miller, WR, Baca, LM (1983). "Two-year follow-up of bibliotherapy and therapist-directed controlled drinking training for problem drinkers." *Behavior Therapy,* 14, 4, 441–448.

[27] Miller, WR, Taylor, CA, West, JC. (1980). "Focused versus broad-spectrum behavior therapy for problem drinkers." *Journal of Consulting and Clinical Psychology,* 48, 5, 590–601. https://doi.org/10.1037/0022-006X.48.5.590

[28] Interview with Andrew Bordt, MEd, October 28, 2025, via phone.

[29] Patterson, Silver Wolf, DA. *The New Addiction Treatment: From Good Intentions and Bad Intuitions to Data, Performance, and Technology.* (Oxford University Press, 2021), 43.

[30] Substance Abuse and Mental Health Services Administration. (2021). National Survey of Substance Abuse Treatment Services (N-SSATS): 2020. Data on Substance Abuse Treatment Facilities. Rockville, Maryland: Substance Abuse and Mental Health Services Administration. Table 4.18b, 89.

[31] Substance Abuse and Mental Health Services Administration. (2021). National Survey of Substance Abuse Treatment Services (N-SSATS): 2020. Data on Substance Abuse Treatment Facilities. Rockville, Maryland: Substance Abuse and Mental Health Services Administration, 31.

[32] Daeppen, J-B, Gache, P, Landry, U, et al. (2002). "Symptom-triggered vs fixed-schedule doses of benzodiazepine for alcohol withdrawal: a randomized treatment trial." *Arch Intern Med.* 162, 10, 1117–1121. doi: 10.1001/archinte.162.10.1117.

[33] Greenberg, E, Zhu, JM, Busch, SH, King, M. (2024). "Acquisitions of behavioral health treatment facilities from 2010 to 2021." *Health Affairs Scholar,* 2, 5, qxae049. https://doi.org/10.1093/haschl/qxae049

[34] Linskey, A. (2023). "Private equity investment is flooding into addiction treatment. Is that a good thing?" *Marketplace.* https://www.marketplace.org/story/2023/01/25/private-equity-investment-is-flooding-into-addiction-treatment-is-that-a-good-thing

[35] https://www.samhsa.gov/substance-use/recovery

[36] Kuerbis, A, Armeli, S, Muench, F, Morgenstern, J. (2014). "Profiles of confidence and commitment to change as predictors of moderated drinking: A person-centered approach." *Psychology of Addictive Behaviors,* 28, 4, 1065–1076.

[37] https://www.psychologytoday.com/us/blog/harm-reduction-or-abstinence/202210/moderated-drinking-creative-strategy-treat-alcoholism

[38] Brown, SL, Brown, RM. (2015). "Connecting prosocial behavior to improved physical health: Contributions from the neurobiology of parenting." *Neurosci Biobehav Rev.* 55, 1-17. doi: 10.1016/j.neubiorev.2015.04.004. Epub 2015 Apr 20. PMID: 25907371.

[39] Koob, G, Volkow, N. (2016). "Neurobiology of addiction: a neurocircuitry analysis." *The Lancet. Psychiatry,* 38, 760–773. https://doi.org/10.1016/s2215-0366(16)00104-8.

[40] Koob, GF. (2008). "Hedonic Homeostatic Dysregulation as a Driver of Drug-Seeking Behavior." *Drug Discovery Today: Disease Models.* 5, 4, 207–215. doi: 10.1016/j.ddmod.2009.04.002. PMID: 20054425; PMCID: PMC2801885.

[41] Zibbell, JE, Asher, AK, Patel, RC, et al. (2018). "Increases in Acute Hepatitis C Virus Infection Related to a Growing Opioid Epidemic and Associated Injection Drug Use, United States, 2004 to 2014." *American Journal of Public Health.*

[42] Shanon, B. (2008). "Biblical Entheogens: a Speculative Hypothesis." *Time and Mind,* 1, 1, 51–74. https://doi.org/10.2752/175169608783489116

[43] https://www.cdc.gov/vitalsigns/pdf/2015-01-vitalsigns.pdf

[44] https://www.rand.org/pubs/research_reports/RR3140.html

[45] https://nida.nih.gov/publications/drugfacts/criminal-justice#:~:text=The%20substantial%20prison%20population%20in,population%20has%20an%20active%20SUD

[46] https://nj.gov/health/eoh/rtkweb/documents/fs/0707.pdf

[47] https://www.niaaa.nih.gov/alcohols-effects-health/alcohol-topics/alcohol-facts-and-statistics/alcohol-related-emergencies-and-deaths-united-states#:~:text=The%20Alcohol%2DRelated%20Disease%20Impact,behind%20

[48] https://www.cdc.gov/tobacco/campaign/tips/resources/data/cigarette-smoking-in-united-states.html

[49] "A Quiet Revolution: Drug Decriminalization Policies in Practice Across the Globe." PDF report, *Open Society Foundations,* 28.

[50] Csete, J, Kamarulzaman, A, Kazatchkine, M, et al. (2016). "Public health and international drug policy." *The Lancet* 387, 10026, 1427–1480.

[51] Bassuk, EL, Hanson, J, Greene, RN, Richard, M, Laudet, A. (2016). "Peer-Delivered Recovery Support Services for Addictions in the United States: A Systematic Review." *Journal of Substance Abuse Treatment,* 6, 1–9. https://doi.org/10.1016/j.jsat.2016.01.003

[52] Madden, EF, Prevedel, S, Light, T, Sulzer, SH. (2021). "Intervention Stigma toward Medications for Opioid Use Disorder: A Systematic Review." *Substance Use & Misuse,* 56, 14, 2181–2201. https://doi.org/10.1080/10826084.2021.1975749

[53] Denning, P, Little, J. *Over the Influence: the Harm Reduction Guide to Controlling Your Drug and Alcohol Use.* (New York: Guilford Press, 2017), 186.

[54] https://www.aa.org/sites/default/files/2021-11/en_bigbook_chapt5.pdf

[55] https://www.ncbi.nlm.nih.gov/pmc/articles/PMC10168602/#:~:text=In%202021%2C%20an%20estimated%2046,hookah)*%20(0.9%25).

[56] https://www.who.int/health-topics/tobacco#tab=tab_2

[57] Lien, L, Bolstad, I, Bramness, JG. (2021). "Smoking among inpatients in treatment for substance use disorders: prevalence and effect on mental health and quality of life." *BMC Psychiatry,* 21. https://doi.org/10.1186/s12888-021-03252-9.

[58] Pettey, D, Aubry, T. (2018). "Tobacco Use and Smoking Behaviors of Individuals With a Serious Mental Illness." *Psychiatric Rehabilitation Journal,* 41, 356–360. https://doi.org/10.1037/prj0000302

[59] *The Health Consequences of Smoking—50 Years of Progress: A Report of the Surgeon General.* Centers for Disease Control and Prevention, 2014, 694–695. http://www. surgeongeneral. gov/library/reports/50-years-of-progress

[60] Lariscy, J. (2019). "Smoking-attributable mortality by cause of death in the United States: An indirect approach." *SSM—Population Health,* 7. https://doi.org/10.1016/j.ssmph.2019.100349.

[61] Doll, R, Peto, R. (1976). "Mortality in relation to smoking: 20 years' observations on male British doctors." *British Medical Journal,* 2, 1525–1536. https://doi.org/10.1136/bmj.2.6051.1525.

[62] Boyle, P. (1997). "Cancer, cigarette smoking and premature death in Europe: a review including the Recommendations of European Cancer Experts Consensus Meeting, Helsinki, October 1996." *Lung Cancer,* 17, 1, 1–60. https://doi.org/10.1016/S0169-5002(97)00648-X

[63] Schelling, T. (1992). "Addictive drugs: the cigarette experience." *Science*, 255, 5043, 430–433. https://doi.org/10.1126/SCIENCE.1734519

[64] Loud, E, Duong, H, Henderson, K, Reynolds, R, Ashley, D, Thrasher, J, Popova, L. (2021). "Addicted to smoking or addicted to nicotine?: A focus group study on perceptions of nicotine and addiction among US adult current smokers, for-

mer smokers, non-smokers, and dual users of cigarettes and e-cigarettes." *Addiction.* https://doi.org/10.1111/add.15634

[65] Stolerman, IP, Jarvis, MJ. (2005). "The scientific case that nicotine is addictive." *Psychopharmacology*, 117, 2–10. https://doi.org/10.1007/BF02245088

[66] Gardiner, P. (2004). "The African Americanization of menthol cigarette use in the United States." *Nicotine & Tobacco Research: Official Journal of the Society for Research on Nicotine and Tobacco,* 6, Suppl 1, S55–65. https://doi.org/10.1080/14622200310001649478

[67] https://www.cdc.gov/tobacco/menthol-tobacco/index.html

[68] Odani, S, Armour, B, Graffunder, C, Garrett, B, Agaku, I. (2017). "Prevalence and Disparities in Tobacco Product Use Among American Indians/Alaska Natives—United States, 2010–2015." *Morbidity and Mortality Weekly Report,* 66, 1374–1378. https://doi.org/10.15585/mmwr.mm6650a2

[69] https://www.cdc.gov/mmwr/volumes/69/wr/mm6903e2.htm

[70] Stolerman, I, Jarvis, M. (2005). "The scientific case that nicotine is addictive." *Psychopharmacology*, 117, 2–10. https://doi.org/10.1007/BF02245088

[71] https://www.cdc.gov/mmwr/volumes/73/wr/pdfs/mm7329-H.pdf

[72] *US Dept. of Health and Human Services. Smoking Cessation,* A Report of the Surgeon General, 2020.

[73] https://www.houstonchronicle.com/health/article/quitting-smoking-and-weight-gain-19753595.php

[74] https://www.cdc.gov/tobacco/campaign/tips/resources/data/cigarette-smoking-in-united-states.html

[75] Guydish, J, Passalacqua, E, Tajima B, et al. (2011). "Smoking prevalence in addiction treatment: a review." *Nicotine & Tobacco Research: Official Journal of the Society for Research on Nicotine and Tobacco,* 13, 6, 401–411.

[76] Morris CD, Garver-Apgar, CE. (2020). "Nicotine and Opioids: a Call for Co-treatment as the Standard of Care. *J Behav Health Serv Res.* 47, 4, 601–613. doi: 10.1007/s11414-020-09712-6. PMID: 32495248; PMCID: PMC7269614.

[77] Morris CD, Garver-Apgar, CE. (2020). "Nicotine and Opioids: a Call for Co-treatment as the Standard of Care. *J Behav Health Serv Res.* 47, 4, 601–613. doi: 10.1007/s11414-020-09712-6. PMID: 32495248; PMCID: PMC7269614

[78] Yoon, JH, Lane, SD, Weaver, MF. (2015). "Opioid Analgesics and Nicotine: More Than Blowing Smoke." *J Pain Palliat Care Pharmacother,* 29, 3, 281–289. doi: 10.3109/15360288.2015.1063559. Epub 2015 Sep 16. PMID: 26375198.

[79] Weinberger, A, Platt, J, Esan, H, Galea, S, Erlich, D, Goodwin, R. (2017). "Cigarette Smoking Is Associated With Increased Risk of Substance Use Disorder Relapse: A Nationally Representative, Prospective Longitudinal Investigation." *The Journal of Clinical Psychiatry,* 78, 2, e152–e160 . https://doi.org/10.4088/JCP.15m10062.

[80] Weinberger, AH, Platt, J, Jiang, B, Goodwin, RD. (2015). "Cigarette Smoking and Risk of Alcohol Use Relapse Among Adults in Recovery from Alcohol Use Disorders." *Alcohol, Clinical and Experimental Research,* 39, 10, 1989–1996. doi: 10.1111/acer.12840. Epub 2015 Sep 13.

[81] https://www.pewresearch.org/politics/2024/03/26/most-americans-favor-legalizing-marijuana-for-medical-recreational-use/

[82] https://flowhub.com/cannabis-industry-statistics

[83] Jonnes, J. *Hep-Cats, Narcs, and Pipe Dreams: A History of America's Romance with Illegal Drugs* (Baltimore: Johns Hopkins University Press, 1996), 128.

[84] Dufton, E. *Grass Roots: The Rise and Fall and Rise of Marijuana in America.* (Basic Books, 2017), 48–50.

[85] https://www.csdp.org/research/nixonpot.txt

[86] Dufton, E. *Grass Roots: The Rise and Fall and Rise of Marijuana in America.* (Basic Books, 2017), 55.

[87] Dufton, E. *Grass Roots: The Rise and Fall and Rise of Marijuana in America.* (Basic Books, 2017), 55.

[88] https://norml.org/blog/2024/09/25/fbi-nearly-one-quarter-of-all-drug-related-arrests-are-for-marijuana-possession/

[89] https://www.endocannabinoidmedicine.com/features/practice-spotlight-staci-gruber-phd-harvards-pot-doc/

[90] Wickelgren, I. (2023). "Smoke Alarm." *Science*, 381, 6661, 936–940.

[91] Fergusson, DM, Boden, JM. (2008). "Cannabis use and later life outcomes." *Addiction,* 103, 6, 969–976; discussion 977–978. doi: 10.1111/j.1360-0443.2008.02221.x. PMID: 18482420.

[92] https://www.forbes.com/sites/willyakowicz/2025/05/02/why-one-time-cannabis-darling-tilray-is-now-high-on-beer-irwin-simon-interview/?ctpv=searchpage

[93] Pollan, M. *How to Change Your Mind: What the New Science of Psychedelics Teaches Us About Consciousness, Dying, Addiction, Depression, and Transcendence.* (New York: Penguin Press, 2018), 58.

[94] Strassman, R. *The Psychedelic Handbook: A Practical Guide to Psilocybin, LSD, Ketamine, MDMA, and DMT/Ayahuasca.* (Ulysses Press, 2022), 35.

[95] Caiuby Labate, B, Cavnar, C. *Ayahuasca Shamanism in the Amazon and Beyond.* (Oxford University Press, 2014).

[96] Strassman, R. *The Psychedelic Handbook: A Practical Guide to Psilocybin, LSD, Ketamine, MDMA, and DMT/Ayahuasca.* (Ulysses Press, 2022), 109.

[97] Liester, MB, Maxon, C. (2024). "The Stoned Ape Theory Revisited." *Psychology Today.* https://www.psychologytoday.com/us/blog/the-leading-edge/202406/the-stoned-ape-theory-revisited

[98] Liester, MB, Maxon, C. (2024). "The Stoned Ape Theory Revisited." *Psychology Today.* https://www.psychologytoday.com/us/blog/the-leading-edge/202406/the-stoned-ape-theory-revisited

[99] https://nyulangone.org/news/vital-signs-podcast-psychiatrists-mission-bring-psychedelic-drugs-mainstream at 03:47.

[100] https://therapsil.ca/docs/what-is-psilocybin-assisted-psychotherapy/

[101] Noller, GE, Frampton, CM, Yazar-Klosinski, B. (2018). "Ibogaine treatment outcomes for opioid dependence from a twelve-month follow-up observational study." *American Journal of Drug and Alcohol Abuse,* 44, 1, 37–46. https://doi.org/10.1080/00952990.2017.1310218

[102] Fell, A. (2020). "New compound related to psychedelic ibogaine could treat addiction, depression." *UC Davis News.* https://www.ucdavis.edu/news/new-compound-related-psychedelic-ibogaine-could-treat-addiction-depression

[103] Hastings, M. (2025.). "What is 7-OH and why is it being targeted in kratom products?" *University of Colorado Anschutz.* https://news.cuanschutz.edu/news-stories/what-is-7-oh-and-why-is-it-being-targeted-in-kratom-products

[104] Koob, GF. (2008). "Hedonic Homeostatic Dysregulation as a Driver of Drug Seeking Behavior." *Drug Discovery Today: Disease Models,* 5, 4, 207–215. https://doi.org/10.1016/j.ddmod.2009.04.002

[105] "The Real Stigma of Substance Use Disorders." *Recovery Research Institute,* https://www.recoveryanswers.org

[106] Kelly, JF, Dow, SJ, Westerhoff, C. (2010). "Does Our Choice of Substance-Related Terms Influence Perceptions of Treatment Need? An Empirical Investigation with Two Commonly Used Terms." *Journal of Drug Issues,* 40, 4, 805–818.

[107] Keyes, KM, Hatzenbuehler, McLaughlin, KA, et al. (2010). "Stigma and Treatment for Alcohol Disorders in the United States." *American Journal of Epidemiology,* 172, 12, 1364–1372.

[108] Stinton, LM, Shaffer, EA. (2012). "Epidemiology of Gallbladder Disease: Cholelithiasis and Cancer." *Gut and Liver,* 6, 2, 172–187. doi:10.5009/gnl.2012.6.2.172.

[109] Sorkin, A. (2012, June 24). "We just decided to." TV series episode. A. Sorkin, executive producer), *The Newsroom.* HBO.

[110] https://www.ama-assn.org/public-health/behavioral-health/what-mate-act

[111] Interview with Arun Gupta, MD, February 12, 2023, LinkedIn messaging.

[112] https://drugabusestatistics.org/

[113] https://www.whitehouse.gov/articles/2025/03/the-staggering-cost-of-the-illicit-opioid-epidemic-in-the-united-states/

[114] https://www.westhartfordct.gov/town-departments/social-services/prevention/recovery-friendly-community#:~:text=The%20Substance%20Abuse%20and%20Mental,which%20individuals%20improve%20their%20health

[115] Kanof, ME. (2003). *Youth illicit drug use prevention: DARE long-term evaluations and federal efforts to identify effective programs.* (GAO-03-172R). US General Accounting Office. https://www.gao.gov/products/gao-03-172r

[116] Ghimire, R, Florence, C, Guy, G. (2026). "Productivity losses from substance use disorder in the US in 2023." *American Journal of Preventive Medicine,* 70, 2, Article 108102. https://doi.org/10.1016/j.amepre.2025.108102

[117] https://www.today.com/video/-think-again-author-adam-grant-wants-everyone-to-reconsider-their-assumptions

## Acknowledgments

I am grateful to these people and organizations.

Aaron and Wendy Goodro
Addiction Recovery Services
Amy Nichols, CARC, CPS
Andrew Bordt, MEd
Arun Gupta, MD
Baldpate Treatment Center
Caron Treatment
David A. Grant
David Pike
Doug Griffin
Evan Boyack
Granite House
Healthcare Resources Center
Henrietta Szutoris, PhD
Institute for Health and Recovery
Jim Wuelfing, BA
John Iudice, LICSW, MLADC
John Kelly, PhD
Joshua Colwell, CRSW
Liberty Health Services
Recovery Centers of America
Serenity at Summit, New England
SOS Recovery
The Anonymous Mushroom Lady
The Grayken Center for Addiction Training and Technical Assistance
William Carrick, MSN

Editor Joni Wilson does so much more than adding or subtracting commas and fixing my grammatical wrongdoings. She brings enthusiasm, know-how, and good judgment. Thank you, Joni, you've made this a better book.

Benjamin Westhoff, initially recruited to write the foreword, provided invaluable creative guidance. This is a better book for Ben's encouragement to say not only what I think but also what I believe. Thank you, Ben, it's been an honor.

Thank you, Bill G., my mentor of over three decades, for always believing in me.

# Index

**Also by Keith Keller…** ***The Infinite Recovery Handbook***

A nuts-and-bolts, one-stop recovery resource.

Made in the USA
Monee, IL
16 September 2026

63312050R00164